Spring, Summer, Autumn

SPRING, SUMMER, AUTUMN

Three Cricketers, One Season

ROB STEEN

The Kingswood Press

First published in Great Britain in 1991
by The Kingswood Press
an imprint of Methuen London
Michelin House, 81 Fulham Road, London SW3 6RB

A CIP Catalogue record for this book is
available from the British Library
ISBN 0 413 64690 4

Photoset by Deltatype Ltd, Ellesmere Port, Cheshire
Printed in Great Britain by
Clays Ltd, St Ives plc

To Anne, my rock and my redeemer,
and Becker, a salty dog.

Contents

Acknowledgements

First on the roll-call is my publisher, Tony Pocock, who hatched the idea. A thousand thanks for your faith, enthusiasm and patience, not to mention indulging my fondness for expensive shellfish. To Ralph, the only member of my family who attends cricket matches. To my parents, John and Shirley, my sister, Jane, and anyone else I know who doesn't: your forbearance during these distracted times was invaluable. To Graham Goldwater, thanks for photographing animate objects for a change. To Huw Richards, thanks for putting me straight on a few things. To other fellow journalists too numerous to list, particularly Peter Smith, Brian Bearshaw, David Foot, David Hopps, Derek Hodgson, Michael Henderson, Nigel Fuller, Francis Ponder and Bernard Webber, your expertise and assistance is greatly appreciated. Being in three places at one time can be tricky. *Mercis aussi* to Peter Edwards, Peter Such, Liz Jones, Christine and James Hughes and the entire Shahid family, plus anyone who picked up the phone in a dressing-room last summer: as messengers you were in the Mercury class. Simon O'Hagen and Tim De Lisle of the *Independent On Sunday*, who never found it suspicious that a Middlesex supporter should want to cover Essex, Somerset or Lancashire every week, were equally helpful. A doff of the cap to the late George Powell, who unravelled the mystery of the late-cut and so turned me on to the most elegant movement in sport, to Paul Filer for fostering that interest, to David Frith and Reg Hayter for encouraging me to express it, and to John Snow, Ken Higgs, J. T. Murray and Tom Graveney, who at the Oval in 1966 first made me aware of the beauty of cricket.

Above all, though, thanks, David, Adrian and Nadeem, for putting up with all those pre-dawn phone calls, inopportune interruptions and cod psychoanalysis sessions. You never expected the Spanish Inquisition, did you? Well, no one expects the Spanish Inquisition . . .

Finally, in addition to Graham Goldwater I must thank David Ashdown (of the *Independent*), Adam Scott (*Independent on Sunday*), *Manchester Daily Mail,* Alan Cozzi, Brian Smith (*Sunday Telegraph*), *The Times, Barbados Times,* South West Counties Newspapers, *Bristol Evening Post, Sunday Express.*

London
March 1991

Rob Stein

1 A Glamour Profession?

6.05
Outside the stadium
Special delivery
For Hoops McCann
Brut and charisma
Poured from the shadow where he stood
Looking good
He's a crowd pleasing man
One on one
He's schoolyard superman
Crashing the backboard
He's Jungle Jim again
When it's all over
We'll make some calls from my car
We're a star.

It's a glamour profession
The L.A. concession
Local boys will spend a quarter
Just to shine the silver bowl
Living hard will take its toll.

(Donald Fagen and Walter Becker,
Glamour Profession)

Glamour is not a word many would use in describing the plus points of their job. Cricket, on the other hand, is at least conceived as a glamorous profession, populated by schoolyard supermen and crowd pleasers eyeing the silver bowl, brutish charisma pouring from many a shadow. Viv Richards is up there with Bob Marley and

Haile Selassie as a Caribbean icon; Ian Botham vies with Merlin as Albion's best-loved magician; Indian women of all castes send perfumed *billets doux* to Sachin Tendulkar; no living Australian is held in higher regard than Sir Donald Bradman.

To a degree it was ever thus, of course, but in this year of 13 AP (After Packer) professional cricket offers mounting piles of the four Fs – fame, fun, fortune and freebies. Yet if the word glamorous implies a certain vacuousness, bringing to mind Joan Collins, Arnold Schwarzenegger and their Hollywooden ilk, it should not here. According to the Chambers dictionary, glamorous means bewitching, alluring, and cricket fits both bills with its finely-proportioned blend of contrasts – art and science, passion and control, grace and danger, frantic action and utter tranquility. As practised by the experts it can offer the most splendid entertainment imaginable. That is why we pay to watch them work.

Not *that* many of us, mind. The Test arena, with its inherent xenophobia and squint-eyed perspective, stages the grand dramas and the Grands Guignols. In England that means galleries of 10,000 or more a day, weather permitting. County cricket, the factory that supplies the widgets for the profitable international machine, yields little triumphs and shallow ruts, not so much fringe theatre as soap opera, rewarding long-time viewers with its intimacy and more credible scenarios, its constancy and humility. Customers, however, are getting harder to find. In 1947 a total of 2.2 million people paid to attend first-class fixtures in the shires; in 1990, Lancashire, one of the biggest draws in the county game, drew 9,429 through the turnstiles to their home Championship games. Even allowing for the 13,300 members (who, on average, turned up less than three times apiece during those five and a half months), their aggregate attendance of 45,496 was pitiful. Granted, more than double that number filed in for the bite-sized portions of the one-day game, but no one could possibly complain of excess demand.

Yet for every spectator who has spent a day huddled under an umbrella watching two men in white jackets take occasional promenades between middle and pavilion, for every one of the nigh-on 100,000 county members, just as many gain vicarious pleasure from poring over a close of play scoreboard, or phoning Cricketcall, or tuning to Radio Five, or turning on Teletext.

Hastened by new technology and affording more expansive information, another contemporary aid has been the growth of local media, one of the by-products of this splintering society. But like train spotting and angling, *The Archers* and *Gardeners' Question Time*, county cricket remains a quiet English obsession, its victims traditionally lured by the unhurried pace and the green space, the artistry of the combatants and the undulations of battle, the conventions and the statistics (boys do so love big numbers). To the unconverted it is a euphemism for boredom, and worse: a letter published recently in the *Bangkok Times* proffered the game as an AIDS antidote, claiming that 'cricket-playing nations are capable of only limited amounts of sexual activity'. We Cyclopes prefer to view it as intrinsic to the national fabric. Dignified, understated and polite on the one hand; petty, formal and unemotional on the other: what could possibly be more English?

But enough romance for now. Let's consider the drudgery, the reality. 'A whole generation of professional cricketers has emerged who don't know the sheer pleasure of lazing around on a free Sunday,' sympathised Brian Brain, the erstwhile Worcestershire and Gloucestershire seamer, in his diary of the 1980 season, *Another Day, Another Match*. Indeed, from mid-April to late September, the county regular, unencumbered by distractions such as Test matches and national scrutiny, can expect to spend between ninety and 100 days on duty, seven-day weeks obligatory, a ridiculous workload for an athlete, even one involved in as languid a sport as this. In fact, allowing for climatic interruptions, a team winning all five major competitions could be on stage for 125 days out of the available 150 or so, a proposition that rendered last year's notions of a Lancastrian 'Grand Slam' somewhat fanciful. Then there are the highway hikes between venues, lengthy, disturbingly frequent and stressful. On Sunday 15 July 1990, Somerset played a Refuge League match in Scarborough. Next stop Worcester for a three-day game beginning on the Wednesday. On the Friday evening they wended south to Uxbridge, where they spent a day before moving west to Neath. A quick 40-over bout, then back to Uxbridge for a further forty-eight hours before returning to Scarborough for three days. Onward to Manchester and, finally, home at the fag end of Tuesday 30 July. Two weeks, eight journeys, six towns and around 1,500 miles of motorway. An extreme example, perhaps, but surely indicative of the extent of unpaid overtime.

The reason for this hyperactivity is clear. Prior to the initial, grudging, financially-motivated absorption of the limited-overs format into the first-class calendar in 1963 – coinciding, symbolically, with the cessation of hostilities between Gentlemen and Players – there was a rigid consistency to the labours of our average shirehorse. Counties played each other at least once, usually twice, taking time off to cane some Oxbridge enthusiasts and crumple against the tourists. The Australians always began at New Road, local derbies adorned bank holidays, Scarborough festivities the end of term. Now the order seems as malleable as putty; Bass, Benson & Hedges, Britannic Assurance, Callers-Pegasus, National Westminster Bank, Refuge Assurance, Seeboard, Texaco and Tilcon must all be kept sweet. Yet there are players who will still spend the greater part of the tax year unemployed, summer bosses unable or unwilling to supply winter shelter. Only in England can cricket support anything remotely approaching 350 professional practitioners; sadly, the level of that support leaves something to be desired.

Admittedly, the pot at the end of this monochrome rainbow does contain that tax-free barometer of loyalty and community affection, the benefit. Cyril Washbrook's £14,000 bonus in 1948, though not exceeded until Colin Milburn raked in £19,473 some twenty-three years later, was left trailing some distance behind by the £96,000 raised in 1986 for Essex's Keith Pont, by no stretch of the imagination anything more than ordinary county plonk. Salaries, though, are skimpy for the majority. Before the start of the 1989 season, the Cricketers' Association, the players' union, attempted to drag the minimum wage for uncapped professionals (over 40 per cent of the workforce) from the derisory depths of £8,500 which was £1,500 below the national mean. So what did these shirehorses get for their £50 subscription? A 10 per cent rise. Some of their capped brethren, furthermore, are only marginally better off. Should we wonder that many a cricketing humanitarian has exchanged his soul for the blood-drenched krugerrand?

Not that there is much evidence of an irresistible force bent on improving matters. Poor labour relations in American sport may have led to stars from the grid and diamond downing tools, but although Frank Hayes, Peter Lever and Barry Wood withheld their labour from Lancashire over contract negotiations in 1975, the nearest the cricketers' union came to mass strike action occurred five years later, when members donned black armbands for the season's opening exchanges. Yet as the potential rewards have soared, so the tolerance of failure has declined. Further truncated by increasingly exacting demands on body and mind, careers are becoming briefer. Fred Titmus's stint spanned five decades, but it is difficult to picture a 48-year-old treading the mill come the next millenium. As that earthiest of cricket writers, Mike Carey, observed, 'most county cricketers play the game for the life rather than the living.'

Welding pride and pragmatism, wit and bluff, courage and persistence, the shirehorse combines many of the assets of that elusive creature we refer to as the quintessential Englishman. Part Noël Coward, part Captain Mainwaring, part Alf Garnett, even a smidgin of Arthur Daley. His canvas is similarly redolent of both Camelot and Milton Keynes. Worcester Cathedral rubs shoulders with the Ladies Stand at New Road, the Jessop Stand with the marketing department at Bristol, dashing Edwardian portraits with database scoreboard at Trent Bridge, peeling walls with squash club at Hove. Even so, only when Durham swell the first-class ranks to eighteen in 1992, will the game discover the North-East Frontier.

But if hanging on in quiet desperation really is the 'English Way', as Roger Waters said on *Dark Side of the Moon*, then the rituals and subtleties of county cricket, the humour and cameraderie, represent our light side. David Shepherd, the umpire, habitually breaks into a jig whenever the score reaches 111, 222, 333 and so forth. When Roland Butcher essays a leg-glance, millimetres stand between anointment and abomination. Such disdain for ridicule exemplifies this quietly jubilant flipside: jubilant that self-expression remains possible, jubilant that loss-leading perennials like the County Championship breathe on.

There was a time, mind, when the oxygen was in danger of running out. C. L. R. James, perhaps the most perceptive of the game's chroniclers, once wrote of 'the grandeur of a game which, in lands far from which gave it birth, could encompass so much of social reality and still remain a game.' Some thirty years later, in

1957, his less smitten pen was chiding cricketers for being 'functionaries of the Welfare State' (an odd statement for a lifelong Marxist). Wistfully he recalled their forebears of the late 19th and early 20th centuries, the so-called Golden Age (surely Romantic would have been more accurate), when Jessop, Trumper and Ranji strutted their stuff on rival bills to Shaw and Lloyd George. 'The prevailing attitude of the players of 1890 to 1914 was daring, adventure, creation,' James asserted. 'The prevailing attitude of 1957 can be summed up in one word – security.' A year earlier, the PEP (Political and Economic Planning) group had published a study in which English cricket was described as an industry 'fighting a losing battle against shortage of capital, shortage of income and shortage of the highly skilled labour the game requires'. Concluding that first-class fixtures should be restricted to weekends, the study, unsurprisingly, was not well received. Its message, though, was undeniable. By 1963 Gloucestershire, accustomed to healthy surpluses during the post-war boom, were sustaining five-figure deficits. Hampshire, who had held their membership fee at one guinea from 1895 to 1951, were now charging three times as much – the same as Hambledon had levied in 1791! The transition from non-commercial institution to nasty, capitalist profit-seeker was proving slow and painful.

We have since moved on, though it is arguable whether the march has been totally fruitful. The urgency essential to one-day competition has helped restore much of the daring, adventure and creation C. L. R. James worshipped, and encouraged the negativity he so rightly despised. Five-figure profits may be commonplace, but Sir Richard Hadlee, discussing his days with Nottinghamshire, noted a lack of ambition among his team-mates, a desire merely to do enough to earn another contract, to make do (hanging on in quiet desperation indeed!), while Peter Roebuck, an atypical county cricketer, has characterised his peers as cautious and predictable. But these perceived character defects are surely pardonable. The sheer pace of change, both within and without cricket, can never have been more hectic than it is now, the desire simply to stay on the rollercoaster ever more fervent as the recession bites.

Which brings us back to C.L.R. and his links between game and social reality. It may be coincidental that England's decline on the international field echoes both a stubborn resistance to change and a receding political clout, but it seems feasible that a dearth of national pride and initiative might have contributed to it. More refreshingly, as the immigration of the 1950s and 1960s bequeathed a multiracial Britain, so Caucasians now stand shoulder-to-shoulder for Queen and country with compatriots of Asian and African stock. Similarly, as the consumer society has gradually got the better of dictatorial communism, so the temptation to sully cricket's comparatively pristine image has grown in direct proportion to the surge in prize-money (which in the past dozen years has expanded tenfold even for the county set). The indiscreet, unforgiving eyes of the TV camera and the tabloid lens certainly make it less easy for the hungry to get away with lapses. Then we have the one-day game, child of the butterfly-mind generation, aimed at a society in a rush, a society that would rather flit between ever-multiplying leisure options than form a meaningful relationship. Still more worryingly, a 1990 survey by the Central Council for Physical Recreation revealed that 75 per cent of British school pupils play less than two hours of sport per week. Resources and playing fields have dwindled with the receding prominence Thatcherism has accorded education, shoved aside by the profit motive. The supply of talent, let alone interest, cannot but deteriorate.

The links are also evident further afield. As Pakistan has emerged from the coat-tails of India and Empire to create an identity for itself, so its cricketers have flourished. As the Caribbean nations, individually and collectively, assert themselves and spread their culture, so their once erratic and divisive cricketing representatives now knit together and overawe rivals with their intense determination not to surrender such hard-earned respect. As South Africa has been ostracised for continuing to uphold that most inhumane of philosophies, apartheid, so its magnificent cricketers have been denied a goal and domestic standards have drooped. As Australia has embraced Americana and espoused a youthful brashness, so cricket there has welcomed the brave new world of razziness and opportunism more enthusiastically than anywhere else. And so on.

The essence of modern county cricket lies in its distillation of these diverse nationalities. Since the quest for imported manpower began in earnest in 1968 (another gambit to attract more revenue),

English cricket has evolved into a veritable League of Nations spanning sixteen counties, Yorkshire the dishonourable exception. Merging creeds and credos, but never submerging them, this has spawned an impressive cast fit to rank with the finest ever assembled. On 24 July 1990 you could have seen Graham Gooch duel with Wasim Akram beneath the turrets of Colchester Castle, nipped off to semi-detached, suburban Uxbridge to compare the contrasting splendours of Jimmy Cook and Desmond Haynes, then whizzed down the M3 in time to catch Ian Bishop and Devon Malcolm jousting with David Gower and Malcolm Marshall at the United Services Ground in Portsmouth. What other branch of public entertainment offers its audience performances by the cream with such regularity, within such close proximity, at such (generally) reasonable prices? Mind you, what other branch supplies so many inconclusive scenarios, or bestows such merit on stalemate and status quo?

The nature and history of the game, its laws and customs, may give county cricket its social distinction (can there be anything more honest in sport than 'walking'?), but it is the players who embody its soul. Code of dress, technique, tactics and demeanour join past to present, stimulating, and so uniting, several corners of this fragmented society. How these travelling troupers respond to life from St George's Day to Yom Kippur captures all these disparate components in microcosm, highlighting the ennui and the graft, diluting the glamour yet never quite managing to erase it. Once it was a complimentary leg of lamb from the butcher or maybe a boil lanced on the house. Now our heroes cruise their domain in sponsored cars, clad in sponsored tracksuits, name writ large on the side of the vehicle for the world to see, left ear engaged to portable phone. The queue to trade places is as lengthy as ever.

And so to the premise of this book. County cricket diaries are not uncommon, but since each season has its own peculiar attributes and peccadilloes, its own issues and points of conflict, its own hue and flavour, so each *Wisden* deserves the accompanying third dimension these accounts provide. The 1990 season also happened to mark the 100th anniversary of the official constitution of the County Championship. Helpfully, it turned out to be more peculiar than most.

Even discounting changes in remuneration and demography, the summers of 1890 and 1990 could scarcely have differed more. At the outset of the Golden/Romantic Age, coloured shirts proliferated on the field, along with bow ties and turned-down starched collars. Diving in the outfield was considered improper. Talk was of the recent authorisation of declarations and the five-ball over. Surrey's magisterial George Lohmann, 'probably the greatest medium-pace bowler ever' in C. B. Fry's estimation, took 220 wickets, the most yet by an Englishman in one summer. In the two Tests possible between England and Australia – the third, at Manchester, was the first ever to be abandoned without a ball being bowled – neither side could reach 200. At Lord's in May, rain, a regular visitor that season, prevented a start in the match between MCC Club and Ground and Sussex until 3.45 on the second day; before the end of the third, thirteen ducks had been sustained, 36 wickets had fallen for the derisory aggregate of 187 runs and Sussex had won.

A century on we found so many runs in the sun that yawns began to greet both. Now it was the bowlers, subjected to a competitive fixture list three times as long, who craved mercy. A television replay was used to settle a disputed umpiring decision. Declarations, for the most part, provided the sole means of achieving a result on the impossibly benign Championship pitches. Fielders, infinitely fitter, turned clean flannels into badges of dishonour. Despite such athleticism, however, the number of new batting records must itself have constituted a record. In decades to come, removed from their context, almost all of them will be marvelled at. A remarkable season.

My criteria for selecting guides were fairly specific. First, each of the four elements of cricket that excite me had to be represented. That meant spin bowling (an acceptable form of deceit), pace bowling (acceptable machismo), enterprising leadership (acceptable Machiavellianism) and elegant batsmanship (acceptable vanity). Sir Garfield Sobers would have sufficed, but since no two current county players cover the requisite territory, it had to be a trio. Together, they should also encompass the age spectrum, and be eligible to play for England, but not actually to have done so. Men, furthermore, who might expose facets other than those depicted by Hadlee and Roebuck. Just under 300 to choose from.

Put plainly, Nadeem Shahid, a youthful Essex all-rounder, was the finest debutant I encountered in 1989, wristy cuts and leg-spin hinting broadly at his Asian birthright, discipline, resolution and correctness mirroring his Ipswich School nursery. A starlet on full-time parade for the first time. More significantly, a pathfinder for a new breed.

Enter Adrian Jones, stage left. Surrey-born, formerly of Sussex, then of Somerset and since returned to Hove. One of the more colourful fast bowlers stalking the boards, he was due to enter his thirtieth year, and become a father, during the summer of 1990. Still aspiring towards a more prominent billing, still fantasising, but primarily occupied with family and future, even to the extent of being prepared to offend the game's overblown notions of fidelity. Have spikes, will travel.

What about a wise owl? A spry 43, David Hughes, captain of Lancashire, a club with as illustrious and deep-rooted a past as any, was also the oldest of our shirehorses. Epitome of the staunch, fiercely loyal English pro, just as his father had been in the leagues. Squaring up to Australia at the MCG had long since ceased to be on his menu, but he had dined at the best tables, and only a Red Rose championship barred him from repletion. Here was a leader not only with a gambler's instincts but also his prerequisite sense of humour. When Mike Atherton came down from Cambridge complete with halo, and trailing rave notices, it was Hughes who playfully sellotaped the sign reading 'God' on the new boy's locker. Another natural.

Three men of dissimilar backgrounds and talents, each with ambitions, all eschewing caution and predictability. Their experiences provide a selection of snapshots from the Year of the Bat. One man in the spring of his career, one in the summer, one in the autumn. Three seasons of a glamour profession.

2 Spring: Nadeem Shahid

b Karachi, 23 April 1969.

Career to start of 1990: Debut v. Leicestershire, 1989. Seven first-class matches. Nine innings, 255 runs at 36.42 (County Championship alone: 245 runs at 49) with one 50 and six catches. Highest score: 52 v. Surrey. Bowled 81.1 overs, 8 wickets at 40.75 (best bowling: 2–40 v. Leicestershire on debut). Victims were Laurie Potter, Winston Benjamin, Nigel Briers, Malcolm Marshall, Tom Moody, Allan Border, Tim Zoehrer, Neil Fairbrother, none of them rabbits. One-day appearances: 1 (v. Northamptonshire in the last Refuge League game, 1989, in which he scored 11 and didn't bowl).

[He] once wrote that the island of Barbados, his birthplace, lacked a hero. As usual, he was under-playing himself. [He] was the first hero of the new nation of Barbados and anyone who doubted that had only to be in the island when his body was brought home in mid-March of 1967. Or in Westminster Abbey when West Indians of all backgrounds and shades of opinion paid their last respects to a man who had done more than any other of their countrymen to bind together the new nations of the Caribbean and establish a reputation for fair play throughout the world.

(Sir Learie Constantine
on Sir Frank Worrell,
taken from *Wisden*, 1968)

Standing shoulder-to-shoulder with his Essex compadre, Nasser Hussain, Nadeem Shahid is a member of the advance party paving the way for a new power base in English cricket. That the Asian influence has been less pervasive than the Caribbean until now is, of course, a reflection of the immigration pattern. In the 1989 *Cricketers' Who's Who* (now such an invaluable asset to the reporter that it is commonly known as 'Sproat', a rare accolade for its compiler, Iain Sproat) among the unflattering mugshots of players qualified to play for England were twenty men of Caribbean extraction. Excluding the anomaly of Dermot Reeve, born in Hong Kong out of Irish stock, four Asians were featured.

The balance, however, is changing. In the 1990 edition of another perennial journalistic crutch, *Playfair*, Nadeem was one of seven county staffers with Indian, Pakistani or Sri Lankan roots and a passport to represent England. The West Indian connection had been expanded by one and the gap was closing. There was also a Spaniard, a West German, a North American, a Ugandan, two Kenyans and a brace of Dutchmen to go with a squadron of white South Africans. The latter's eligibility for Test selection rankled both with those who favoured an England-for-the-English national team and with those who objected to a system which granted expedient brotherhood and financial compensation to the beneficiaries of apartheid.

That said, who but the most overt patriot can fail to delight in the marvellously cosmopolitan troupe that now graces English cricket? If sport has any sociological function it is surely to bring people together in a common cause. Yet racism remains a barely blunted thorn in the side of peaceful co-habitation in British sport. Remember the bananas hurled at the England soccer international John Barnes during his early days at Liverpool, and the failure of Howard Gayle to 'make progress' at that same institution, the refusal to invite Keith Connor, a former Olympic medal-winning triple jumper, to become a national athletics coach, a post for which he had applied, and the barbs aimed unerringly towards Viv Richards at Headingley down the years.

For all their claims about the Asians of Bradford taking time to develop and their stubborn, self-defeating yet vaguely admirable persistence in refusing to sign anyone not born within the shire boundaries, Yorkshire County Cricket Club does more than most to perpetuate the us-and-them mentality. When Phil Carrick was summarily sacked as captain after the 1989 season, his crime was to have had the nerve to propose that the club should abandon the policy. More damningly, no black or Asian born within the county boundaries has represented the White Rose. Talij Dutt, captain of the local Al-Faiah Cricket Club, when informed of the county's attempts to uncover Asian talent, railed, 'That's just the Yorkshire people trying to show the Asians that they care, which they don't.'

The prejudice seems to flow from the very top. The former England captain and current chairman of the Yorkshire cricket committee, Brian Close, put his jaundiced feet in his mouth last May, shortly after Yorkshire had taken the unprecedented step of recruiting a player qualified to represent another land. It was OK, though. Craig White, an opening bat-cum-off-spinner and member of the Australian Academy of Cricket, was as palefaced as his name implied. Anyway, in a BBC documentary entitled *The Race Game*, Close referred to 'bloody Pakistanis' and spoke in terms of 'our lads' and 'them'. The resulting, carefully-worded apology came only after a series of midnight telephone pleas from the Yorkshire chairman, Britain Walsh, who later stressed that although Yorkshire had circulated an invitation to all 6,000 clubs in the county to send their best coloured youngsters to nets at Headingley, only twenty-nine aspirants had turned up. Yorkshire, Walsh said, had also had leaflets printed in five languages encouraging youngsters to get involved in organised cricket, as well as sending out talent scouts to seek out promising coloured players.

If, as Close claimed, these initiatives were being ignored, how could one blame the invitees? Being on the outside can dim one's respect for, and desire to link arms with, those manning the exclusion zone.

Barely a month after the *Race Game* kerfuffle, Lady Hill, wife of Sir James Hill, was present at a one-day International at Headingley: 'My husband and I were appalled by the constant stream of lewd and incredibly offensive remarks about coloured people, in particular, coloured women and Jewish men . . . Among these middle-aged louts was a man who had held high office in the cricketing world but could certainly not be described as a gentleman.'

By the autumn of 1990, the twenty-three-strong, all-powerful Yorkshire general committee would convene to debate the 'Tykes only' issue once more, faced by an ageing, dwindling membership (9,300, down on 1978 by 30 per cent) and anticipated record losses of £70,000. That at the end of a summer in which Martyn Moxon and his men gained but one Championship victory without resorting to collusion with the enemy, one which also saw the death of Sir Leonard Hutton, perhaps Yorkshire cricket's greatest servant. Hutton, though, had to lead England before Yorkshire were persuaded to drop their stance on professional captains. Shortly after he died, two senior county officials had chats with India's ridiculously stylish middle-order bat and captain, Azharuddin, who had expressed a sliver of interest in turning out for Yorkshire. Having broken a seemingly indestructible barrier himself, Hutton could have wished for no finer tribute than for his passing to have coincided with the deletion of another brick in the wall.

Unfortunately, and more than a little predictably, the general committee produced a heavy majority in favour of retaining the exclusion zone. Some ground was conceded, mind: residential qualification was now acceptable. But even that adjustment, merely a clarification in certain eyes, provoked outrage. 'It's a bloody disgrace. Anybody who was not born in this county – no matter who they are – should not be allowed to take the field for Yorkshire,' whined Fred Trueman, 'Our Fred'.

It was against this insidious background that Nadeem entered the first-class fray in 1989. Born in Karachi twenty springs earlier, he spent three months there with his grandparents before joining father Ahmed and mother Salma in Surrey, where the pair had met and formed a bond in the winter of 1961. When Ahmed, a plastics moulder, changed employers in 1976, the Shahid clan, which by now included sisters Kulsoom and Kashwi alongside Tafweaz, Nadeem's elder brother, upped and accompanied him to Ipswich. 'Study hard, that's my boy,' was Ahmed's oft reiterated priority for his slender, facially striking younger son. Nadeem dutifully fulfilled those wishes at Ipswich School, but from the moment he attended an English Schools Cricket Association Under-15 course at Dover under the sage tutelage of Les Lenham, cricket became increasingly distracting.

At that stage he was 'a No. 11 slogger'. 'When Nadeem went into the net all the boys used to queue up because they couldn't wait to bowl at him,' recalled Bob Cunnell, who would later captain Nadeem when the pair played for the village of Copdock a few miles from Ipswich. Bowling took precedence. One lesson from that ESCA course took root. Lenham advised him to extend his run-up in order to allow himself 'more time to think'.

Later that year, however, a sudden spurt saw Nadeem soar a foot in height within the space of a few months, prompting the embryonic leg-break bowler to run home awash with tears. 'I thought I'd lost it. Because of my height I could only bowl toppies.' He needn't have worried. Although he recalls being bowled by a Hussain leg-break while playing for Suffolk Under-16s, the two protégés were to progress in opposite directions as bowlers. The next step provided a brush with reality. Applying himself increasingly to his batting, he became, at 16, the youngest player ever to represent Suffolk. This Minor Counties bow came at Fenner's against Cambridgeshire; he wound up with a pair and made only one further appearance, two summers later in 1988, scoring 58 and 33 and taking 2–64. Still, a trip to Barbados with Ipswich for the Sir Garfield Sobers International Schools Cricket Tournament brought the first rave review. 'Roland Holder, Brian Lara, Nadeem Shahid and John Meadows . . . are names which may be on the lips of countless cricket fans in a few short years,' wrote one semi-prescient reporter from the *Barbados Times*. 'Ipswich's most impressive player is Nadeem Shahid, a right-handed opener in the classic style [who] also bowls a tight leg-spin.'

Progressing towards true all-round status, Nadeem began to make inroads into the representative arena. In an English Schools South trial against Surrey 2nd XI, he numbered Keith Medlycott and David Ward among his prey in a return of 6–50. The invitations followed: Public Schools, MCC Schools, NCA Young Cricketers, ESCA. In 1987 Nadeem won the annual *Daily Telegraph* schools bowling award, repeating the feat (the first so to do) the following year just as he was on the verge of signing for Essex, that original amble to the wicket now usurped by a jaunty, elbows-to-the-fore action.

Not that his batting, more austere and technically correct than Hussain's brew of heady audacity, was lagging too far behind. In the same year he missed that same newspaper's schools batting award by a handful of runs. Ditto the following year, when Nick Knight, a fellow member of the English Schools team and now an Essex colleague, pipped him by 92 runs after the highly correct, if sometimes over-ambitious, right-hander had marked his A-level year with more than 1,000 runs in addition to 103 wickets. 'Nick's an opener – and he had three more innings than me.' The alibi is presented in factual terms, not as a gripe. The rivalry between the two, though keen, has always been extremely amiable.

Nadeem's precocious self-assurance, sometimes belied by a stammer, received its first serious examination when he made his Championship bow against Leicestershire on 17 June 1989, emulating other Suffolk-raised fruits such as Ray East and David Larter. His contribution to a match stifled by a cautious declaration from the acting Leicestershire captain, Nigel Briers, one that provoked ill-tempered barracking among the normally fair-minded Chelmsford regulars, was encouraging enough. Denied an innings by the success of the Essex top six in coping with what *Wisden* described as 'a bland pitch', he made his mark by dismissing Laurie Potter and Winston Benjamin to emerge with 2–40 from fifteen overs, comfortably the most incisive analysis in the Leicestershire first innings, then followed up by accepting a return catch from Briers in their second, drawn-out dig.

My own first sighting of Nadeem came in the next Championship fixture against Hampshire. Although totally ignorant of his existence when I set off for Ilford, within ten minutes of taking my seat in the press tent I had discovered, courtesy of *Playfair* and the kindly, wisecracking local reporter, Nigel Fuller, that Essex had a new leggie who played for Colchester and East Essex in the Paladin Plastics League, one who could evidently bat a bit and field with distinction just about anywhere. For this romantic, there could be no more tempting invitation to keep my eyes peeled. However, even though John Childs's canny left-arm spin was to bring him matchwinning figures of 12–74 on a helpful though scarcely spiteful surface, Nadeem did not bowl in the first innings and was given just six overs second time up.

Consolation came by way of an astute 40 that helped Essex recover from 96 for 5 on the first morning against a rampant Malcolm Marshall and eventually total 277. More than that, Nadeem unfurled a late-cut of such delicious daring that the nape of my neck was suddenly layered with goosebumps. Though he disguised the fact well, that assurance took time to surface. 'I was very nervous when I came in to face Marshall. I can't even remember walking to the crease. The sun was reflecting off the sightscreen and I didn't see the first ball at all. "Dusty" Miller told me it was a big in-swinger, but the main thing was that I survived, somehow.'

The following morning, readers of the *Daily Telegraph* spluttered as they picked up my over-the-top ramblings about Oriental wristiness and timing of impeccable quality, under the mistaken belief that they were reading a match report. Had I been old enough to have seen Ranji or Duleep, their names would surely have been invoked along the way.

Yet I make no apology. One of the delights of reporting sport lies in uncovering a gleaming nugget that none of your rivals has yet located. 'We think we have outgrown it, but in truth we can hardly wait for the next shy and shining, extraordinarily talented young man to come along and make the game thrilling for us again.' Roger Angell was referring to baseball, but such sentiments are no less applicable to cricket, or any other sport for that matter. Sharing that enthusiasm is the next rewarding step. More than anything else, though, cricket, and sport, is too peripheral to the serious business of survival to withhold the observer's right to fantasise without fear of disillusionment.

Judgement vindicated and an impression made, Nadeem made four further appearances in Essex's remaining fifteen first-class fixtures, a number that reflected the strength of the first-choice batting order and the county's predilection for seam rather than failure. Aside from scores of 10 and 0 going in at No. 3 against the irresistible Australian tourists, his lowest score was 27 not out. In the ante-penultimate Championship game at Northampton, Brian Hardie, acting as captain with Graham Gooch and Derek Pringle serving England at the Oval, set the hosts a reasonable 264 in seventy-three overs. For Essex, victory was critical to their chances of overhauling Worcestershire and overcoming the Southend Factor (the already infamous 25-point slapped wrist administered by the TCCB, seemingly for Southend Council's inability to find a decent groundsman, but to all intents and purposes a sop to the chorus demanding that a scapegoat be found for the proliferation of substandard surfaces).

When that walking ignition, Wayne Larkins, kick-started the chase, the gamble metamorphosed from risky to doomed. The one hope was to disconnect Larkins. Fulfilment appeared nigh when he swept Childs towards Nadeem at deep square-leg. But with the mid-afternoon sun rendering judgement hazardous, the arcing projectile assumed the menace of an invisible grenade. Ripping through the fielder's hands, it exploded on his nose. Nadeem collapsed, blood stained the outfield, lengthy medical attention ensued before his withdrawal – and Larkins strode on to set up a Northamptonshire victory. Little mention was made of the sun in the papers the next day, most of the reporters preferring to hark on about the consequences of Nadeem's dropped catch rather than the causes. 'To my surprise, a couple of days later I received letters from people sympathising with the lack of recognition paid to the influence of the sun. It was all "no wonder you can't trust newspapers" sort of stuff. The fact is that I lost the ball in the sun. I kept thinking to myself – and there was plenty of time for thought because the ball was up there a long time – "if you stay here and wait till it comes out of the sun, you'll catch it and you'll be a hero". The next thing I knew the ball had landed on my nose. The doctor said he couldn't do anything for me until the bruising had subsided. I couldn't breathe, eat or swallow that night.'

Remembering that Alan Lilley had been absent from duty for six weeks a couple of years earlier with a similarly displaced proboscis, Nadeem assumed that Keith Fletcher, the Essex coach, was just having his little joke when he told him to turn up at Chelmsford the next day for the game against Surrey. In common with the colleagues who finally sharpened the edge of those three seaxes into a winning one at the end of the 1970s, Fletcher is noted for his capacity to infuse competitive instincts with a jocular approach that keeps the game in its proper place. Nadeem had been fortunate to join a club, and a dressing-room, where bonhomie comes, if not before, then certainly on the same rung as success. On this occasion, however, any humour was unintentional.

'I saw a specialist at eight in the morning who told me that although the nose, which had ballooned out to here, was broken in two places, and that if I got hit again the bone would rise up and cause brain damage, I could play provided I felt comfortable. At catching practice Pring said that if I caught everything I could play. I did, but I still never seriously thought I would.' Even when he was given the go-ahead, Nadeem refused to take out any insurance. Being one of those silly sorts who disdains the protection of a helmet grille ('it hinders a clear view of the bowler; if you're confident, you'll never get hit') he broke his promise to the medic and went out to bat on the second day of the Surrey match without one.

His reward was a maiden half-century in senior cricket, top-scoring with a feisty 52 to take Essex to within manoeuvrable distance on the first innings. Later, a more fluent 31 supplied the final lever towards the victory that ensured all of Essex could spend the winter crying into their pint pots. But for the Southend Factor, the county would have won the Championship by a clear 18 points. Even for a snotty man of Middlesex whose inexplicable nausea for his native county had found substance in the XR3-driving, lager-louting wide boys who now besmirched its London boundaries, it was impossible not to share those grievances. Nadeem, meanwhile, had left enough of a mark in the dressing-room to warrant the award of a nickname: Prince.

The close season saw Nadeem burrow down to Perth for six months. Sydney and Tasmania were his original destinations, but a plane strike complicated matters, and Mark Waugh recommended the western state for its reviving climate. Gosnells, a local first-grade club for whom Nadeem played at weekends, paid his air fare, found him digs and a sponsored car and secured him a clerical job in a public trust office. A solitary domestic life proved beneficial, setting in train plans to leave home when he returned.

In cricketing terms, the experience was equally rewarding, even though Nadeem found himself at odds with the Australian analysis of grade cricket standards. 'They weren't as high as they claim. It was a cross between minor county and 2nd XI, but games are very hard-fought and there's a lot of sledging. I found myself answering back to senior players like Graeme Wood, which is something I wouldn't dare do here.'

Mark Ramprakash, another precociously talented young Englishman with coloured antecedents, was banned from playing in Melbourne for three weeks after responding testily to racist abuse on the field, but although Nadeem, too, let his fury show on one occasion, pigmentation was not the provocateur. 'In one game I kept smacking this offie over mid-wicket with the spin, and Ken McLeay eventually came down the wicket to me and stood face-to-face and swore at me. The basic drift was, how could I play shots like that. I told him where to go.' A firm fist to go with such erudite hands? This boy would surely go far, even if he did begin the 1990 season without a girlfriend to whinge to in the evenings. 'She couldn't stand the game, and it was taking up too much of my time for us to see each other regularly anymore. Cricket won, I suppose, but then maybe she wasn't the right one?'

3. Summer: Adrian Jones

b Woking, 22 July 1961.

Career to start of 1990: Sussex debut, 1981. Awarded cap in 1986 after taking 21 wickets at 29 apiece to accompany 43 one-day victims, the most in the country, including 7–41 v. Nottinghamshire in the John Player League. Somerset debut/cap, 1987. Also played for Border in 1981–82 and Orange Free State in 1986. First-class record: 284 wickets at 29.66. Best bowling: 7–30 v. Hampshire at Southampton, 1988 (including a spell of 7–18 in 12 overs and the first seven batsmen to fall). Five wickets in an innings eight times. Ten wickets in a match once. 714 runs at 10.98 in 115 matches, remaining unbeaten in 46 out of 111 innings. Highest score: 43* at No. 11 v. Leicestershire at Taunton in 1989. 34 catches.

From clamouring Caribbean palm-fringed ovals
with Sobers strong and smooth as Mount Gay rum,
casually batting, rummaging through bowling,
dimming even the tropical sun;
To writhing, wracking Bangladesh birth,
all riots, hardship and blood on dry earth,
matches played on political whim,
Bhutto's anthem, Ayub Khan's funeral hymn;
Then schizophrenic Australians, bottles and cans,
Pommy bastard, 'on yer mate, let's shake hands,
Lillee and Thomson, the Chappells and Co.,
white flannelled undertakers happy you should go.

(Extract from
Sometime, When I'm Older by John Snow)

The fast bowler is the white-flannelled hitman hired to wipe out meddlesome batsmen. Yet John Snow's technicolour verse refutes the theory that these fascinating buggers are all brainless macho men. Did not Robert George Dylan Willis spend much of the 1982–83 tour of Australasia submerged in his bath listening to Van Morrison, that most poetic of Irish bards? Was it not Frank Tyson, that tearaway scourge of Harvey, Miller and Morris, who recently compiled an insightful treatise on cricketing psychology? In the summer of 1988, I ghosted a newspaper column for Michael Holding, generally deemed the prince of modern pacemen (with Lillee as king), and discovered a sharp mind, a generous spirit and a gentle demeanour. Walking around the back of the stands at the Oval with him during the fifth Test against the West Indies, I was bowled over by the number of people, predominantly black males, who turned and yelled encouragement or stretched back to shake his hand. He was a soul brother to them all.

However, without 269 Test wickets, and without the methods Holding utilised to get them, this goodwill may not have been as pronounced. No matter how much we hail his physical abilities, his pantheresque approach, his aesthetically pleasing delivery action and his skill – and there is no more exhilarating sight in cricket than all these components in harmony – the fact remains that one of the basic functions of a fast bowler in this age of helmets and high stakes is to intimidate. Why else does the short-pitched ball that rears past the nose or thuds into the chest qualify for acclaim from slips and spectators alike? Unlike others, this delivery does not content itself with merely curbing the run flow or inducing a mishit; it achieves such ends, and sends out a message to the rest of the order, by making the target apprehensive, by threatening his body, by challenging his manhood.

After the violent 1974–75 Ashes series, arguably the precursor of today's bruising conflicts, Jeff Thomson expressed astonishment that no fatalities were suffered. Within a couple of years Mike Brearley was sporting a skull protector and Dennis Amiss a motorbike helmet. The licence to go head-hunting had been granted. Yet this ploy is sanitised by the same commentators who spend the remainder of their time posing as bulwarks of decency. In baseball, if the pitcher so much as kisses flesh, the batter automatically walks to first base. Cricket's sole safeguard, Law 42 (d), is possibly the least observed regulation in sport.

Anyway, that's the peacenik's view, one that did not prevent me from developing a friendship with Adrian. We first met in Haywards Heath in early 1987, the occasion a pub lunch on *Wisden Cricket Monthly* and an interview. From the magazine's perspective, the aim was to discover from Jones, then whiling away the winter working for Abbey Life insurance, why he had just left Sussex for Somerset, and thus find out the real story behind the civil strife at Hove. But as soon as this tousle-haired, handsomely built, regular churchgoer announced that Imran Khan had lauded him as 'the best white fast bowler in the world' (despite his having taken less than 100 wickets in forty-nine first-class matches at that juncture), I realised that the story might very soon be him, not Sussex. Disarmingly frank, hugely desirous of success and terribly conscientious; for some reason not at all what I'd imagined.

Woking-born and the middle child of three, Adrian basked in the glow of a close, supportive family. His father, William, 'a very clever, brilliant man', ran a stationery and office equipment company in Sussex; it was mother Emily who nurtured Adrian's affectionate manner. 'It's my father I aspire to, though. He's a self-made man. I have never heard anyone say a bad word about him. He was the eldest child whose father died young, so he could only ever rely on himself.' William, a useful all-rounder in Surrey club cricket, was followed into the office equipment field, not by daughter Denise, now a British Airways hostess, but by Adrian's brother, Glynne, a sales manager. 'He's the real sportsman. He plays rugby and cricket for Horsham, and he's got all the talent. He also has far more enthusiasm than me, and he may kick himself one day for not trying to play professional cricket.'

After leaving Seaford College with eight O-levels and two A-levels, Adrian had been less modest, although he did try to guard against any failure to make the grade by qualifying as an NCA coach and obtaining a consumer credit licence. Comfortably over six feet tall and tilting the scales at more than 13 stone, he was an imposing physical specimen whose powerful frame was put to equally good use whether opening the bowling (right-handed) or batting (left-handed), although even then he was one of life's natural long-legs. After dabbling with the Red and White Cricket Club in Haarlem in Holland, he made his Sussex debut against Cambridge at Fenner's in

1981. Among his three victims was a budding accumulator by the name of Robin Boyd-Moss, who but for injury might well have been the first-drop England spent most of the 1980s seeking after mindlessly discarding Chris Tavaré.

Further outings came against Sri Lanka (Duleep Mendis was one of five to succumb), Gloucestershire, the Australians (another nap hand, this time featuring the likes of Kim Hughes and Graeme Wood) and, in the last match of the season, Yorkshire. Sussex embarked on that fixture knowing that victory, accompanied by a spirited Glamorgan display against the leaders, Nottinghamshire, would result in their first County Championship title. In the event, although Adrian took 4–33 to sweep Yorkshire aside on the first day at Hove, Richard Hadlee had already nudged Glamorgan halfway towards a two-day drubbing. At the end of that second day the news came through from Trent Bridge. If Ranji, Dexter and Tony Greig couldn't drag Sussex to that elusive pennant, what right did John Barclay, Imran Khan and Garth le Roux feel they had to break the chain of failure? Sussex celebrated regardless, many of the players sprinting bare-buttocked around the boundary after the close. Second place was worth celebrating too.

If Adrian's hostility and unstinting effort had drawn compliments, his figures were just as noteworthy: had he bowled in a couple more innings, his 17 wickets at less than 17 runs apiece would have left him fourth in the national averages. Some well-timed blows from the depths of the order also found favour, particularly among the fading deck chairs. Yet it was to take Adrian another four seasons to get anywhere near carving a regular niche for himself. With bowlers of the quality of Imran, le Roux, Geoff Arnold, Ian Greig and Tony Pigott all ahead of him in the pecking order, opportunities were scarce. Talk of his being injury-prone, though essentially unfounded, began to rumble. There were three Championship call-ups in 1982, five the following summer and eight the next, when his 20 wickets left him second in the county averages. There were eleven games in 1985 and another score of victims, but it was 1986 that proved his watershed. If 21 wickets at a fraction under 30 sound rather ordinary, then 43 one-day removals were certainly not. Enough to earn Adrian his county cap and to have other counties sniffing around his door when it became impossible to deny the mounting internecine ructions at Hove. Somerset stepped in with a tempting package and our boy was gone.

There was little evasion on Adrian's part when I asked about the causes and consequences of the civil strife that had forced out the then-Sussex manager Stewart Storey, along with the spunky Sri Lankan Gehan Mendis, one of the most promising and forthright openers in the country. But when the odd sheepish pause did occur, it became abundantly clear that loyalty and regret would allow his mouth to go only so far the way of his heart.

We met up again at Canterbury eighteen months later. I was walking Becker, our cocker spaniel, around the boundary. Kent, chasing the Championship, had just overwhelmed Somerset and I had already filed my story. With nary a hint of despondency, Adrian ambled over and began playing around with Becker. He said that his wife Liz had spent her childhood with dogs because her father was a breeder. They would have liked one but work got in the way. Listening intently to all of this, I playfully suggested that if he wanted to be a temporary parent, Becker would be ideal. I was planning a five-month trip to Australia with Anne, my soon-to-be-betrothed, but foster parents with a yen for over-active spaniels were thin on the ground in London. Much to my astonishment, Adrian responded enthusiastically. A week later we confirmed matters and two months after that we met on Salisbury Plain for the handing over ceremony. Another twenty-one weeks and we were there again, reversing the process. In the meantime, through Becker, we had become friends.

For Adrian, the 1989 season had been his best yet: 71 first-class wickets costing 28 apiece, a record surpassed only by Neil Foster and Paul Jarvis among English fast bowlers (as opposed to brisk medium). Then there were the 45 one-day victims (at 20.68), two more than his closest pursuer Wasim Akram. Beneath these figures lurked further reasons to feel that higher recognition might not be out of the question. All bar 8 of his 69 Championship victims were in the top eight of the order, 52 from among the first half-dozen, including 17 who had represented their country. He was also responsible for half of Somerset's four victories, taking 6–37 against Hampshire and 7–30 against Leicestershire. The frequency of legbefores and disturbed stumps bore testimony to pace and precision, counterbalanced by a goodly smattering of loose deliveries that cost plenty. A free spender rather than a careful one. Although a strike rate of a first-class wicket every 51 deliveries lagged behind the penetration of England's premier warheads, Graham Dilley (47) and Foster (50), 72 per cent of Adrian's scalps were specialist batsmen, a superior ratio to either. Compelling figures.

The action remained deceptive, that strange tippy-toed approach seeming to conceal more deliberation and control than hitherto. Bouncers were few, but the venom was indisputable and there were plenty of hasty fullish-length air-to-surface missiles that either left the prey late off the seam or thudded into his pads. The number of batsmen he clean bowled or lbw-ed far outweighed those he had caught, evidence of a commendable accuracy. Few bowlers, moreover, had quite such unquestioning self-belief.

Even so, during a tortuous summer that saw eleven specialist English seamers beat an indelible tattoo on the meat of Australia's finely-tuned bats, Adrian was ignored. This oversight was unquestionably due at least in part to what was perceived in many quarters as an overly abrasive temperament. Somerset's captain of 1989, Vic Marks, a wry, all able farmer's son and Oxford graduate who retired at the end of the season to become cricket correspondent for the *Observer*, concedes that his charge posed a few headaches.

'Jonah is very gifted and he tends to get good players out – Hick and Gooch in key one-day games, for example – but there were times when he blew a gasket. I remember Ray Julian rejecting one appeal and Adrian responding with a loud noise. He tends to reveal his frustrations, yelling or going red in the face. I don't think it's calculated, he just gets steamed up. You can't put Elastoplast over a bowler's mouth. He likes to be the focal point, to be in the limelight. He thrived on it when Neil Mallender was injured. He's also quite a dominant personality in the dressing-room, and he's very popular off the field.

'He can be difficult to captain. I found him easy-going when I wasn't leading the side, but felt less at ease when I was. He likes to test a captain's strength, to see how far he can go. Yet he was our most prolific bowler. He causes problems but he does the business. To do himself real justice he need to be fitter and take wickets more cheaply, but he's as good as anyone.'

Eric Hill, summing up Somerset's unremarkable 1989 in *Wisden*, was less specific. 'Adrian Jones led the bowling, playing in every match in spite of some injuries and occasional trouble with some authorities for his huge enthusiasm to get rid of batsmen.' One of those occasional troubles occurred during the game against Kent at Bath in mid-June. Rendered all but impotent by stultifying heat and a dormant pitch, he finally had cause to exercise those powerful lungs. A member of the Dennis Lillee School of Strident Appealing, Adrian let one go, spinning round to face the umpire, Alan Whitehead, and thus make the plea more personal. All to no avail. Rejected, he muttered some expletive to himself and then loped back to his mark. Unfortunately, some bright spark in the press box, apparently bored by the dead-end fare before him, saw fit to inflame the incident into an exchange of views. Another nail in that reputation.

Neil Mallender, aka 'Ghost', is the quieter of the Somerset opening bowlers. More often than not he gives Adrian choice of ends, rooms with him on away trips and shares driving chores. 'I am a compromiser, but Adrian wants to expose anything where he feels hard done by. He's the shop-steward type. He may not fire the bullets but he certainly loads them up, and so the players follow him. When Neil Burns, our wicket-keeper, asked Alan Knott to come for some coaching sessions at Millfield School, Adrian had to ask for Lillee.' Adrian's reasoning in this instance seemed impeccable: 'I asked if this was to be a new club policy and whether that meant the batsmen and bowlers were also likely to have the luxury of specialist coaches. People like Knotty cost a great deal.'

Adrian and Liz had every reason to feel content in Taunton. A spacious new red-brick home, hosts of other young marrieds nearby to mix with, a peaceful environment. All this and hubbie a local cult hero. During the last game of the season Adrian had been introduced to a Somerset member who also happened to be the vice-president of Hughes and Hughes Ltd, a company selling laboratory equipment and pest control, based in Essex. Four days later he took possession of a contract as a sales rep (he has since been asked to become a director) for Jarvis-Allen Ltd, an offshoot housed in Wellington and thus conveniently close to home, much to Liz's delight. So ended a period of uncertainty.

'Somerset try hard to find their players work during the winter, but it's very difficult because it isn't an industrial area. Jobs are obtained mainly through the goodwill of companies who build up relationships with players. That said, counties in general could do more to help. If we had regular winter jobs and thus two incomes, we wouldn't be such a financial burden. Of course, there's still always South Africa. Jon Hardy goes every winter because he married a South African girl, and I spent two winters in East London from 1981 to 1982, playing for Border and coaching at Selborne College, then returned later to Orange Free State in 1986 and Pretoria in 1988. But despite the fact that Jimmy Cook keeps trying to tell me to come and play for Transvaal and bowl at the Wanderers, I won't go back again. I still want to play for England and so I naturally don't want to risk the five-year ban, but my experiences in 1986 and 1988 were nightmarish anyway. There was no real accommodation on either occasion, promises were made and not kept, and, on the second occasion, my sponsor went bankrupt, I wasn't paid and I was forced to go home early. The only reason Liz and I got out as quickly as we did was because South African Airways kindly waived our return fares. The press here made a good deal of noise about that and Ali Bacher wrote to me expressing his surprise. If you are white, it is a very nice country to live in.'

His immediate future confirmed, Adrian switched his attention to the longer term. Talk of a five-year contract with Somerset had evaporated into a twelve-month agreement, not exactly a gesture designed to generate loyalty. Word of the contractual haggling reached the papers and soon the offers began to flood in. Yet money, Adrian insists, was not the be-all and end-all. 'Money was certainly not the motive for me wanting to play for Sussex again. I have a feeling for the club, for the county, but more than that, for the players. I would have fitted in nicely and they would have been a useful side again. I'm not just saying that to blow my own trumpet, but if they had another strike bowler they would be stronger. The prospect of going back home to be near my family was appealing too. But Kent were also interested, offering me a handsome package far in excess of what I was getting in Taunton. Glamorgan too, and Surrey, who have always been interested in me. I've known Chris

Waller, Geoff Arnold and Ian Greig from my Sussex days, and the Oval wickets can be of help to quicker bowlers. It also helps being in or around London if you're seeking recognition.

'In some quarters it was suggested that I was using the press to sell myself, but I rang up the Somerset chief executive, Peter Anderson, to assure him that I didn't want the publicity. He should have issued a statement denying all the rumours, but he never did. In the end, though, Liz became pregnant and that effectively made up our minds. Once having made the decision to stay, it was an enormous relief. Taunton has been good to us. We bought our first house there, I've been successful and popular with the members because of the effort I put in. I have a little fan club at long-leg. I also do a lot for the club during the off-season, opening things, picking out raffle tickets and the like, but although I'm flattered to be asked, I only do it for people I like. Cricket is my job. It's no different to being an accountant or an estate agent. And doing things like that is part of my job, to a degree. If we can help by pleasing people, why not?'

But how easy was it for Adrian to switch loyalties from Sussex to Somerset? It was certainly quicker than once was the case. Tom Graveney was given little option but to part with Gloucestershire in 1960. Michael Marshall relates in his illuminating tome *Gentlemen and Players* how Graveney was awarded his cap in an ignominious little ceremony conducted by Basil Allen, who threw it across the dressing-room in full view of Graveney's colleagues. 'You'd better have this,' said Allen. 'You'd have got it much sooner if you hadn't been so big-headed.' When Cambridge came to Bristol a couple of years later Graveney had the effrontery to call David Sheppard 'David', whereupon Allen spun round. 'He's Mister Sheppard to you,' barked the old growler, omitting to tack a 'boy' on the end. (Graveney was two years the elder, but a professional as against a gentleman undergrad.)

In 1960, less than a year after he had led Gloucestershire to the runners-up slot in the Championship, Graveney, the professional, was elbowed back to the ranks in favour of an inexperienced amateur, something that even his forbearance could not stomach. Yet the regulations then in force compelled him to spend the next summer spectating before he was permitted to don the cap of another county, Worcestershire in this case. As recently as 1972,

Bob Willis had to miss half a season before he could turn out for Warwickshire after moving from Surrey.

The guilt factor, too, is less prevalent now. Money has seen to that. And it is to the game's credit, as well as to the credit of the spectators and administrators who plug in that electric blanket of belonging, that movement between counties remains a relatively minor, if growing, source of news. Of 305 men and boys who took part in the 1989 Championship, only fifty-six had previously spilt a pint of Greene King down more than one club blazer.

True, Worcestershire won the Championship that year with a ratio of fourteen loyalists to five interlopers, a proportion that only Somerset and Gloucestershire (both of whom finished in the bottom half of the table) exceeded. That Kent (21–1) and Yorkshire (22–0) commandeered two of the last three places says precious little for the benefits of local produce, yet Essex and Middlesex, the dominant counties of the post-Packer era, are renowned for their home cooking. Furthermore, the England team chosen for the first Test against the West Indies in 1990 featured eleven one-club men; coincidence or not, high fidelity carried the day and the hype insisted that a real team had been born.

The well-travelled English county cricketer is an unusual beast. Allan Jones, now a first-class umpire, dropped in on four counties, but there have been few as fickle. Sometimes, though, a change of scenery can be beneficial to a career. Chris Broad left Gloucestershire for Nottinghamshire because he felt his efforts were not attracting enough attention and that switching to a more visible club would enhance his Test prospects. But maybe it was merely coincidence that his international debut occurred during his first season at Trent Bridge. John Childs was a 33-year-old underachiever when Essex re-leased him from Gloucestershire, yet he could have worn an England cap long before he finally did four summers later.

Temptations are few. The homegrown county pro is rarely a target for those under-the-counter, back-of-a-cab sweeteners so beloved by football clubs, if perhaps only because the priority lies with financing overseas imports. In the opinion of Adrian and a good many of his contemporaries, they are fettered by a gaoler referred to as The Benefit, which is basically an opportunity to sell your body to a county for ten years in exchange for a near six-figure golden handshake. Should you leave your original county six years after your debut, as Adrian did, you run the risk of not playing long enough to get another chance to secure your future.

The advent of major sponsorship is beginning to ease the squeeze, enabling Worcestershire to spring such coups as the signing of Botham and Dilley, and permitting less well-endowed clubs like Somerset and Glamorgan to hang on to their assets. This, Adrian believes, should not preclude serious contemplation of a fully-fledged transfer system. Not that he finds it desirable, just that that may be the only solution if things get out of hand. 'At the moment we're moving towards an us-and-them scenario. If you've got the money, as some counties have, then you can afford to go for the best and so you'll keep on winning trophies, while the poorer counties have to live off what's left. I'd favour the American football draft system, whereby the lower you finish, the earlier your pick of the best young players is. Then again, we don't exactly have cricketers pouring out of our colleges, do we?'

A limitation on one registered overseas player per county was due to enter the equation in 1991, conjuring up visions of an almighty free-for-all as domestic talent becomes more valuable. Adrian's concern for a more equitable arrangement is therefore even more pertinent. But should he end the 1990 season at loggerheads with Somerset, there seemed little likelihood of him simply grinning and bearing it.

4 Autumn: David Hughes

b Newton-le-Willows,13 May 1947.

Career to start of 1990: Lancashire debut, 1967. Awarded cap in 1970. Benefit, 1981. Also played for Tasmania, 1975–77. Toured South Africa with D. H. Robbins's party in 1972– 73 and West Indies with English counties' team in 1974–75. *Wisden* Cricketer of the Year 1988. Lancashire captain, 1987 to date. 421 first-class appearances. 626 wickets at 29.86. 5 wickets in an innings twenty times. 10 wickets in a match twice. Best bowling: 7–24 v. Oxford University in The Parks on 23rd birthday in 1970 (match figures 11–78). Bowled thirteen consecutive maidens at Bristol in 1980. 10,071 runs at 21.79, including eight centuries. Highest score: 153 v. Glamorgan at Old Trafford in 1983. 1,000 runs in a season twice (1,303 in 1982 was the best). 308 catches. One-day record: 242 wickets, including 169 at 21.11 in the Refuge Assurance/John Player Leagues; 4,620 runs including 801 at 36.40 in the NatWest/Gillette competitions.

Leaves of brown they fall to the ground
And it's here, over there leaves around
Shut the door, dim the lights and relax
What is more, your desire or the facts.

(Van Morrison, *Autumn Song*)

He may be known as Yosser in dressing-rooms the length and breadth of the land, but there is an immense disparity between this vigorous and fiercely proud Lancastrian and the tragic oaf invented by Alan Bleasdale to characterise the casualties of Thatcherite England. The son of a former Bolton League professional, Lloyd Hughes, David was born in Newton-le-Willows in South Lancashire as Denis Compton and Bill Edrich were moving into their gluttonous stride in that sun-drenched, run-saturated season of 1947. Educated at the local grammar school, he represented the town in the Manchester Association before following Lloyd into the League, turning out for Farnworth, rather than his father's old mates at Walkden. At 18 David fulfilled his boyhood ambition, joining Lancashire Club and Ground as a left-arm spinner who might one day put bat to ball pleasingly. At a shade under six foot tall and favoured with strong, supple fingers, he soon demanded attention and within two years was the leading wicket-taker for the 2nd XI. His first-class debut came during that same Summer of Love, 1967, against Oxford University at Old Trafford, his inaugural victim obliging with undue haste before lunch on the first day as Jack Bond caught another D. P., Toft, an elegant opener who would stroke 145 in the Varsity match a week later. David claimed a second wicket before the close, but the students were by then well on their way towards a declaration, almost unthinkable these days. David's involvement from then on was minimal. Listed at eight, he was never needed at the crease, while his second innings bowling stint amounted to a single, costly over.

Although that turned out to be it for that summer, he would at least glean the satisfaction of another chance, unlike David Saunders van der Knaap, an 18-year-old Johannesburg-raised off-spinner and late middle-order bat. Van der Knaap, if *Wisden* is to be trusted, took 2–69 in the match, as did David, dismissing Toft and Watson in the second innings; and so ended the briefest of trials. Although he is listed in the Lancashire Yearbook for 1968, and in various histories of the club, the South African's county career record remains a complete blank, since he is quoted as having neither batted nor bowled. For the next dozen years, 'D.S.' would play for Transvaal, as powerful as any Test side during that period, alongside the likes of Clive Rice, Ali Bacher and Jimmy Cook.

David's introduction to serious county cricket came at Canterbury on 4 May 1968, Lancashire's ambitions for the season already halved by their Gillette Cup exit at Trent Bridge a week previously. He made a single first time up, bowled by Asif Iqbal, one of seven once and future Test players on the Kent roster. No disgrace in that, given Lancashire's demise for 69 on a rain-affected pitch, followed as it was by an equally derisory Kent total of 83. David fared better in the second dig, adding 48 with Ken Shuttleworth for the ninth wicket. Then, when Kent were nearing victory on a less hazardous surface, came the first notch on the locker door: M. C. Cowdrey caught Higgs bowled Hughes 28. A spirited start.

Although he contributed some twinkling 20s and 30s at fifth wicket down behind David Lloyd, Barry Wood, Harry Pilling, Farokh Engineer, Ken Snellgrove and Jack Bond, David found himself back in the 2nd XI by June, stymied by seaming pitches and inordinately damp weather. His first Roses innings brought an unbeaten 30 as Lancashire slithered towards an innings defeat against the county champions in the first week of June. By the return fixture in August, a benefit match for that sterling servant Ken Higgs, Hughes was playing in front of 21,000 and ejecting Ray Illingworth. Southport was the scene of his first 'five-fer', the last five to fall in the Derbyshire second innings, Messrs Harvey, Eyre, Taylor, Smith and Jackson, craggy names in a journeyman team. More illustrious were the half-dozen at Weston-super-Mare: Roy Virgin, Greg Chappell, Bill Alley, Roy Kerslake, Graham Burgess and Roy Palmer. After 9 wickets there, 29 at 22 for the season, embellished by a maiden 50 at Edgbaston against the spin of Lance Gibbs, Eddie Hemmings and Bob Barber: progress had been made.

In 1969 Lancashire had their first outright victory in a major competition since the 1934 Championship. John Player's County League was made for that Lancashire side. Plenty of forceful strokeplayers, a battery of accurate seamers and, crucially, a batch of bits'n'pieces players, men who, like the average club regular, could bat a bit, bowl a bit and be depended on to do something or other of use. A positive attitude to the new arrival was also influential. Jack Bond, a captain who relied on commonsense and a personable nature rather than leadership by example, welcomed it as a way of 'letting off steam', claiming that it could be 'the making of cricket. We may not like sacrificing first-class principles in order to provide a spectacle, but it is worth a try.' The idea, he stressed, was to 'enjoy ourselves; if we do that the crowds must surely enjoy themselves too.'

Victory in three-quarters of their Sunday sorties gave Lancashire the title by a point from Hampshire, the gap represented by the predictable abandonment of the first 40-over Roses contest – the sitting tenants who occupy that dirty old cloud above Old Trafford never did respect new-fangled contraptions. David played his part, 10 wickets at 26.6 and a cost of less than 4 runs an over, a precious sense of economy between those young ears. He also averaged over 25 with the bat at a brimming Old Trafford, where 6 of his wickets came; a sense of occasion too.

David also made his 60-over debut that summer. This time Lancashire entered the fray in June as opposed to April, but their fate was no different, Yorkshire easing home by 7 wickets in front of a near five-figure crowd at Old Trafford. David strode in rather gingerly at 111 for 6, Lancashire's top order having been lured to the abyss by Don Wilson after starting out with all the urgency of a comatose snail. David's unbeaten 29 did no more than delay the inevitable, but, combined with nine tight overs, it constituted another in a sequence of encouraging beginnings.

The following year David built on them. He removed Lancashire's bulkiest obstacle in the Gillette semi-final against Somerset by dismissing Virgin, then clean bowled (or 'teased out' as *Wisden* put it) the menacing Sussex middle-order of Parks, Greig and Graves in the Final to keep the long-acknowledged one-day monarchs down to a manageable 184 for 9. David also imposed himself on the decisive John Player match at Old Trafford, where, watched by 33,000, the first full house Lancashire had had since 1948, he dispatched Sharpe and Hampshire leg-before as Yorkshire strove to step up the rate, Red Rose duly retaining the 40-over title.

Lancashire also came within 22 points of a unique treble, finishing third in the Championship behind Kent and Glamorgan. David took 66 wickets, nearly a fifth of the county's aggregate haul, following up with 73 twelve months later as Lancashire fell even shorter, 14 points to the rear of Surrey and Warwickshire. Not for another sixteen years would they get that close to the honour the club so craved. Gold medals are all very well in the sprints, but even today they mean zilch when compared to winning the marathon.

It transpired that David, as a bowler anyway, had peaked too. In the estimation of John Kay, writing his annual post-mortem in *Wisden*, he had yet to learn 'to spin the ball viciously'. He was also still a trifle expensive for comfort. This was the Underwood era, after all. The nearest David would get to wider recognition was a tour of South Africa with D. H. Robbins in 1972–73, when he might reasonably have expected to be on the subcontinent with Tony Lewis and the England team. One local observer described the visiting spin attack as short on 'guile and penetration'. Of such comments, particularly when they appear in the tablet of stone slabbed down between *Wisden*'s yellow covers, are reputations made and broken. In David's case, they scarcely served as good PR.

Not that his expectations were especially high. 'With Underwood and Gifford plying their wares on uncovered wickets in the early 1970s, what chance was there? I played in a couple of MCC trials and thought I acquitted myself well, but Underwood was always there. I think I was close to selection for Tony Lewis's tour to India, but they went for experience and took Gifford. I missed the first three months of 1973 with suspected cartilage problems in my knee, which necessitated cortisone injections and a plaster cast, and that was effectively it. But if I'd have been the David Hughes of 1970 and 1971 [he took 82 and 79 wickets during those two summers, becoming the first slow left-armer to top the Lancashire wicket-taking lists since Malcolm Hilton in 1956] in 1990, I'd have been pushing Keith Medlycott, Phil Tufnell and Andy Afford. It is my one sadness in cricket that my bowling never reaped any rewards in international terms.

'I always felt I was a bowler first and foremost, but the advent of the John Player League left me going in for a slog at No. 8 or 9. The reputation I derived may well have detracted from people's view of me as a bowler. Once Bond left, David Lloyd succeeded him as captain and wanted to bowl slow left-arm himself; then Frank Hayes replaced him and he was more pace-oriented. Wickets at Old Trafford helped the seamers then. Having deteriorated since the early 1970s it was now going sideways. The ball was leaving juicy marks on the pitch and seaming all over the place. Bert Flack, the groundsman, lost control. Simmo [Jack Simmons] kept it tight, and I lost out to the extra seamer. Now the pitches are back to par under Peter Marron's guidance. He completely relaid the square and it's simply magnificent.'

Magnificent was just one of a host of complimentary adjectives bestowed upon David in the wake of his fifteen minutes under the full beam of the national spotlight. The date: 28 July 1971. The stage: where else but Old Trafford? The show: Lancashire against

Gloucestershire in the Gillette Cup semi-final. There were more notable events afoot. Labour were trying to force an election to determine once and for all whether Britain should join hands with the six members of the EEC. The editors of *Oz*, a radical underground newspaper, would be found guilty the very next day of publishing an obscene article, despite the claim of one witness for the defence, the comedian Marty Feldman, that the Bible was heavier on such supposed immoralities. *Gimme Shelter*, a film portraying the circumstances surrounding the death of a fan at a Rolling Stones concert two years earlier, later cited by Don McLean as 'the day the music died', was released in London. 'You could call it the epic of a self-destructive nation . . . what you can't do is ignore or deny it,' wrote Derek Malcolm in the *Guardian*.

Neither, though, could the Great British Public, particularly those with a sporting bent, ignore or deny the import of proceedings at Old Trafford. At Lord's the day before John Snow had barged Sunil Gavaskar, by some distance his physical inferior, to the floor during the first Test between England and India, albeit accidentally. In the *Daily Express* a cartoon by the inimitable Roy Ulyett depicted the consequences of violence spreading to the cricket field, concluding with the prediction that: '. . . Harry Levene will be the next President of MCC'. Forget drug-crazed hairies and the prospect of bedding down with a bunch of foreigners. It was the potential degeneration of cricket that was really rotting the very fabric of Life As We Knew It.

The one-day bastard son had yet to establish the grip it holds now. The first limited overs international had taken place as recently as the start of the year (*Wisden* even refused to allot the contest the courtesy of a full scorecard). Only the 1968 60-over Final, moreover, had truly managed to instil excitement into a one-day showpiece. Even then, some disciples were sacrificed when Alan 'AC' Smith led Warwickshire to victory in the half-light after ITV had offended a sizeable audience by truncating coverage of the vital overs. Even in 1990, commercial television has yet to be entrusted with relaying domestic Tests or the principal one-day games (internationals and the NatWest), indicating the gravity of the offence. It was nonetheless becoming self-evident, as various batty bonus point schemes were experimented with in the

Championship, that English cricket needed to come up with an alternative ruse to entice Paul and Paula Punter through the turnstiles. Guaranteeing a result in a day had been a step in the necessary direction, but the bug had yet to catch on in the way sponsors and administrators had hoped. At the start of the 1970s, Nottinghamshire were the only first-class county not in the red.

Lancashire and Gloucestershire, as well as the other two Gillette Cup semi-finalists, Kent and Warwickshire, therefore took the field that Wednesday with a couple of additional burdens: to restore faith in cricket as a guide to The Proper Way and to help ensure its future. With Clive Lloyd and Mike Procter on opposing sides, however, Manchester seemed the likelier venue to offer salvation. The Guyanan, Lloyd, long on stature, languid of stroke and lithe in the field, had been the chief catalyst, in a playing sense, for Lancashire's rejuvenation. Gloucestershire, though yet to win anything, were similarly indebted to Procter. The feline menace of his batting, his javelin-like throws and frugal bowling made Lloyd one of the first great one-day players. Procter, if anything, had the edge. One of the best fast bowlers of his generation, a ferocious, yet never incorrect, hitter and a sound fielder. Had South Africa not been thrown off the Test circuit, Prockie would now enjoy a standing commensurate to that of Sobers and Botham. If any manager can extract maximum effort and consistency from Northamptonshire in 1991, he can.

Yet Lloyd was more than just an inspiration to his team-mates. Learie Constantine notwithstanding, he was the first West Indian sportsman to emerge as a focal point for the immigrant population of Britain. Sobers didn't hang around at Trent Bridge long enough to achieve that kind of ripple effect, and besides, he had already been everywhere and done pretty much everything by the time he arrived in 1968. Lloyd had only recently annexed a place in the West Indies middle-order when he first turned out for Lancashire. John Conteh was still a Liverpool labourer, Viv Anderson had yet to sign apprentice forms with Nottingham Forest and the young Daley Thompson probably thought 'decathlon' was a new kind of choc bar. Them were the days when people of Conteh's hue were referred to in the *Daily Express* as 'cafe-au-lait-coloured'. Little wonder Lloyd was welcomed as a blood-red Lancastrian long before he was granted citizenship.

Not that Lloyd and Lancashire entered their duel with Procter and his assistants in exactly the mint of condition. Eighteen hours earlier their Championship game against Somerset, never in the breeziest of health, had died a protracted death. The torpor had driven Eric Todd of the *Guardian* to pen the following lament: 'The sight of Brian Close studying the speculative off-breaks of Harry Pilling with the same concentration he once gave to the leg-breaks of Richie Benaud was the most striking commentary on a game which, for sheer futility and boredom, seldom can have been surpassed.' Clearly, something had been held in reserve, not least by David, who bowled four overs for 9 runs and didn't take guard.

The gates were locked half an hour before the first hurrah and, at 11 a.m., ringed by an audience of 23,520 paying receipts of £9,738, Ron Nicholls and David Green embarked on the Gloucestershire innings. Undeterred by the loss of an hour through rain, the visitors, hustled along by Procter's 65, reached 229 for 6, a total whose merits are enhanced all the more when one considers that only four counties had ever made more than 250 batting second in such games. That season, the highest had been Lancashire's 217 for 4 against Worcestershire in the second round. David, unusually, had been unable to slow the momentum, having Roger Knight caught improbably at long-leg but giving up more than a quarter of the runs. Harnessed by Procter and the underrated left-armer, Jack Davey, David Lloyd and Barry Wood gave Lancashire a steady rather than vigorous launch, but 105 for 1 declined to 163 for 6, John Mortimore, a spindly former Test off-spinner still to relinquish his powers of persuasion, bowling 'Hubert' Lloyd and compelling Engineer to hit his own wicket to expose the Lancashire odd-job men. Rendered more murky than normal by the smoke belching from a nearby chimney, the light was considered bad enough at 7.30 for umpires Bird and Jepson to consult for a second time, then give the order to carry on. Stretching forward to locate the ball more in hope than expectation, and withstanding a 'fierce bodyline barrage from the South African [Procter]' (James Lawton in the *Express*), Bond and Simmons rustled up 40 in seven overs to bring the target within compass. But when Mortimore bowled Simmons with 27 needed and six overs remaining, the fast-reducing visibility appeared to be drawing a curtain on the chase.

At 8.45 the lights of Warwick Road station were in sufficient evidence to evoke Piccadilly Circus; the 8.30 special to Bristol had got fed up waiting. Mortimore to Hughes to start the 56th over, Lancashire requiring 25. Feet splayed in the neo-classical fashion of the thrasher, David drilled the first ball for 4. The next soared for 6. Home hearts were pumping, Mortimore's waning. A couple of scampered, more orthodox 2s, then another boundary-bound blow. With 7 wanted and the issue now settled, David propelled the last ball of a famous over gleefully to the outer reaches for a second 6. Sedate and secure now, Bond prised a single from the fifth delivery of Procter's next over, and Lancashire were there. At 8.55, the crowd released a roar, part relief, part disbelief. And the Beeb stayed with it to the joyous end.

Meanwhile, at Canterbury, David Nicholls of Kent, a batsman broader yet no loftier than Gavaskar, administered the gentlest of barges to Warwickshire's lofty seamer, Bill Blenkiron, who reeled away in mock anguish. This time the witnesses howled with laughter. Within a few short hours the legacy of Snow's clumsiness had been laid to rest.

The next day David tarted himself up for the cameras and posed with a bottle of champagne poised over twenty-four glasses, one for every run of that 56th over. A few weeks later he encored, bashing an unbeaten 25 in the last four overs of Lancashire's innings in the final against Kent. Asif Iqbal then caressed Lord's into backing Knott and company before Bond cut him down with a flying catch at extra-cover that for any player, let alone a supposed non-athlete of 39, was stupendous. The following summer a third wham-bang competition, the Benson & Hedges Cup, came into being. Now fings were definitely not what they used to be.

Moving on another decade and a half, we find David ready to give up the game. He had seen just about everything county cricket had to offer. A snowstorm at Buxton in June; a Danish fast bowler, Soren Henriksen by name, holding back the waves of a Worcestershire onslaught; Lancashire bowled out twice in a day by an equally unimpressive Northamptonshire at Old Trafford, then creaming highly-ranked Leicestershire at Grace Road in the very next match; conceding an English record fourth-wicket stand of 470 at Southport and still beating Warwickshire by 10 wickets; White

Rose drawing Red blood in the Championship, in Manchester. Converted from a bowler who could bat into a valued member of the middle order who could bowl if absolutely necessary, he had scored 601 Championship runs at 20.03 per innings in 1984. His output with the ball, mind, gave even those figures a respectable sheen, seventy-six overs bringing one wicket at a cost of 219 runs. Lancashire, coincidentally, conducted their worst Championship campaign in 110 years that summer: one win in twenty-four, 4 points clear of their first bottom-place finish. David made half as many appearances in 1985, improved his average to 24 and reduced his bowling output to 126 deliveries as Lancashire finished fourteenth, denied a consoling Benson & Hedges Cup triumph this time. Arguably, this was the real slough of despond. Fourteenth in the Sunday League, bottom in their Benson & Hedges zonal group and ejected from the NatWest in round two, Lancashire were proceeding towards realms of humility even Yorkshire had yet to dredge.

David was 39, a young, enthusiastic and totally dedicated 39 but nonetheless consigned to 2nd XI obscurity and out of love with his employers. Though as popular a figure as ever, his imperturbable nature had been stretched to the limit by the persistent feeling that Lancashire's plans did not include him. He had even gone as far as to write a letter of resignation. Distracted by Lancashire's domination of the 2nd XI competition, he held it back and ultimately alleviated the shame of another highly undistinguished summer for the county by leading a team containing likely young lads such as Mike Atherton and Graham Lloyd to a morale-enhancing triumph. Within weeks he had been appointed captain in succession to the retiring Clive Lloyd, a decision that so astonished one former skipper that he proclaimed it to be the worst appointment the club had ever made and threatened to return his treasured cap and blazer as a token of his disgust.

The nomination of the widely-respected Alan Ormrod to coach and manage helped David offset such discouragement, and the pair set about repairing the hull of *SS Lancashire*. Before the start of the 1987 season, David spoke to each member of the first-team squad in turn, spelling out what was required: utter commitment and perfect behaviour on and off the field. If the intention was to re-emphasise the importance of pride as a performance fuel, the ploy succeeded.

Second in the Championship, their best placing for twenty-seven summers, was the immediate result, followed by the Refuge Cup in 1988 and the Refuge League in 1989. More encouragingly, for the first time since 1960, Lancashire strung together three successive top nine finishes in the Championship. Although still a gutsy, fly-papered livewire close to the wicket, David did little statistically to help usher in this new era, as three 50s in ninety-one innings and 14 wickets in 124.1 overs underline. Jibes about a return to fashion for the non-playing captain could be heard, but were drowned out, more often than not, by gratitude for his galvanising influence. In fact, when *Wisden* named him as one of its Five Cricketers of the Year for 1987, his reaction was aptly modest: 'Perhaps I have underestimated my own contributions'. Just as no other team sport allows captains to command a regular place more or less regardless of personal form and achievement, so no other team sport depends so much on the skills of leadership.

'When I took over the captaincy in 1986, our Championship record was appalling. What was worse, we were playing negatively. I simply tried from the start to play attractively, to try and have games of cricket with people. I also inherited an unmanageable staff of thirty-one players, one full of uncapped players in their mid-20s being pressed by youngsters. I felt we needed more experience and youth, but of course I found it difficult to think in terms of hiring and firing. Now we've a staff of about twenty-five, seventeen of whom are 24 and under.

'In 1987, we were motivated by the feeling that we'd been mocked for a long time. We hadn't won the Championship outright for fifty-three years, and I wanted to leave cricket with Lancashire being feared again. We finished 4 points short and caught the imagination of the Lancashire public. In 1988 we finished ninth in the Championship mainly through injuries to our overseas players at vital times, but won the Refuge Cup. In 1989 we won the Refuge League, but the same injury problems beset us for four Championship games in July and August when we were without both Patrick Patterson and Wasim Akram. Given the quality of our staff and the type of fellows they are, we *should* be winning things.

'We made three really good signings in Wasim, Trevor Jesty and Phil DeFreitas. The first time I saw Wasim, he whipped out five

Australian batsmen through sheer pace, Kepler Wessels and Kim Hughes among them, to win a one-day international in 1985. Two years later we signed him on a six-year contract, which is still unheard-of. Even then, with Hadlee in decline as a batsman, Botham and Dev as bowlers, I saw him becoming the new leading all-rounder in world cricket, and that's what he is. But one of the problems with overseas players is that the sheer quantity of international cricket means that they can't possibly give of their best at all times.

'Not least because I was brought up in a side with Engineer and Lloyd, I've always been a supporter of overseas players. There can be no finer learning process than batting with Clive. Paul Allott had his best county season when Michael Holding was with us in 1981. I'd like to see counties allowed to sign two overseas players, one from each discipline.'

Of course, matter was creeping up on mind's shoulder as 1989 gave way to 1990. For the first time since 1968 Lancashire would begin a season without 'Flat Jack' Simmons, but if that constituted a hint, David did not take it. He is not, however, the type to kid himself. Whereas the physical demands of the game were once sufficiently lax to allow Wilfred Rhodes to play Test cricket at 52, David acknowledged that he could not expect to see much service in the new decade.

'I feel as if I'm in my last couple of seasons now, but I'm in a situation where the enthusiasm and love are still there. In a game that now demands ever-increasing fitness standards and therefore requires much more from you physically, I feel I've kept very fit. Indeed, there's a definite incentive for me to outfield the younger guys. I can't find anyone else who fancies fielding short-leg in the three-day games, still less a natural for the position, so I carry on there.' To anyone who has ever evaded his captain's line of vision when he requests volunteers for 'Boot Hill' duty, such devotion to self-inflicted discomfort is the stuff of Custer and Horatio. Worthy as hell, and quite bonkers.

Mike Atherton, the bookies' favourite to lead England into the 21st century, was unaccustomed to being given orders when he joined the Lancashire staff, having been in charge of teams since he first attended Manchester Grammar. His admiration for David's leadership is thus all the more pertinent. 'It's an age-old argument as to whether a player can be worth his place for his captaincy alone, and I'm sitting on the fence, but I've learned from his tough, enterprising approach. He believes we should win every game and he's mortified when we don't. But he brings players up with an attitude of not being scared to lose. His strengths include experience, obviously; he's been through good times and bad. He shows faith in you too; as a bowler I'm a bit inconsistent, but he always lets me set my own field.

'He is also very good at setting targets and declarations and, perhaps most important of all, his man-management is sound. Neil Fairbrother and I had an argument in the middle during a game against Hampshire and then carried it on when we got back to the changing-rooms. Someone else may have let it run on. Instead, he took us into the captain's room and sorted it out immediately. He gets on with, and mucks in with, all the Lancashire players. We play golf and drink together. He doesn't treat you as a junior, either. At team meetings he's happy for the younger guys to have their say and he expects you to play like an experienced player whatever your age. And you don't notice the age gap in the field because Yosser's still an exceptionally agile fielder and because he's still bubbly and young at heart.'

As befits a self-employed local dignitary, David spreads himself during the off-season. There's an insurance brokerage in Bolton and consultancy work (under the aegis of the David Hughes Consultancy) for Stuart Canvas Products, the leading manufacturer of covers in county cricket and originators of the 'bubble' covers at Cardiff, Chelmsford, Worcester and Old Trafford. He is also a member of the editorial board of, and a monthly contributor to, *Cricket World* magazine and has his musings translated into a weekly column for the *Manchester Evening News*. In addition, along with Clive Radley and Tom Graveney, he helps fillet out deserving causes for investment managers Whittingdales, who struck a deal with the TCCB in 1989 to support bright young cricketing things during the off-season (and thus dissuade them from skipping off to South Africa); Martin Bicknell and Nasser Hussain were the initial selections, incidentally. A free, perceptive talker who could gabble the *Test Match Special* team under the table and still keep his marbles intact, David would dearly love to be a commentator one day, although he pictures himself moving towards the rear of the spotlight. 'If I stayed in cricket I imagine myself on the administration side, commercially, organising and man-management. I'll help out if someone wants to know about bowling left-arm slow, but I'm definitely no full-time coach.'

Any further considerations of future plans are generally tucked away in the farthermost regions of David's mind. Still infatuated with playing up and playing the game. Once bitten, forever smitten.

5 Another Season

Another season, another chance
Another reason to dance this dance
Another endless motorway trance
Another flirt with glory?

Another year, another start
Another tussle with this artful art
Another test of soul and heart
Another bid to play a part?

Another bat, another box
Another pair of boots and socks
Another saga of crocks and clocks
Another spell with fortune?

Another wicket, another run
Another catch – perhaps some sun
Another dose of friends and fun
– another season's work is done.

Thursday 12 April, West Hampstead

Spring is sprung, the grass is riz, wonder where the cricket is. These days, with seasons seeming to begin almost before the first cuckoo, impatience is unnecessary, in 1990 less so than ever. Play is scheduled to commence on 14 April, three days before the end of England's tour of the Caribbean. In 1980 the whistle went on 23 April; in 1970 on 22 April. The finishing post, some 160 days distant, is as unusually late as the start is early. Heigh-ho, away we go.

Time was when pre-season training was a lap or three at the height of the April shower season, a few nets and some elbow exercise at the local hostelry. For the really dedicated there was the swift perusal of *Wisden* and *Playfair* to check the winter's comings and goings, sound off about the nominations for the Five Cricketers of the Year and confirm how many people had a career record inferior to yours. Or, if that search proved fruitless, how many had endured a worse time the previous year.

'Training is almost a twelve-month operation now,' David assures any disbelievers. 'And, come November, those Lancashire players who don't go on tour are each given a personal fitness programme. At the end of January we start to meet a couple of times each week and the level of activity mounts from then on as the season draws closer.' Not unsurprisingly, David feels that pre-season tours can also help improve a side's performance during the subsequent months. For Lancashire, the practice of packing the boys off somewhere warm and vaguely exotic began when a Liverpool firm offered to underwrite a trip to Jamaica in 1988. They kindly repeated the offer the following winter and then the club stepped in to finance a short tour of Zimbabwe. The 1989–90 close season had brought an even more ambitious trek: three and a half weeks to Perth, Tasmania and Singapore. If Lancashire were in trim, then so were the county books. Spurred on by expectation of a victorious year, members have been signing and re-signing, raising subscription income towards hitherto unattained levels. For the third season on the trot, the membership list is set to close, this time at 13,300. Better still, women are now entitled to become full members. MCC, sadly, remain staunchly reluctant to take note.

Nadeem remained near the source of the Fremantle Doctor until the end of March, seeing plenty of the middle. Whilst there, he received instructions from Essex on how to maintain fitness and underwent a six-week course on his tod, rising at 6a.m. for an hour of running and circuit training before breakfast. Upon his return he was plunged into three weeks of even more intense bodily abuse. Cracking the whip was Colin Tomlin, an athletics coach who had put the England party through their paces at Lilleshall before their Caribbean crusade, honing the players into the fittest combo ever to leave these shores. Every day from 9 to 4 the Essex first team squad pounded the Chelmsford perimeter and the neighbouring park under his stewardship, doing timed runs of three and five miles as well as circuit training, and even undergoing bleep tests to assess heart rates.

Adrian, meanwhile, has been hard at it in his local sports club every lunchtime since mid-January. Cycling, running, lifting weights, anything to oil that motor for the sapping routes that lie ahead. 'Because of my asthma I need to work harder than ever on my stamina if I want to fulfil myself and give myself a chance of playing Test cricket. I feel as if I may have been given an opportunity before now and I know I wouldn't have let either myself or my country down. But then I think the same could be said of many players in county cricket this coming season. There are so many good players.'

That much is beyond dispute, but then a year ago some had been made to look a good deal better than they were. That – 1989 – was the year of the granite seam, the fifteen-strand Reader concoction that reduced even the very best batsmen to clueless gropers while elevating some decidedly fortunate medium-paced mediocres to the ranks of the unplayable. But opinion is divided over whether seam or surface was the more villainous. That Worcestershire finished the season topping the Championship and propping up the Pitches Table of Merit – a drop of one from their position following another Championship triumph twelve months previously – appeared to direct the finger of suspicion towards the groundsmen. Or, rather, those whose instructions they obeyed, sometimes over-zealously.

Something Had To Be Done. And, of course, suggestions have not been slow in coming forward. A poll conducted by *The Cricketer* magazine produced some revealing insights. Chris Broad, arguably the most dependable left-handed English opener since John Edrich, but recently exiled for five years along with another fifteen bounty hunters for wintering in South Africa, claimed that 'there has been too much skullduggery from captains and committees'. A Glamorgan regular said he had 'hardly played on a good wicket for the last three or four seasons'. Norman Gifford, the Sussex coach, stressed the need for 'a programme of re-laying throughout the country'. Tim Robinson, another Nottinghamshire Test player contemplating a shadowy future, narrowed down the variables into a question of priorities: 'There should only be one aim, either to improve cricket standards and the England team, or to win at all costs.' Coming from one of the more negative county captains, such sentiments sounded rather rich, but there was little to quarrel with in Robinson's analysis.

Four-day cricket was held by the majority of county captains and many other prominent voices to be a step along the road to reaffirmation, but thus far the tool has been wielded half-heartedly. The counties, concerned that a full four-day programme would mean a cutback in both sponsors and the even more lucrative festival weeks, set their stall out to foil any attempts to mess with a trusty formula. 'The TCCB talks complete cock and balderdash', proffered one Derbyshire member after hearing the board's cricket chairman, Ossie Wheatley, advocate a four-day Championship. Compromise, as ever, won the day. A meaningless combination of six four-day games and sixteen three-day games per county became law in 1988. Neither one thing or the other. But since the real duration of a match is determined by outside forces, pitches most of all, the decision not to tamper with the balance this 1990 season, reached by a majority of twelve to six at the TCCB spring meeting, bothered few outside the ruling classes. More than anything this seemed to be a nose-tweaking exercise, the board's cricket committee of Micky Stewart, A. C. Smith, Wheatley and Ted Dexter (who had hotfooted it from Zimbabwe to attend the pow-wow), seeing its latest proposal for a four-day Championship thrown out by a fourteen to four margin. For once, a regrettable revolution.

The TCCB's predicament is plain enough. In 1989 they unveiled their nuclear deterrent, a 25-point deduction for counties who failed to prepare a satisfactory surface. Essex fell foul of the tripwire and so effectively lost the Championship. Nottinghamshire, too, were punished, but many more could have followed suit. The expected reversion to even-handed pitches had not occurred to the degree expected, and the whole process was further sabotaged by the accursed Reader ball. Now, in reducing the number of strands in the seam by 40 per cent, and emphasising their intention to monitor pitch behaviour even more closely, the TCCB have filled bowlers with trepidation, those relying on movement off the wicket more than any. It will not be enough to produce a featherbed. It must be a straw-coloured featherbed (or was that beige with a hint of lemon?), topped off by a soupçon of grass. The official definition of the 'perfect' pitch, upon the advice of Harry Brind, the TCCB pitch inspector, is one capable of 'helping the batsmen, but with some pace in it'. In the effort to correct the balance between bat and ball, these were fine sentiments that purported to reward the virtuous rather than the middling. For once, apparently, a worthy regulation to add to the pile. However, the impression that the pendulum might swing the other way is inescapable.

It is futile to point to the game's healthy financial state as any compensation. In 1978, the Packer Revolt prompted Cornhill, a fairly anonymous insurance firm, to sponsor, and tack their name on to, England's home Tests. It was the first true indication of what English cricket was prepared to do in order to flourish as a viable business, and the surge in commercial awareness and marketing activity that ensued was inevitable. Receipts for international games, a large percentage of which are distributed among the counties, remain primarily responsible for the five-figure-plus surpluses that are becoming par for the course. But how much longer can they maintain a level high enough to sustain an industry? England's 4–0 humbling by Australia in 1989, capping a four-year winless run on home soil, augured ill. But lo, in the second of this infant decade's sporting shocks, Gooch led an England shorn of Broad, Dilley, Foster, Gatting, Emburey, Botham and Gower to victory at Sabina Park in February, mangling a myth in much the same way as Buster Douglas had felled the unfellable Mike Tyson in Tokyo around the same time. I was in Zimbabwe with the England A party at the time, but even in Southern Africa it was as if Mafeking had been relieved and Waterloo taken on the same day. In sporting terms, only Headingley 1981 and Wembley 1966 had given rise to such partisan fervour and unsuppressed joy back in Blighty, natural reserve flung to the winds like an unwanted raincoat at the onset of summer. The next Test, in Trinidad, would have provided an action replay but for rain and some shameless go-slow tactics by the half-beaten hosts, who had got their breath back by the time the Guyanan Test had been washed out and did much as they pleased in the last two games to claim the series. Honour and hope in defeat, then, but ultimately still losers. England have now emerged victorious from just one of their last ten series.

If anything, though, the most significant goings-on of the winter occurred in New Zealand and Pakistan. Amid the serenity of Lancaster Park, Christchurch, surrounded by swaying elms, emerald parks and roving hills, there took place a pantomime of the lowest order. Playing for Canterbury against Wellington, the Shell Trophy at stake, wicket-keeper Lee Germon faced up to the penultimate over with his side 8 wickets down and nearly 100 short. In order to tempt Canterbury back into the debate, Germon was allowed to mash 68 off an over from the obliging Kiwi Test batsman, Bert Vance, who stood at the crease to purvey lobs, and also gave paceman Ford a boundary, in the course of a 22-ball travesty of the sport that altogether cost 77 runs. In fact, there should have been 23 deliveries in the over, since Vance served up 17 deliberate no-balls, but an understandably perplexed umpire lost count. So much time had elapsed, moreover, that Vance and his colleagues were deprived of 4 penalty points. To cap it all, Ford blocked the final ball of the match, leaving Canterbury 1 run short of the victory that would have given his team at least a share of this particular damned urn. Sadly, because of the rapidity with which the scoreboard had been changing, incorrectly for the most part, Ford's two-fingered gesture was inadvertent.

Better news by far had come four months before, in Karachi, when one black Englishman, John Holder, and one white one, John Hampshire, took charge of the first Test between India and Pakistan, thus beginning the first series in which neutral umpires had officiated from gun to tape. Along with thuggish bowling, though only fractionally more reprehensible than fictitious fare of the Christchurch kind, poor or biased umpiring is the bane of cricket. A trail worth blazing.

The prognoses for Nadeem, Adrian and David are just as mixed. Age before beauty, so let's start with David. Leading a Lancashire side studded with stars and starlets and eight internationalists is all fine and dandy. Being favoured to win everything bar the ICC Trophy is quite flattering, if a mite optimistic. Lancashire may have been the sprightliest scorers among the counties in 1989, but there is no front-rank spinner to speak of now Flat Jack has gone, while the possible loss of three of their number to national service – Atherton, Fairbrother and DeFreitas – will be hard to gloss over.

For David, justifying his place in the side is going to be difficult at times. Lone voices may do little to disturb the peace, but they can make a disturbing racket. Take Frank Hayes, an apparently embittered ex-Lancashire captain and longtime colleague. Last summer Hayes launched into a tirade against David via the *Manchester Evening News*. The victim, though hurt a trifle at first, shrugged it off. 'I don't take too much notice of criticism. If it's constructive, then fair enough. I feel under pressure for Lancashire to do well, and I want to do well personally. But if people have been looking to criticise Lancashire recently, they have looked at my contribution first. I'm not going to be around much longer and my Test dreams are over. I took on the job of captain on a one-off basis, so I do it my way. I'm now in my fifth year and I don't feel I'm denying a youngster my place.'

Andy Hayhurst, newly ensconced at Somerset after leaving Old Trafford a little huffily during the winter with one year of his contract to run, might beg to differ. David: 'I didn't want him to leave, but if a player wants to leave, I won't stand in his way. Yet while he was with us the opportunities were there for him to battle for the No. 5 slot as an all-rounder, along with Steve O'Shaughnessy and Mike Watkinson. He played for us throughout the 1987 Refuge League campaign, through half the following Championship season, then he was given a chance at No. 3 last summer when Atherton was up at Cambridge, but by the time he broke his thumb, which ruled him out for the rest of 1989, he was back in the 2nd XI. I wish him the best of luck, but not against us.'

The fact remains that skippering matters more in cricket than any other land-based sport. David's contributions with bat and ball, allied to his seaworthiness as helmsman, make him rather more than the fringe player Hayhurst was. 'I'm trying to do a good job as captain. It takes a long time to come to terms with captaining one of the two premier counties and what that means in terms of expectation and support. And, not surprisingly, Lancashire are concerned about my successor. As to the immediate future, I find myself with a difficult decision to make. My contract is up at the end of the season; should 1991 be my last year? With the make-up of our staff I realise I will have to bowl more because we are very inexperienced on the spin bowling side. We'll just have to see how the season goes.'

As Lancashire limber up in the paddock, their chief worry is Akram and that deep-rooted groin problem of his, the cost of being a fast bowling all-rounder who tramps the boards from January through December. 'He's our strike bowler, so I'm delighted he's fit and, so I have been assured, will be available from early May. The batting looks slightly stronger if anything, with Mike Atherton available full-time for the first time. He'll be our first quality No. 3 since Pilling. To an extent spin is probably our weakest department.' *Plus ça change*. Just before the 1971 Gillette semi-final, Bond said the very same. With John Emburey barred from national consideration and so available full-time for Middlesex, along with the fast-improving Phil Tufnell, such a shortcoming may be brutally exposed in the Championship. 'Simmons's retirement has given us a difficult gap to fill, not only in the one-day games where we had long relied on him to close an end up, but in the Championship too [between 1972 and 1983 Simmons was Lancashire's leading first-class wicket-taker *five* times]. The sad aspect is the decline of our left-armer Ian Folley. Maybe talk of him getting an England tour in 1987 got to him, although I doubt it. That would motivate me more rather than induce relaxation, say. He had no luck at all in 1988 and didn't play a game last summer, when he was going to be our senior spinner. Now he has totally lost any command over line and length. He's OK in the nets, but he can't seem to translate that confidence to the middle.'

That there are no plans to play Folley this summer, barring a considerable improvement, has not only compounded the depletion of resources signalled by Simmons's retirement, but also forced David to change tack. 'In the latter part of the 1970s and early 1980s the policy at Lancashire appeared to be to give our four spinners 250 overs each per season, but you don't get value from them that way. In 1987 and 1988 I gave Folley and Simmo long stints, but those two are no longer in contention, and this season we have Atherton, Dexter Fitton and myself to lob it up, so I'll have to spread the workload.'

For his part, Adrian is staring at a heavy workload. Happily, the arrival at Taunton of Hayhurst, an all-rounder but more adept with the bat, has been accompanied by the acquisition of two bowling all-rounders. Ian Swallow, late of Yorkshire, will bowl off-spin in place of Marks and add depth to an already formidable tail. Despite being blighted by deformed fingers, this skimpy slither of flesh and bone from Barnsley is also an exemplary fielder. The other new kid in town is Roland Lefebvre, a physiotherapist from Rotterdam reputed to be the best all-rounder in the Netherlands, and a skilful manipulator of the seam and equally deft at the mechanics of swing. Somerset hope he will be the second-change seamer they need so direly to support Adrian, Mallender and Graham Rose, another man of two parts. There is certainly room for improvement. Only Kent, with 53, gathered less than Somerset's 54 bowling bonus points in 1989.

The batting, at least, is rather chunkier. It will again be led off by the willowy 37-year-old Transvaalian schoolmaster, Jimmy Cook, the latest in a line of brilliant Somerset batting imports, stretching from Greg Chappell to Steve Waugh via Sunil Gavaskar, Viv Richards and Martin Crowe. In 1989, Cook rustled up 2,241 effortless runs and eight centuries in his maiden English season, and there should be no shortage of sizeable numbers for the genial David Oldam to ink into his meticulous scorebooks this term. The studious Peter Roebuck should be a Test opener, and might have been were he not an intellectual; Richard Harden (the only Somerset-raised member of the squad) is on the brink of flowering, and the new captain, Chris Tavaré, is too fine a batsman to have earned as few as thirty-one caps. Since only Gloucestershire and Glamorgan scored at a more sluggish rate than Somerset in 1989, mind, a trifle more urgency will be in order to give an average attack sufficient time to wheedle out opponents. The high point of 1989 was a narrow defeat in the Benson & Hedges semi-final; realistically speaking, something along the same lines is the likeliest outcome of the coming campaign. Still to reconstitute fully after the traumatic clearout of 1986, Somerset will acknowledge that their prospects of landing the County Championship at the ninety-ninth attempt are no better than slim.

On a personal level, Adrian recognises that this could be one of his last chances to curry favour with the all-seeing selectors, one of whom had been spotted giving him a fleeting once-over last summer. Few, precious few, are the bowlers who have depended largely on sheer pace and still contrived to woo a selector when stranded on the wrong side of 30. For the sharpest prong in the Somerset attack, there should be plenty of scope to put in a bid.

Time is the last of Nadeem's vexations. He has oodles of the stuff. The question is whether he has the wherewithal to fidget in the wings. At full throttle, Essex are driven by the strongest first five in the land. From the top, Graham Gooch, John Stephenson, Paul Prichard, Mark Waugh and Nasser Hussain, backed up by wise old birds like Brian Hardie and Alan Lilley, plus a gaggle of up-and-comers headed by Adam Seymour and Nick Knight. True, Stephenson did struggle on the England A tour of Zimbabwe, while Prichard has rarely tapped any consistency since a broken finger robbed him of a crucial season in his development. But Nadeem believes that his best opportunity lies with injuries, or else some unimagined purchase for his leggies. Ironically, Hussain, his closest friend at the club, represents the widest loophole. Having broken his wrist in the Caribbean, he is not expected to take up his post for at least a month.

More encouragingly, Neil Foster will be available all summer long for the first time since 1982, while newcomers Steve Andrew (a pacy slinger who failed to live up to expectations at Hampshire) and Peter Such (whose off-breaks were sparingly employed by Leicestershire) should add lustre to a nicely varied attack. With Derek Pringle bothered by back problems, Stephenson yet to do his talent justice on a loftier stage and John Childs's controlled left-arm spin strangely unfashionable, Test summonses are likely to be restricted to Gooch. The portents are excellent for Essex, less so for Nadeem as he peruses the 2nd XI fixture list.

For all three of our guides, there are issues further afield worth pondering as the days tick down towards the first 'Play' of the 1990s. How will Gower make out amid the more upwardly mobile environs of Hampshire? Will Viv Richards be able to get off his sore backside and resurrect Glamorgan like some latterday Wooller? Is Derbyshire's newly-acquired all-rounder from the veld, Adrian Kuiper, really as brutal a hitter as Gatting and the rebels reported? Can Bobby Simpson forget his responsibilities as Australia's coach and lubricate Leicestershire? Can Eddie Barlow, another Test bulwark-turned-manager, brighten gloomy Gloucestershire? Is Graham Thorpe anything like as fine a batsman as his press from

Zimbabwe inferred, or will the bowlers suss him out during that difficult sophomore season? And what about Malcolm Devon, as the chairman of selectors once dubbed Derbyshire's answer to Frank Bruno? A decade-and-a-half after John Snow's final curtain call, dare we believe that England now have a shock bowler again, someone capable of getting his retaliation in first?

And what about the other new regulations? Fines for sloppy over rates, hitherto paid by the counties, are to be covered entirely by the players. On the up side, they will at least have the advantage of being able to bowl three fewer deliveries per hour in order to meet the new stipulated mean of eighteen overs. Gee. Zonal winners in the Benson & Hedges Cup can now be drawn against the runners-up from their zone in the quarter-finals, which seems a bit silly. The popular explanation is that, this way, there would be less chance of another cock-up when the draw for the last eight was broadcast live by the Beeb; in 1988, two zonal rivals were paired together erroneously. The convex bat, meanwhile, came and went the way of Dennis Lillee's aluminium creation. Developed by Chris Cowdrey and manufacturers Zenith for the sole purpose of 'slogging', as they put it, the weapon has been banned from use in first-class games. You can picture the scene at that spring meeting. 'Any more business, chaps?' 'Well, yes, Ted. There's this curvaceous sort of bat old Cowders has come up with. Supposed to give the ball a bit of extra welly. Sounds like it could be fun. I take it we can just give it the old thumbs-up and nip off to the Tavern?' 'I should say not. We can't very well have slogging in the Championship. We must have standards.'

From whatever perspective David, Adrian and Nadeem look at the coming twenty-odd weeks, slogging is precisely what they will be doing. Slogging up and down the highways and byways, slogging over blips in form, slogging through a fixture list that sometimes demands them to cope with three different formats of the game in as many days. But there are acquaintances to make and renew, favourite haunts to haunt once more, self-improvements to be carried out, dreams to chase. Lead on, Macduff . . .

6 April

Wednesday 18 April, The Parks

Oxford University v. Somerset

'What I wouldn't give to have my years at Oxford over again; without the radio, without all things nuclear; when all was laughter and friendship, and a ghastly war was just over, and all the geese were swans; when the sun always seemed to shine . . . May all who play cricket in The Parks love it as much as we did.'

So gushed Raymond Charles Robertson-Glasgow, 'Crusoe' to his friends, a tall medium-fast bowler who played for Charterhouse, Oxford University and Somerset between the world wars, but was probably better known for scribbling delightful epistles on the game on behalf of the *Daily Telegraph*, the *Sunday Times* and the *Observer*. Unfortunately, even his romantic soul would have had difficulty in locating the sun, actual or metaphorical, when the 1990 season opened at The Parks.

OK, so you can still get in for free to soak up the vapour trails emitted by C. B. Fry, Plum, Lord Ted and 'Tiger' Pataudi, but the justification for keeping the Oxford University Cricket Club – and its Cambridge counterpart – within the first-class clique has been running out of steam for some time. Of the thirty players to see action for England in the 1989 Tests and one-day internationals, three were Blues; in 1982, five of the eighteen Englishmen who did battle with India and Pakistan were of Oxbridge extraction, along with two of the Pakistanis, Imran and Majid. As examinations grow more rigorous, and fixture lists expand, so the matchless quality of the pitches at The Parks and Fenner's has come to be regarded as the only saving grace for an anachronism.

Last week's opener pitted Glamorgan, still awaiting the arrival of the King of Antigua, against a motley crew of German,

South African and Australian students, and even the odd Brit. If that little match-up scarcely stirred the blood, then the weather positively froze it. Thermal underwear, leg-warmers and cups of hot coffee were standard issue. Alan Butcher needed Araldite to keep his cap on (helmets are felt to be superfluous against today's uninspiring undergrads). The bails could have done with similar assistance, and at one point play was interrupted as a particularly fierce squall gusted the covers twenty yards inside the square-leg boundary. The German TV reporter shuddering in the pavilion could have been forgiven for wondering why this cricket business was held to be the English summer game. As Butcher and Hugh Morris ploughed on through gales and showers to put on 123 for the first Glamorgan wicket, Horst began to scoff. 'Maybe they should be batting with umbrellas, no?' Ha-bloody-ha. By the time the ghost was finally surrendered just before 6 o'clock, Horst had shuffled off, none the wiser. There was one ounce of consolation, mind: in Antigua, where the West Indies and England were debating the final Test, conditions were only vaguely better.

Things were barely more temperate the following Wednesday, when Somerset took their turn on the flat mattress. Temperatures did rise, however, when one of the umpires. Alan Whitehead, realised that Adrian was playing. Whitehead, the same official whose inflated brush with Adrian had cost the player a fine at Bath ten months earlier. Adrian: 'Had the match taken place later in the season, then I would almost certainly have given way to one of the younger seamers, Jeremy Hallett, say, but match practice is all that counts in April and this is an excellent chance to bowl and practice your field placings. I was all for it, although they [Oxford] just want to get the game over with and nip down to Oriel College for a drink. Whitehead is no problem for me, but I think I am for him. Before the start he said to Jack Bond, the other umpire, "Jones should bowl at my end because it will help him more, but I shouldn't think he'll want to after what happened last summer." Bondy told him that I wasn't the type to bear a grudge.'

Sure enough, before the game began, Adrian walked over to Whitehead, shook him by the hand, said hello and asked him how he'd been keeping. Whitehead, who has been on the first-class panel since 1970, longer than anyone bar David Constant and Peter

Wight, later confessed to have been taken aback by such bare-faced affability. 'I'm sure,' said Adrian, 'that he would've carried it on otherwise.'

Reduced to an innings and a half, the main bout revealed little. Tavaré made 83 in his first knock as skipper, Harden 99 and Somerset 328 for 6 before Adrian's 2 early wickets shoved Oxford towards a perilous 14 for 3, whereupon Mark Crawley, who had taken 6-92 and scored an unbeaten 103 against Glamorgan, effected a revival, reminding Lancashire followers that young brother John was not the only Crawley with talent. Oxford finished on 144 for 5, the second and third days yielding but seventy-seven overs all told. When one particularly vehement appeal from Adrian failed to find favour with Whitehead's co-officiator, Jack Bond, the umpire turned around and congratulated him on his thespian abilities.

A ruffle-free start for the new captain, then. 'There is a new regime with Tav in charge. He is a brilliant cricketer, better than people know. Many of our supporters just think of him as scoring excruciatingly slow 50s for England, but the style he adopted in Test cricket bore no relation to the way he normally bats. A couple of days ago he did a flip-chart presentation, highlighting the mistakes we made last year, primarily in the one-dayers, and what we were going to do to remedy them. No one had ever done that at Somerset before. He doesn't need to crack the whip. We've got so much respect for him, for his experience, that we know what's needed. It was difficult for Vic, particularly during his tenure as captain last season, when Robey and Tav were the only people in the side he really knew. But with Birky [Birkenshaw] in his second year as manager and a better spirit in evidence, I think Tav's enjoying himself. He is not an inspiring man, mind you, and he often seems to be verging on sheer boredom. A cerebral rather than motivational captain.'

Sunday 22 April, Taunton

Somerset v. Worcestershire (Refuge Assurance League)

When Ian Botham returns to his former stomping ground nowadays, cameras and notebooks are no longer poised, aching to convey any lingering undercurrents of bitterness between him and Roebuck, over whose locker he was once supposed to have slapped a sticker reading 'Judas'. The Taunton diehards who once lionised Botham remain in his pocket, willing him to wield his wand, though not with quite the intensity of old. The first serious match of Somerset's season, a Refuge League altercation with Worcestershire, thus passed without untoward incident. In the event, 'The Legend' assisted Tim Curtis in an opening stand worth 86, then dismissed Tavaré and Harden during an economical spell of medium-paced swing.

Curtis, a bit of a grinder but capable of putting his foot down when required, proceeded to 124, Graeme Hick, a young man with a penchant for shredding Somerset attacks, weighed in with an undefeated 78, and Worcestershire raised 237 for 2, which was 33 more than their hosts could muster. Adrian kept a tightish rein but went wicketless. 'It was a lottery. Sunday cricket is a batsman's game, and I'm not a containing bowler. I take wickets. My runs-per-over rate is not very good, but I do take wickets because I attack.'

Since Gooch and his charges had acquitted themselves so well in the Caribbean, the now annual Campaign for the Reinstatement of Ian Terence Botham remains some way short of fever pitch, but there are still many of his peers who feel his international days are far from numbered, Adrian among them. 'Botham seems a bit subdued, but I think he'll play for England again, simply because he wants to. He's still the best all-rounder in the country.'

Wednesday 25 April, Ipswich

Kulsoom Shahid was away in a nearby laboratory, product testing for Harris, purveyors of sausages and other popular vegetarian fare. Younger sister Kashwi was behind a desk in the local TSB. Their elder brother, Tafweaz, was playing with somebody else's money too, tapping away on a calculator in an accountants' office. Their other brother, Nadeem, was packing his bags at chez Shahid, preparing to pop off to Lord's to play a game of cricket tomorrow with Graham Gooch, Mike Gatting and Desmond Haynes.

Even though readers of *The Cricketer* had recently nominated him in their imaginary England Under-24 team, it was difficult to conceive how Nadeem could have been accommodated in the Essex 1st XI had Nasser Hussain's broken left wrist not been six weeks from total recovery. The effervescent Brian Hardie was still valuable as opener or No. 5; John Childs, the wiliest slow left-armer in the country, would normally expect to play in the Championship, and Peter Such had been signed as a second spinner to replace Geoff Miller. Yet there was no significance in Nadeem's omission from the team that opened the season with a surprising loss to Kent in the Refuge, then rebounded in the Benson & Hedges to settle an old score by defeating Nottinghamshire, their vanquishers in last season's 55-over final. (Or perhaps that should be 'Gooching Nottinghamshire', given the captain's weighty contribution in his second innings after breaking his left hand in Bridgetown.) Quite rightly, Essex prefer to work on the techniques of their brightest young batsmen before easing them carefully into the swamp of one-day cricket, where discipline and textbook values are quickly submerged in favour of improvisation and haste.

For that vital first Championship game, however, Nadeem had been summoned as one of two changes, displacing Alan Lilley, while a fourth seamer, Steve Andrew, stepped in for his Essex debut in Childs's stead. Against a Middlesex side deprived through a rib injury of their bowling fulcrum, Angus Fraser, yet still eminently capable of matching Essex stride for stride, Nadeem thus had a dual function. Just as he liked it. In Childs's absence he would be the sole spinner, while his presence at No. 6 would lend ballast to an erratic middle order. 'I know there is no chance of my winning a permanent place in the side just yet, but I reckon I might play 75 per cent of the time this summer. All I need is a good start. Nasser's injury has given me an opportunity to impress as a batsman, but I'm encouraged all the time as a bowler, so I'm sure I've been selected for both.'

Entering the holy portals in St John's Wood Road holds few tremors. Indeed, the thrill appears long gone. 'I've played at Lord's five times already, for MCC Schools and the National Association of Young Cricketers in 1987, then three times for MCC Schools the following year, so I've even been in both dressing-rooms. Maybe I'd be a bit more bowled over if I was fascinated by the history, but I'm afraid to say it doesn't do much for me. I don't read cricket books; not many players of my generation do as far as I can tell.'

David and Adrian are no different. David has a fairly extensive knowledge of cricket's heritage, but he rarely reads about the game any longer, especially not in the press. One reason for this is that he has no time for the constant comparisons made between generations of Lancashire players. The sum total of literature on the game in the Jones household is contained in a neat pile next to the downstairs loo. A 1983 *Wisden*, covering Adrian's inaugural season for Sussex, plus a couple of Sproats.

Nadeem was therefore unlikely to get too het up when he saw the unsightly metamorphosis at the Nursery End. The embryonic Compton and Edrich Stands opposite the pavilion, a mass of rocky rubble at present, are so far behind schedule that there seems little likelihood of Lord's being at full capacity for its major forthcoming attractions. Older collars are warming up as news of the world's biggest sightscreen spreads.

No such disenchantment among the Essex members, mind. For the first time in the club's history there is a waiting list for membership, the box office having been closed at 9,000. Only Lancashire could pride themselves on a similar excess of demand over supply. That said, Essex have lost one member, an irate subscriber who submitted his resignation in the off-season, enraged by Neil Foster's decision to winter in South Africa under a flag of convenience alongside a band of apologists and wise monkeys. At a dinner a couple of weeks before Foster embarked on that ill-fêted, ill-fated expedition, I queried his motives. Of course, the very idea of apartheid was awful, but, given his perennial tussles with injury, he obviously wanted to secure his family's future while he still could. As a 'rebel', he would earn as much in two years as he could if he played Test cricket for the next five, calculations courtesy of the player-manager David Graveney, a qualified accountant. Yet he also expressed a desire to see apartheid first-hand, rather than rely on the second-hand views of others. 'Have you ever been there?' he wondered, with a justifiable degree of facetiousness. I told him that I would no sooner have spent a penny on South African soil in the climate at that time than switch allegiances from Middlesex to Essex. Hearing about evil is sufficient.

In the opinion of Essex's sardonic, pragmatic secretary, Peter Edwards, employers cannot be held responsible for staff morals, particularly when they are not paying them all year round. It is difficult to argue with that, except to point out that if the counties made greater efforts to keep their summer labourers off the winter dole queue, then the players might not be forced into such an invidious position. Apart from Bill Athey, a Thatcherite adorned by a Union Jack tattoo, cricket folk do not wear their politics on their sleeve. In public, most dismiss the subject with a blend of feigned ignorance and distaste, with a heavy bias towards the latter. Why should they be prevented from working in South Africa when half the business world was still bedding down with the Bothas and de Klerks? As I grudgingly conceded to Foster that evening, for those of us who never face such quandaries, it is rather too easy to get high and mighty.

Thursday 26 April, Old Trafford

Lancashire v. Worcestershire (County Championship, 4 days)

Would you Adam'n'Eve it. The opening day of the Championship season at Old Trafford and the rain is not on some soggy plain in Spain, but here. Now for the truly bad news. As proof of the depths of negativity to which county cricket can sink, this takes the proverbial biscuit. Even before the bell had clanged Lancashire's bout against Worcestershire into action, gloves were off and headguards on. David was infuriated. 'Before we'd bowled a ball Phil Neale said to me: "I'm not prepared to play a game with you." As plain as that. He said he thought we would be up at the top of the table at the end of the season, and, hopefully, Worcestershire would be there too, so he doesn't feel inclined to give us a chance. I told him I understood his feelings and accepted them, but it is disappointing, very disappointing when a thing like this happens. The public don't know, of course, but they're still getting a raw deal. I mean, he could have waited until the middle of day three to tell me.'

Though excessive, Neale's caution was at least logical. Lancashire, along with Middlesex, were the county most likely to pilfer the Championship from Worcestershire (or, given their chairman's hands-on approach, perhaps that should be Fearnleyshire). Yet not only had Neale and his squad been the mean machine of the past three summers, the only parts lost since last September had been two rather rusty rivets, Paul Pridgeon and Steve O'Shaughnessy, the former Lancastrian. The incomers, meanwhile, comprised no more than a quartet of youths, one of whom, admittedly, did happen to be Dean Headley, grandson of the Black Bradman. In all fifteen members of the squad had been in harness since the onset of a run that, albeit triggered by the bat tycoon's chequebook, had yielded the following enviable record: two Championships, two Refuge Leagues, a NatWest Final and semi-final, a Refuge Cup Final and two Benson & Hedges quarter-finals. Their frontline bowling consisted of four England seamers and the England A slow left-armer. Their batting was headed by the most prodigous young blade the game had known, and by the lustiest leather-flogger seen in a generation.

So what on earth was this admirable, astute captain of theirs doing conceding the initiative before the season was a week old? Massaging Lancashire egos to furnish them with a false sense of security? Or was the swagger that had enabled Worcestershire to surmount debilitating casualties last summer no longer quite as pronounced?

David and Neale had a further parley on the fourth and final day. Having been denied the opening three sessions, each side had batted for a day. Worcestershire recovered well to reach 360 for 7 on a supine surface, David stepping up after Fitton and Atherton had been found wanting to remove Damian D'Oliveira (155) and Steve Rhodes (72), the nuisances responsible for pushing their side from 86 for 5 (Hick 33, Botham 17) to 312 for 6. Mendis, Atherton, Fairbrother and Jesty all made 50s, as Lancashire batted circumspectly against Richard Illingworth's tight line and occasional turn before David declared 60 behind. His opening gambit when the Monday summit got under way, or so the press box was informed, amounted to 320 in eighty overs, 'which was equivalent,' wrote Michael Austin in the *Independent*, 'to asking for a blank cheque.' Neale, he concluded, 'laughed [Lancashire] out of the bank with "not negotiable" stamped on their foreheads.' Neale dug his heels in for a second time and, after a relatively ponderous third innings enlivened latterly by Hick's century and a Botham half-century, he dared Lancashire to have a crack at 292 in forty-six. Mendis and Fowler opted for batting practice, and the plug was pulled with eight overs remaining. Best to tip out the dirty water before starting the washing-up.

Saturday 28 April, Lord's

Middlesex v. Essex (County Championship, 4 Days)

By the third afternoon against Middlesex, Nadeem's nerve ends were beginning to fray. His solitary contribution until then had been a wayward, blushworthy over on the second day, the obligatory last one before lunch, naturally. For a leg-spinner more than any other bowler, the line between good and bad is communion-wafer-thin and, making the mistake of trying to cram in too many variations, he was carted for a dozen runs and spent the remainder of the innings stooping at silly-point or darting around in the covers. Overly conscious of the need to make an impression, he began to sweat profusely as his time to bat approached.

'I was worried, mostly about whether my feet would move. Because most of the first day was rained off, I'd had plenty of net practice, both in the indoor school and in the middle, where couples would take turns to bat for forty minutes. But there's no real competition in that, so I suppose I was a little jittery. Mike Garnham came into the dressing-room and calmed me down, and then, almost as soon as I went in, at 223 for 4, we found ourselves at the crease together. And at the end of every over he came down the wicket for a chat. It helped, but I still didn't bat well. Maybe it was the slope, but I missed too many shots.

'Still, when I came off at the end of the innings Fletch congratulated me, so perhaps I'm too critical. I only seem to remember the bad strokes. I have a tendency to hold my shots, watching how I hit the ball rather than where it's going, so I miss singles. Nasser will square-cut yorkers for 4 because he trusts his eye, but I trust my technique. Fletch says I won't score 100 in two hours with a good technique at this stage of my career, so at least I'm not expected to smash the bowlers around. Not that many batsmen are going to be smashing the Middlesex bowlers around this summer. Williams skids it on to you and is quicker than he looks, and Cowans was not as quick as I thought, so I found his deliveries stopping on me. There was also more bounce than I'd imagined, and I kept on being hit on the legs and thighs.'

Comfortable it wasn't, but Nadeem's unbeaten 34 did help raise an unbroken sixth-wicket stand of 73 with Garnham and so enable

Gooch to declare 76 behind at 300 for 5. The onus was on Middlesex to take the initiative on the last morning, but despite a cracking 100 from Haynes, his fourth of the month, they were never quite able to regain the stirring momentum of Saturday evening, when Gatting bludgeoned seven boundaries in his chunky unbeaten 32. This was partly attributable to Gatting's subsequent absence with a swollen ankle, partly to a splendidly sustained spell from Foster, who started by challenging Mark Ramprakash to hook and induced a top edge. When Keith Brown, 'the new Radley', nudged Andrew to second slip, Middlesex had lost their middle order inside eighteen overs, consigning any thoughts of an early closure to the plughole.

With Haynes in his counting house, however, no possibility can be safely discounted. So when Gooch unexpectedly called on Nadeem for the 51st over, ten minutes before lunch, his instructions were explicit: forget the fancy stuff and keep it tight. He could well have been influenced by the remarkable goings-on the day before at Hove, where the Sussex leg-spinners Ian Salisbury and Andy Clarke produced a joint analysis of 16–0–63–5 to pave the way for a Refuge League win over Surrey. Another anti-clockwise twirler, Mike Atherton, had also been prominent, deluding three Nottinghamshire batsmen. But whatever his motivation, Gooch had made an important gesture of faith towards Nadeem, who duly reimburses him. A warm-up delivery to Andrew turns square. Encouraging. Floated towards Paul Downtown in a whirring blur of arms and knees, the first two genuine balls are on a good length. Nadeem brushes the ground with his fingers after each, a common quirk based mostly on superstition. The third delivery is slightly shorter, inviting the drive, but Hardie intercepts at extra-cover. Downton gets it right next time, bisecting extra-cover and mid-off for a boundary. The fifth ball is shorter still, but punched straight to the inner ring, and Downton is so surprised by the full-toss that follows that he contents himself with a push to mid-off. Well, 4 off is considerably better than 12.

Nadeem returns to the attack after lunch, this time from the Nursery End. Haynes ploughs a short leg-side ball for 4 but otherwise shows respect. At the end of the over, Gooch walks over and gives the bowler a reassuring pat on the back. Just a single off the next over; then, in Nadeem's sixth, Haynes launches into a flighted delivery that appears to dip a little as it arcs in, then turns a shade away. The only thing wrong with the shot is that Foster catches it with a headlong dive at cover. The advent of John Emburey, a marvellously elegant off-spinner and ingenious batsman whose concept of crease style seems limited to holding the blade the right way up, provides the cue for a fascinating duel. At one point he finds himself turned square, legs apart, and thick-edging to point on the bounce. In the last over before the declaration, though, Nadeem suffers as so many have suffered before, Emburey almost doing the splits as he slogs consecutive 4s over wide mid-on.

Nonetheless, with figures of 1–33 from his eight overs, Nadeem had cause for contentment. 'I was surprised Gooch called me up after the way I bowled in the first innings, but at least I had more time to settle. I tend to get tense when I bowl, so I often drag the ball down when I first come on. But Gooch was really helpful. Every time I bowled a bad ball he came up and told me not to hurry. One supposed googly went down the leg-side, and I told him I couldn't believe it. His answer was, "All I want you to do is contain". It was the first time I'd seen Haynes in the flesh. He has so much time for his shots, but he plays a lot straighter than most West Indians I've seen. I think I got the balance right against him, though, and it was a great experience simply bowling to such a great batsman. So even though wickets didn't really matter by the time I got him, it still felt good.'

Set 313 in fifty-five overs, Essex speed away as if determined not merely to catch the 8.15 shuttle scheduled to spirit them up to Glasgow, but also to take in the 4.40 performance of *New York Stories*, currently showing in Belsize Park. There are times when Gooch rolls back the years and takes the mothballs out of his rip-roaring former self. This was one such. Now more bank clerk than bank robber, he can still shred an attack at twenty-two paces, and, even more than it had during his first innings 137, his pomp suits the circumstances to a T. After taking six overs to find his bearings, he decrees that Williams simply has to go. Hooks, pulls and all manner of violence pour forth from that mighty plank of willow: 38 in twenty-five balls. Refusing to buckle, Williams searches high and low for a bucket of cold water and at last finds one as Gooch edges another orbit-aimed drive to

Downton. The game expires at a stroke. Stephenson and Prichard decorate the last rites, Essex calling it a day at 163 for 3.

Although he has a ticket for the flight, Nadeem is not in quite as much a rush as his colleagues when stumps are drawn. While they head for the country that sired those cricketing opposites, Jardine and Denness, he has been redirected to Cambridge by Fletcher, who believes he will gain more from a long bowl for the 2nd XI than sitting idly by as a reserve batsman for the Firsts.

Sunday 29 April, Taunton

Somerset v. Gloucestershire (County Championship, 4 Days)

Look ma, top of the world. Well, the best in the west then. Thanks primarily to Adrian's 6–75, Somerset are heading the Championship after one game. All right, so Gloucestershire are the sort of team that can induce an outbreak of assertive smiles in most rival dressing-rooms. Setting aside Kevin Curran, a Zimbabwean with an Irish grandmother, and Courtney Walsh, a Jamaican, Jack Russell is their one player of international calibre; Tony Wright, the new captain and the third man to hold the post in as many seasons, has made seven centuries since his debut in 1982; doubts over the long-term future of that Sonny Liston of fast bowlers, the endearing David Lawrence, have heightened since his breakdown playing for England A in Zimbabwe; two of the elder statesmen, David Graveney and Bill Athey, are living under the cloud of their involvement in the 'rebel' tour to South Africa. Their secret weapon is Kevin Jarvis, formerly an England 12th man when with Kent but now 37 and no longer likely to beat young batting guns to the draw. Eddie Barlow, that avuncular sergeant-major who revitalised drowsy Derbyshire during the late 1970s, has his work cut out with this lot. But a win is a win is a win . . .

Until the final day, the contest had been ebb and flow. Gloucestershire recovered from 39 for 3 to 133 for 3, but lost their last 4 wickets for 5 runs to subside for 197, Mallender ghosting his way through the tail after Lefebvre had swung through the abdomen of the innings. Walsh had Cook caught behind for 16, Jarvis accounted for Tavaré almost as cheaply and Somerset slid to 196 for 5 before Burns (166) and Rose (85) bowled them along to 409 for 6. But an eventual lead of 241 was not earned without further discomfort for Adrian, who had failed to get among the wickets.

'I know I should expect it by now, even though I'm a No. 10 or 11, but when Courtney Walsh bowled me a short ball I didn't move. The first thing I knew about it was when I saw the paint flaking off my helmet. I nicked the next ball down to third man and, as I completed the single, Courtney tapped me on the shoulder without saying a word, as if to say "Are you okay?". Athey asked me if I was all right. I said yes, then he came back with, "You know something, twenty years ago you'd have been dead." Comforting, huh? Even so, the next couple of deliveries were short and around my chest and shoulders.'

Adrian stopped Athey in his tracks later that day, bowling him for 39 as Gloucestershire made a better fist of things second time around. By stumps, however, they still lagged 3 runs behind with 5 wickets down, and Sunday was set fair for a favourable denouement. 'During the first innings, I'd angled the ball in, but things didn't really come right and I ended up with nought for plenty. On Saturday I trapped Hodgson lbw with a quick ball, then got a fast yorker through Athey, who was our chief target. This morning Rosey got rid of Syd Lawrence early on, but Jack Russell hung on with Jeremy Lloyds for a while before I bowled him a short one and he came down the wicket as he did in the Windies, got a bottom edge and was brilliantly held by Tav. Then I got my own back on Courtney, coming round the wicket and having him caught at short fine-leg off a bouncer. Lloyds shored up one end superbly and fully deserved a 100, but I got him for 93 when he pulled a bouncer to deep-square. Good bowling that.

'David Graveney was the last to go, gloving another short one from me to first slip, and we were left with 99 to get and bags of time to get them, although Hardy and Cook didn't dally and they knocked off the runs at nearly 4 an over. To start the season like this is magnificent for us, and good for the membership drive too. I'm not a believer in averages because I feel your value lies in how many wins you set up, or, in this case, clinch for your county. By now I should be good at storing batsmen's weaknesses and that knowledge helped me today.'

The president of Adrian's fan club greeted him on his return home. 'Liz (heavily pregnant) was out in the garden looking like a beached whale. She'd been following the game on Teletext and was very happy for me. She's not a great fan of cricket. My parents travel over the south-east to see me play, but although Liz watches me only occasionally, mostly in one-day games, living close to the ground enables her to pop in more often. And when she does it gives me a motivational tonic. She's still the greatest supporter I could ever have. The only date that means anything right now is 11 May, the day the baby is due.'

7 May

Tuesday 1 May, Taunton

Children can never wait for anything. Ms Amy Jones has moved into Adrian's life ten days ahead of schedule. 'At 3 a.m. this morning the contractions started and so we went to the hospital. At 7.30 I rang Tav and told him, and he said it was OK for me not to play against Derbyshire. But Liz had a long and difficult labour and Amy didn't arrive until 9 o'clock this morning. While she was in hospital I went home and watched the progress of the game on Teletext. I received lots of calls from the players, which was marvellous considering they were involved in an important Benson & Hedges game. Tav asked me if I wanted some more time off but I declined. Nice of him to offer, though.'

Nice indeed. During Game Two of the 1990 baseball World Series, the Cincinnati Reds' pitcher Tom Browning, not needed that night, was forced to sneak away from the dugout in his work togs in order to be at his expectant wife's bedside. When his manager, Lou Piniella, discovered Browning's absence, he went loopy. Still, the Reds won.

So did Somerset, rattling along to a daunting 310 for 3 after Cook (66) and Hardy (109) had led off with 126. Peter Bowler, left-handed and acquisitive, and John Morris, burly and full of bravado, answered with centuries and a stand of 210, but Derbyshire were restrained 8 runs short of victory. Adrian had something else to celebrate.

Friday 4 May, Cardiff

Glamorgan v. Somerset (County Championship, 4 Days)

Amiss, Barrington, Border, Boycott, Chappell (G.), Chappell (I.),

Graveney (T.), Greenidge (C. G.), Harvey, Haynes, Kanhai, Leyland, Lloyd (C.), May, Mead, Morris, Pollock (G.), Ranji, Washbrook, Zaheer. A score of scorers. Twenty of the finest batsmen to take guard. None, though, ever did what Jimmy Cook accomplished today as he extended his overnight 236 to 313 and still refused to budge.

To those of us for whom a 50 for the club is enough to fuel a winter's worth of breast-beating, a triple century is inconceivable. Think of all that concentration. I am always bored into submission once I've been in for half an hour. Not Cook, though. Bored at times, submissive, never. In a shade under eight and three-quarter hours he collected forty-three boundaries and threatened Viv Richards's Somerset record of 322 but was ultimately denied the opportunity to storm its barricades by Tavaré's sensible lunchtime declaration. Richards for one, confined to the dressing-room by a stomach upset, was as grateful as his new, rather more footsore team-mates.

Adrian saw it as the work of a supreme artist. 'That was a piece of cake for him. He told me he was actually bored at times. He's the best bat in the country. He makes it all look so simple: he doesn't bludgeon the ball, he accumulates. Glance at the board and he's got 70. Next time you look he's got 120; the next time, 150. I'm sure he would have passed Richards's record, but Tav genuinely wasn't aware of it. There was little point in batting on anyway. Even in a four-day game, if you get 800 you don't give yourself many options, but with 400 or 500 you do.' And so it transpired. Morris and Michael Cann, opening the Glamorgan innings in the injured Butcher's stead, put up 120 before Adrian removed them both within the space of 7 runs. Maynard prospered briefly before Swallow drew him into a typically impetuous biff to mid-on, prompting one matronly spectator to blow her considerable top. 'I'd put him across my knees if I was his mam,' she wailed.

Glamorgan closed at 198 for 3, behind by 337 and struggling, but evaded the follow-on on the Saturday courtesy of an unconquered 125 from Geoff Holmes, one of the less celebrated South Africa blacklistees and walking proof of the recent dilution of Welshness at Sophia Gardens. When the faithful Geordie first played for the county in 1978, eleven of his fifteen fellow workers were Welsh; now Holmes is one of seventeen 'foreigners' among the twenty-six-strong

Glamorgan staff. Anyway, Somerset added to their lead of 123 with some urgency, Hayhurst becoming only the third Somerset batsman since 1953 to score a century on his first-class debut for the county.

Set 368 off what evolved into seventy-seven overs, Glamorgan showed little inclination to do more than test the water. Steve Barwick, leading them for the first time and probably too steeped in failure to risk defeat, held back his biggest bazooka, Richards, at No. 5 and by the time he had raised a bat in anger, Glamorgan required 180 at close on 8 runs an over. Richards strove manfully, and Maynard atoned with 64 from seventy-two balls, but when Swallow stepped over a disused hocky touchline to catch King Viv off the bowling of his erstwhile nemesis, Roebuck, the game's final, imperfect cadence was marked by unwarranted chants of 'cheat' from home supporters convinced that the touchline was the boundary.

Fangs drawn by the somnolent surface, Adrian bowled only seven overs in the second Glamorgan innings. 'Viv told me that, as far as he was concerned, this new ball is no good for batsmen either. He says it becomes so soft by the time he comes in at No. 5, that he finds it difficult to put the correct weight behind his shots. It's still harder for bowlers, though. This damned thing looks like a grapefruit after forty overs, and is just as squishy.' Adrian tempted providence by asking Richards his views on the press who had clambered on his back like ravenous nits in Barbados a month earlier. The West Indies' captain's response to criticism by James Lawton of the *Daily Express* had been to march up to the press box as his colleagues were taking the field, and threaten the offender. Unseemly? Yes. Yet in the circumstances, not entirely unjustified. 'He said they were all bastards, or words to that effect. I can't say I blame him either.'

The heavily-trumpeted reunion of Richards and Roebuck had passed without incident, although the 'pop' papers did their utmost to drum up a dram of controversy. 'They picked up on the fact that when Viv was bowling on the first day, Robey bent down to pick up a shot from Cook that had dribbled harmlessly towards the non-striker's stumps. He handed it to Viv, and it was bloody headlines the next day. Hardly any mention of Jimmy's 300, or Tav's 100, but a great big pic of Robey handing the ball back. After the game Viv came in to the dressing-room and said to Robey, "Pete lad, I'll see you. Goodbye, all the best'', that sort of thing. There was no animosity. In fact they were very friendly towards each other.'

Friday 4 May, The Oval

Surrey v. Lancashire (County Championship, 4 Days)

Drifting through the Hobbs Gates ten minutes before lunch I confidently expected to catch the fag end of the Surrey first innings. At 396 for 6 overnight and with only Ian Greig and Keith Medlycott of the semi-recognised batsmen lingering, who would have thought otherwise? Instead, I reached the door at the near end of the Long Room, peered over a couple of shoulders and saw Greig push Atherton for a single and so reach what the quickest scoreboard in the business revealed to be his double century. A swift calculation, a bit of eavesdropping on some excited, incredulous chatter among the members, and it is apparent that I have missed one of the more astonishing slabs of unfettered strokeplay witnessed within these walls for some considerable time.

Until today, Greig had perhaps been best known as the younger of two smart South African brothers. Albeit every inch Tony's equal as England captaincy fodder, if not quite in the same exhibitionist class as batsman, bowler or man, he had had good reason for optimism when the hottest potato in British sport (England's football manager, Graham Taylor doesn't actually have to play, does he?) was put out for tender last August. Sir Humphrey Appleby would have given his eye teeth to have engineered the ensuing farce. One of those nauseating bureaucratic exclusion clauses so beloved of the civil service mentality pervading English cricket's upper echelons stipulated that even though Greig junior was qualified to play county cricket as an Englishman, a 1988 close season coaching appointment in Australia meant that he was ineligible to add to the two England caps he won against Pakistan in 1982. When is an Englishman not an Englishman? Apparently when his elder brother is a known affiliate of Kerry Packer. 'I'll go to my grave wondering whether the selectors would have picked me as captain for the Caribbean if that qualification hitch had not come up,' a baffled Greig later confided.

Now, though, it was the gross or so spectators dotting this cavernous arena who were befuddled. Only six centuries had hitherto issued forth from Greig's breezy bat, and none in his three years at Surrey, but this Oval pitch was a duffer's delight. Resuming at 56, he heaved, hooked, hacked and hoicked 145 out of the 187 runs ladled out before lunch. In his first extensive twirl for some years, David, barely recognisable under one of those elasticated baseball caps that have recently become such a rage among the players – and so enraged the elders of the press box – had felt the full force of the mistral. Greig's post-prandial blast was even fiercer. For an hour he buckled his swash and hurtled to 291, thrilling blows all.

The Lancashire players were less captivated. Patterson padded around the boundary with the enthusiasm of a recruit from Elvis Costello's *Oliver's Army*: 'I would rather be anywhere else but here . . .' Mendis, shaggy hair flopping far below his collar, moseyed around the infield, waiting for the declaration and the chance to strut his own stuff. David bobbed in with the effervescence of a boy a third his age, left arm classically high, to induce an edge from Martin Bicknell and so halt the eighth-wicket stand at 205, only 1 run after the pair had tippexed out the 1898 liaison here between Len Braund and Tom Hayward, again against the Lankys and until now the longest-standing record partnership for Surrey. Then, with a rare sense of symmetry, Greig carted him for 6s over long-on, then straight, then over long-off, from successive deliveries. Jesty's well-judged running catch feet from the boundary permitted David a measure of revenge and ended the frolics with Greig scenting 300. His departure 9 runs short (235 off 173 balls in 190 minutes today) was accompanied by the declaration, but if David had derived any pleasure from jettisoning this troublesome fellow, he did his best to disguise the fact. A peek at the old scoreboard explained all: Surrey 707 for 9, the highest Championship total since Kent mugged Essex for 803 for 4 at Brentwood in 1934.

An hour later Atherton and Mendis are progressing with unexpected *élan* following the early exit of Fowler, of all things run out charging for a second with another 513 needed to save the follow-on. 'I'm in a situation,' David says wearily, and not a little testily, 'where we've got to make 558 to avoid the follow-on. I don't think we're going to lose, but I must say I would have expected Greig to declare at 500. Why not? I know there aren't many spectators here, but they want entertainment. They can't get as much fun from watching a team make 700 as 400. Greig played absolutely magnificently, mind. That was one of the finest innings I've ever seen – and I've seen Barry Richards. What surprised me was that he was able to go on so long. I've seen him hit explosive 70s and 80s before, particularly at Hove one time during his Sussex days, when we pitched short and he walloped us. This time I told the bowlers to pitch it up, but it didn't make any difference. The boundaries have been brought in because of the building works, so this isn't one of the biggest Oval outfields, but his shots back past Patterson were terrific.' So, too, were some of Mendis's lean-to cover drives as Lancashire shifted along to 179 for 1 by stumps.

Saturday 5 May, Chelmsford

Essev v. Leicestershire (County Championship, 4 Days)

It is not often that a batsman listed at No. 6 in a four-day match has to spend the entirety of his team's first innings resisting an impulse to sneak away for a kip. Nadeem was well on the way to just such an experience. Although he had compensated for some under-length offerings on the first day by picking up Jon Agnew and Martyn Gidley, two of the Leicestershire lower order, the soporific nature of Andy Atkinson's pitch had already been exposed by Chris Lewis. More is expected of this accomplished young all-rounder's whippety bowling than his batting, yet here he was, all but tripling his career-best with an unbeaten 189 out of a total of 520, the most by the Grace Roadsters for forty-three years. Today, Gooch and Prichard dunked their paws in the honeypot with even greater relish. Essex followers have never witnessed anything remotely like it.

At 2.30 the 300 stand plops into the scorebook. At 2.40 Prichard bids adieu to his previous best scorc of 147. A few minutes later the pair supercede the Essex second-wicket record of 321, set by Ken McEwan and Gooch himself against Northamptonshire at Ilford twelve years ago. Another quarter-hour and Gibb and Horsfall's county all-wicket record of 343, extant since 1951, vanishes as Gooch whacks Agnew over mid-wicket. Gooch finally goes twenty-five minutes before tea, caught flashing with intent for 215, the alliance worth 403. Other historically greedy English second-wicket pairs, Hobbs and Hayes, Bowley and Tate, Shrewsbury and Gunn, had all fallen by the wayside, though the Jameson-Kanhai 465 remained a distant peak. Prichard has more to prove, and a new grip to prove it with, neccesitated by the finger injuries that have threatened to fracture his career. Far from overshadowed by his more strident partner, he carries on ransacking until 5 o'clock before slicing a weary loft to cover on 245.

Nadeem is becoming increasingly dubious about joining the pig-out. Gooch shuffles the order, promoting Garnham to No. 6 when Lewis bowls Waugh for a spindly 43. The wicket-keeper is promptly cut down by the same lively hand and in strides the leggy Foster, armed with a lifetime best of 74 and a proven propensity for profitable swinging, but hardly this profitable. Shortly before the close Essex cruise ahead of the 692 they had totted up at Taunton in 1895. Leicestershire prick the bubble by winning Sunday's Refuge clash by 5 wickets, but come Monday Foster is back on the beat, pounding to his maiden century in seventy-nine balls before Gooch declares at 761 for 5 upon his dismissal with Nadeem still waiting for his Godot.

More even than the concurrent antics at the Oval, the fact that two fast bowlers here reached three figures for the first time seemed the most indictable feature of a surreal round of matches. There is enough time for Tim Boon and Nigel Briers, the visiting openers, to repel a tidy spell from Nadeem and saunter to their second century stand of the game, the first time a Leicestershire twosome had given their team such a send off since 1965. The result, as at Kennington, has long ceased to be of any significance.

There was one bowler who managed to excel in his chosen field, however. Such, the sad-eyed blond from Dumbarton, twirled his high-flown off-breaks with patience and probity to ease aside the top three in the Leicestershire first innings, a get-stuffed-mate in anyone's language. A modest, erudite soul of 25 whose willingness to pay a hefty price for his wickets would have served him rather better in the 1930s. Such, though previously selected for Young England and TCCB XIs, seemed to have been drifting out of the game until leaving Grace Road for Chelmsford. After five increasingly useful seasons at Trent Bridge spent in the bulky shadow cast in more senses than one by Eddie Hemmings, he joined Leicestershire. There, a rabbity batting technique and an inability to compromise his art for the purposes of containment, two fatal anachronisms, restricted opportunities. In eight years on the circuit he had been permitted just four innings and 104 overs in one-day combat, yet there remain few more heart-warming sights in the game than to see a creature of Such's disposition wheeling away. Essex, a county that could afford to buy wickets, might prove to be the haven he had been seeking. On the evidence of a match in which a wicket had consented to fall every hour and a half or so, his capacity for long spells could be indispensable.

News is spreading of an outbreak of the lethal watermark disease among the white willow trees of East Anglia, where 90 per cent of the wood used to hew the world's cricket bats is grown. Right now, no one, save the batsmen, appears to give a fig.

Monday 7 May, The Oval

Surrey v. Lancashire (cont.) (County Championship, 4 Days)

And now for something not that different. Spurred on by Fairbrother's hectic triple hundred (Cook had been there and done that already, so excuse the lack of amazement) Lancashire swing their way to 745 for 3, then on to 844 for 6 with a that'll-teach-you grimace writ large over every determined helmeted face. Ever prepared, the ground staff have a hook on which to hang the extra digit, but England's first score of 1,000 remains elusive, Surrey sweeping away the tail for the addition of 19 (David not out 8). As a coda to a silly symphony, this is truly a loony tune. After 071 and 081, London now has two more three-figure numbers to remember: Fairbrother's 366 (the highest score by an Englishman this century, the third highest ever mounted in England, the second highest by a left-hander anywhere and Numero 12 on the all-time list) and Lancashire's 863, the second highest total in Championship history, the third most brimful score ever made in England and the ninth largest in the history of the game. That top nine, incidentally, excludes North Zone's 868 against West Zone at Bhilai in 1987–88, of which 68 represented penalty runs awarded for the fielding side's failure to maintain the requisite over rate. On this Persiled pitch, with this de-seamed ball, Lancashire's gluttony surely warranted a few penalty runs in Surrey's favour.

'Give my regards to the boy,' Sir Len Hutton said when asked for a comment on Fairbrother's achievement in superceding his own 364 here in 1938. Others viewed all this number-gorging with a more dubious eye. As Matthew Engel noted in the *Guardian*, the billiards scores of the past few days suggest that cricket is now approaching the same perilous position the potting game was mired in when Walter Lindrum invented the nursery cannon; he gradually wrecked the sport because no one could stop him scoring. Still, the TCCB should be over the moon. After all, Persiled pitches and de-seamed balls were among their contributions to the search for A Better English Batsman. Sir Len's chief concern was over four-day matches: 'It makes it hard for the bowlers and we don't have many as it is.' Engel's response was characteristically pithy: 'If cricket goes on like this, there will not be any [bowlers] at all; they will go and take more interesting jobs. Latrine attendant, say.' The batsmen's creed was straightforward enough: never mind the quality, feel the width.

When one of the more foreseeable stalemates of the modern era finally arrived, David was in less magnanimous fettle than he had been last Friday. What did the general who ordered the bloodiest massacre on an English field for fifty-two summers have to say in his defence? 'I still don't understand why Greig batted on when he must have known the way the wicket would develop. I thought it would stay the same, which it did, but while I can understand it if he thought it would break up, if that was the case I don't think he read it very well. There was no point in carrying on with the game after we'd saved the follow-on, but there was also no point in declaring then because they would simply have batted for the rest of the game. Why give them the batting practice? Greig would have had to set us 350–400 off eighty-five overs to make us a realistic challenge on such a wicket, but by Surrey batting into the second afternoon, opportunities were reduced.'

Having justified his game plan, at least to the satisfaction of the Lancashire dressing-room, history beckoned David into its lair. 'At 665 for 3 over the weekend, 1,000 was quite realistic. Our highest score, 801, was the first target, then Yorkshire's 887. Jesty being unable to bat today because of a tweaked hamstring didn't help, but we achieved the first. To get 863 in an innings is phenomenal, and I was proud of the professional way we tackled the task of saving the follow-on. Despite the state of the ball and the pitch, that speaks volumes for our application, and it will have done wonders for the batsmen in terms of bolstering their confidence. Mendis made it all possible by the way he began the innings, but there was no real thought of records until after we'd saved the follow-on.

'Personally, I'm not one for records, and my only fond memory will be of Fairbrother's 366. A lovely man. His mother is quite volatile and aggressive and Neil has inherited that, but he's learnt from his experiences and he is more mature now. You need to have a sound temperament and strong mental discipline, as well as ability, to make 366. Mind you, he was stuffed by having a Sunday game in the middle; but for that he would have been more mentally attuned today.

'After a Sunday game my legs are shot and sometimes I feel my age. Then I look around on a Monday morning and youngsters like Austin and Hegg look even worse than I do. That does me a power of good! Yesterday we chased 268 here and won with seventeen balls to spare! The adrenalin was pumping and everyone was on edge. Then you relax. We were mentally and physically drained this morning and Neil said he just couldn't get going, otherwise I'm sure he would have passed MacLaren's 424.

'It was still a great knock. He used to drill short balls pitched off-stump over square-leg, then he became tentative for a while, partly, I suppose, because of his bad luck as a Test player. He made his debut against Pakistan at Old Trafford three summers ago, and when he went in the light was bad, there were twenty minutes to go to the close and he was lbw fourth ball playing no stroke. He failed in his next two Tests, against Pakistan and New Zealand that winter, and then spent two days with his pads on at Wellington as the rain pissed down on a perfect batting pitch. Then, the following summer, Monte Lynch got in ahead of him for the Texaco despite the fact that Neil had made centuries in three competitions at that stage of the season. I got into a fair bit of trouble with the club for telling the press what I thought of that. I said it was regional favouritism. I always want to push Lancashire players in terms of international recognition, so I suppose I could be accused of bias at times, but that made no sense at all.'

Outside his twenty-minute flit at the crease, David had had no cause, between 3 p.m. last Friday and mid-afternoon today, to flex a muscle in this match (for the sake of convenience, let's persist with the concept of this event as a contest). He spent most of these leisure hours under the main, still manual, scoreboard. 'I was trying to get away from the noise coming from the building going on next to the pavilion. The dressing-rooms are sited next to the new West Stand and the continual drilling wears you down. We were more aware of it in the field, mind you; I had to shout at the top of my voice just to get someone twenty yards away to shift to his right. I tried to keep busy. I found myself watching golf on someone's TV in between writing letters and composing my *Cricket World* column. Some of the younger lads, Atherton, Hegg and Fitton, joined me for a spell. They loved what was going on in the middle.'

David was somewhat less enamoured. 'What has happened here since last Thursday fuels my argument against four-day cricket. I've been landing myself in trouble with Lancashire for saying this in the press, but we've been producing Test cricketers for a century or more from three-day cricket. We do want less cricket, and sixteen four-days would reduce the workload by seven or eight days, but the boredom can be unbelievable. And what happens in a wet summer? You might be lucky to get a dozen knocks from your Test players. The Australians scored 500s and 600s last year in the Tests, but there were plenty of other big scores on supposedly bad pitches. Let's wait and see whether there is a genuine upgrading of pitches at the non-Test venues. I guess the crowd enjoyed Greig's knock, and I suppose I did too. It was quite thrilling. Maybe people do come to see individuals? Maybe that's why they come to Championship games? But an entertaining contest must be the key. I try to be attacking, but if I can't win I'll do my best to stop the other side winning, which I guess is every captain's attitude.'

In four one-day games since losing to Middlesex in the Refuge on the opening day of their season, Lancashire had looked unstoppable. Funnily enough, only the Combined Universities, in the Benson & Hedges, had threatened that swanky mode (and the students' brave challenge owed much to Mark Crawley, one of Lancashire's own). In the competition that really mattered, however, Neale and now Greig had erected highly effective roadblocks. The cancer is not the four-day format, which seems an eminently good idea, not least since the need for prefab finishes would correspondingly weaken. The reluctance to risk defeat in any walk of life reflects a sour spirit, something that one would never normally accuse Neale or Greig of possessing. Yet in one of the few branches of the entertainment biz that does not always penalise failure, the circumstantial evidence incriminates them now.

Tuesday 8 May, Taunton

Somerset v. Minor Counties (Benson & Hedges Cup)

Amy was stricken with jaundice, and Adrian was finding it hard concealing his concern, let alone keeping his mind on the job. Again he was offered some time off, again he declined. After the Benson & Hedges zonal game against the Minor Counties, he could have been excused the odd misgiving. Despite picking up an early wicket, he was shown scant respect by the part-timers as 63 runs flowed from his eleven overs, most of them coming during an unbroken seventh-wicket stand of 80 between wicket-keeper Andy Fothergill and the former Surrey all-rounder, David Thomas, that spanned the last eleven overs.

'I don't really know how it happened, but maybe I tried too hard. Because they've scared people in the past you set out to dominate the whole game. The standard isn't very good, but somehow they contrive to do very well at times. After all, they have beaten first-class opposition four times in the competition, and they might have done even better if their selection process had been more even-handed. They could be fielding guys like Andy Needham, John Carr and Andy Miller, all ex-Middlesex, but there's something in their rules that prohibits it. Don't ask me how or why.' Not that chasing 241 was ever going to exercise Somerset overmuch, Hayhurst (76) taming an attack boasting three one-time Oval seamers to set up a 6-wicket win with twenty balls to spare.

Wednesday 9 May, Old Trafford

Lancashire v. Hampshire (Benson & Hedges Cup)

From the *Guinness Book of Records* to Edward Lear. After rain had lopped nearly five hours off yesterday's play in the Benson & Hedges Group C game between Lancashire and Hampshire, Lancashire proceeded unhindered to 352 for 6 today, thus passing Essex's competition record 350 for 3 against the Combined Universities in 1979. However, a mid-afternoon shower convinced the umpires, those two bookish Dons, Oslear and Thompsett, that there was insufficient time left in which to bowl the remaining forty-eight overs before the scheduled 7 p.m. close. Oslear and Thompsett played it straight, disdaining any thought that the tea interval might be included in the reckoning. And so Lancashire's hefty total, not to mention Fairbrother's 145, the broadest one-day score yet fashioned in a Lancashire outfit, and his third-wicket stand of 244 with Atherton, another county best, were expunged from potential posterity before the scorers had completed their sums.

A fresh, 18-overs-a-side contest began. Lancashire, a little deflated, made 147 for 5. Hampshire, with Gower and his brutal batman, Robin Smith, in such command that they elected to reject a bad light offer, were rolling merrily along at 99 for 1 from twelve overs at 7.15 when a heavy shower brought the whole shebang to an end. Two matches, two (almost certain) winners and one point apiece. With impeccable timing, for once, the shower soon blossomed into a downpour, cleansing the memory.

David swallowed this messy state of affairs more comfortably than many would have done. 'The rules are as fair as they can possibly be, and it is sad that the records have gone by the board, but we could have made 100 instead of 352 and then we would have benefited from a fresh start. If light and weather permit, I don't see why we can't go on to 7.30 or 8, although whether we should have played on in that light is another matter. We couldn't see the ball; we were in greater danger of it hitting us than the batsmen were, but it was Gower and Smith's decision to bat on. There has been a move in recent years towards playing games in ridiculous conditions, particularly on Sundays. Remember that England-Australia one-day match at the Oval in 1977, when the Aussies won at 8.15 amid a torrential downpour? But because of the risk of injury I don't think it is fair to expect too much of players in this respect. We are entertainers, but there is a line.

'What I'm interested in discovering is what happens to the over rate fines Hampshire were liable for after our first innings? Before the start of play today the umpires asked me whether I wanted to take lunch between innings, and I told them no. I would have had thirty-five minutes at Hampshire before lunch. Understandably Mark Nicholas didn't want that, so he spent the whole of the morning session bowling the remaining twenty-eight overs of the innings. The umpires allowed it because the match had been interrupted, but will those fines be rubbed out along with our total? Probably.

'And there's another old potato. I cannot understand why players vote for over rate fines anyway. It would be different if we were paid 150 grand, but the West Indies are on higher wages and yet we play their game at Test level. I know they were fined in Australia a couple of winters ago, but that seems to have been a one-off. We don't hit them in the pocket. Why do we consider the general public in county cricket, but not in Test cricket?'

When the minimum over rate was reduced by three balls an hour in March, the rider about players being liable to pay any fines in their entirety, rather than share the burden with their employers, received little attention, partially because the Cricketers' Association representatives who negotiated the deal with the TCCB failed to properly communicate the changes to their colleagues. The culpability of the clubs themselves is beyond question. The make-up and creed of a team is to an extent down to management; inadequate sightscreens, insufficient marshalling, building works and all those other external elements that conspire to hold up play, totally so. Grumbles can already be detected, however, as realisation dawns of what all this means in this year of flat seams and flatter pitches. Less enthusiasm to bowl, a paucity of high-class spinners and steamy days are combining to make even the new mean a difficult one to maintain.

In seven weeks or so the returns for the first half of the season will be totted up, a worrying prospect for some. That teams are not assessed on the season as a whole seems a trifle unfair, but at least this system works against inane late-summer orgies such as the one that once saw Graham Gooch and Keith Pont dob down forty-eight overs in an hour against Middlesex in a bid to lift the Essex rate.*

*In hindsight, the change can be seen to have worked. Only four counties were fined in the whole of the 1990 season, one of them twice (the TCCB refused to name names, but Hampshire who duly paid up for their misdemeanours at Old Trafford, can be counted on as one). Yet by December the Board's cricket committee, at the behest of the Cricketers' Association and the captains, was meeting to consider reverting to the original formula of shared responsibility and 18.5 overs per hour. 'Round and round we go in the circle game'.

Yet the concept of penalising teams who fail to bowl a certain number of overs in a day is an odd one. On the surface, the underlying premise that the customers get better value for their shekels if they see more deliveries at least suggests a desire to discover what turns on a crowd, which is more than can be said of most other sports. Do the football authorities, for example, ever think to outlaw the back-pass, or limit its use? The only reason for the long overdue restructuring of the off-side law, and the mere proposal, ludicrous though it is, that goals be widened, was the award of the 1994 World Cup to the USA, that most reluctant of footballing apostles.

In the consumer age the message is simple: bore your audience, and you can be sure there's someone else who can bore them a little more cleverly. In the kingdom of the fickle, the one-eyed traditionalist is doomed. Yet it is highly doubtful whether the decline in Test match attendances, or, for that matter, county attendances, is attributable to any shortcomings in the balls per hour ratio. Indeed, the West Indies, those arch exponents of drawn-out torture, drew almost as many to their tour of Australia in 1988–89 as did England two winters earlier. However, on a more parochial level, the principal function of these fines – to curb the inherent negativity of slowing the over rate – is utterly laudable. So why the double standards?

What really rankled with David right now, though, was an incident on Tuesday involving Mendis and Kevin Shine, the hasty young Berkshire-born right-armer who would emerge with the quixotic figures of 11–0–73–3 from the original Lancashire innings. 'Mendis received one bouncer from Shine, then later in the same over he hooked another short one, over shoulder height, and was caught at long-leg. Mendis ran down the wicket and said, "Wasn't that a no-ball?" It should have been a no-ball [under one-day rules], and it was really the square-leg umpire's responsibility because he had a better view. I'll make reference to it in my umpire's report. There is no point in losing my temper over any of this, but it could be helpful to the game if I reported my thoughts about what went down. Umpire's reports are meant to be with the TCCB twenty-four hours after a game, but one or two things have happened here that might delay me a bit.'

Given that he sits voluntarily on the TCCB umpires' committee, filing a captain's report is not as much of a chore for David as others might find it. 'It's a good report but it takes quite a time to fill in. It's not just a question of marking the umpires then folding the paper and sending it back. You have to mark them from one to five – from "very poor" up to "very good" – for attitude, dress, conduct, the way they get on with the players, even down to light, ground conditions and so on. It's quite comprehensive.' His average mark has always been four, 'good', and he could not recall submitting too many twos.

His assessment of Oslear and Thompsett would be privy only to the TCCB, but it seems reasonable to assume that only generosity would have prevented him from making an exception in this instance. Had he ever awarded a five? 'Once, at Lytham in 1987, after a very low-scoring game. [Lancashire beat Sussex by 54 runs in a match containing two 50s, 562 runs and three career-best bowling analyses, David himself scoring 60 for once out to emerge as the most successful batter.] I thought Nigel Plews and Peter Wight did exceptionally well in the circumstances, making some superb decisions on a slow wicket that made lbw judgements, for one, terribly difficult. The TCCB like us to have a rapport with the umpires, even to tell them you're going to mark them down. I don't think that's necessarily a good thing. I always go and thank the umpires after a game, and at Lytham I congratulated Wight and Plews, but I don't feel inclined to go to umpires and say, "Look, you had a poor game, and I'm going to mark you down." Human nature is human nature and people don't respond too well to criticism. All I try to do is to be as constructive as I possibly can and so help the umpires to become better.'

At the end of each season these reports are collated and a table of umpires for three-day and one-day cricket compiled to decide the international panel for the following summer. 'By and large during my period as captain, Dickie Bird has probably been the most consistent. Plews, Barry Meyer and David Shepherd have been up there as well, but the marks for all twenty-four umpires have been very tight. We really do have a lot of good ones. The key? Commonsense, an ability to work as part of a team, an understanding of players and a feel for when to be flexible and when to be rigid.'

Thursday 10 May, Headingley

Yorkshire v. Lancashire (Benson & Hedges Cup)

From the ridiculous to, at least from a Lancashire standpoint, the sublime. For Yorkshire, rendered a paler shade of white by the Combined Universities yesterday, it was pure pathos. On a pitch that seamed and afforded irregular bounce under the perennial Leeds morning cloud, the very same, moreover, that had been used on Tuesday and Wednesday, Yorkshire spiralled from 35 for 3 to 88 for 9 and only surfaced with 141 thanks to a bellicose 42 from Paul Jarvis at No. 10. Poor old Keith Boyce. The most vilified groundsman in the country – and one of the reasons why Headingley is no longer automatically entitled to host a Test every summer – explained that since four of the pitches on the square had recently been relaid, three one-day games had had to be catered for by two strips, hence the double-up. Tricks were still being played when Lancashire went in, and they faltered when Fowler chipped Stuart Fletcher to mid-off and Fairbrother was beaten off the pitch two runs later to leave his side on 88 for 4. However, Mike Watkinson, that man of many parts (but, in the selectors' estimation, master of none), bulldozed to 43 from twenty-nine balls to follow his earlier 3–31 and ran away with the match award, Lancashire docking 18.5 overs early. 'If Yorkshire were offered at this moment a two-headed coin for the toss, they would call wrongly,' lamented Derek Hodgson, the county's estimable biographer, in the *Independent*.

To the astonishment of this soft, peacenik Southerner, one denied any experience to compare with the birth-to-earth, womb-to-tomb rivalry that has fuelled Roses contests since Richard III offered his throne in exchange for a horse, David preferred to sympathise than gloat at the end of his 'quite incredible' week. Things, as they say, change. 'I was brought up in a school of thought that regarded Roses games second only to Test matches, yet to current players it's just another game against second-rate opposition. That's another tradition that is disappearing. I have taken my players down the Old Trafford steps and indicated the history of the place, but I bet some of them think I'm mad. We allow 13-year-olds to play in the middle of the square there while the 2nd XI play at inferior venues, so the magic is lost to the kids. But neither does it give me any pleasure to see Yorkshire struggling. Watching their batsmen scratch around today, pushing half-cock at balls just short of a length, heads not over the ball, was sad. Yet when I arrived at Lancashire there was a legacy of Yorkshire hammerings, though since the 1970s things have turned completely around.

'Back when I started we were being watched by crowds of 15,000 for a day of a Roses match, but I couldn't count more than twenty still here for the awards ceremony today. Maybe that's because, in the only county where cricket really is the national game, their representatives are so uninspiring? You can see how badly drained of confidence this present Yorkshire side are, and I really feel for Phil Carrick. He and I have had parallel careers; I'm a couple of years older, but we're both slow-left armers who can bat, we've both captained our counties, we played together in South Africa and we've become good friends. But what can he and the rest of the team do with that square of theirs? They are at a disadvantage playing at home because the Headingley wickets never come up to par, either for three-day or one-day games. There have been very few days over the years there without cloud cover, so there's always movement in the air, but that hasn't been the cause of the problems. I've never seen the ball turn there, even when it's been wet, but you get exaggerated sideways movement, prodigious at times, and uneven bounce, which are the most disconcerting things a pitch can offer. A couple of years ago 23 wickets fell in a day there against Nottinghamshire, and that was put down to the atmospheric conditions. Preparations for this game were hampered by the weather, and consequently both of the available pitches needed more time and attention. One was mottled, the other covered in grassy patches. Yet since Leeds no longer play their league games there and Yorkshire use more outgrounds, maybe the opportunity is there to relay the whole thing as we did a few years ago at Old Trafford. The square was 100 years old and our previous groundsman, Bert Flack, produced pitches with too much sideways movement during the 1970s. Put nine inches to a foot of new soil down and lay in some chippings. That's the Peter Marron recipe.'

David's comments on today's antics were based on a relatively detached perspective. He did not pick up a bat, nor propel a delivery.

Yet again. In Lancashire's six legitimate one-day affairs up to now, his quota had been three overs against Middlesex in the Refuge.

Thursday 10 May, Lord's

Middlesex v. Somerset (Benson & Hedges Cup)

Backstage at the Lord's Tavern. In one corner of the bar Mike Gatting holds court, seemingly oblivious to the possibility that, even on his own manor, some punter might well throw a pint of beer over his head. A withering glare greets a couple of cracks about the way he had run himself out, just as Middlesex were threatening to construct a formidable total, but most of the Middlesex and Somerset youngsters surrounding him pass on the hot potato with due care and attention. If the establishment view of Gatting is dim, then the respect of his peers serves as ample compensation.

In another corner, competing with the infantile blast of Sky TV, Adrian occupies his throne, puffing on his pipe like some latterday King Cole. Players from both sides flock round. Eyebrows are raised, quips and asides attempted, but most of the courtiers are stuck for a sufficiently witty response. His denials that this could be construed as a form of affectation are relaxed enough to be credible. What time did he have to be in bed, I ask. 'Doesn't matter. I've only got two overs to bowl tomorrow.' Just over a mile away in Belsize Park, Jack Bond, one of the umpires, stands alone outside a Chinese restaurant, cutting a forlorn, lonely figure as he peruses the menu.

It had been an average sort of day, no more. Under joyless skies, Middlesex, unbeaten, like Somerset, in Benson & Hedges Group B, had been forced to combat a soggy outfield, some suicidal running and a fine, penetrative spell from Mallender. They reached 183 for 6 off forty-eight overs by the close. Adrian began with three slips, all-out warfare in the context of limited-overs cricket, but failed to make an incision. He did have Desmond Haynes in some trouble early on, though, conceding a couple of streaky boundaries and then drawing a shriek of self-reproachment when the opener drove crisply but straight to mid-off. 'Dessie!' he exclaimed, to which Adrian retorted with a cry that contained more frustration than vehemence: 'C'mon, you were lucky with the other two, so it's about time I had a bit.' Haynes let it drop.

Although the running out of Gatting and Roland Butcher seemed likely to keep Middlesex's total within bounds, a flurry of blows from the tail wrung 64 from the final seven overs the following morning. Somerset, however, were sunk by a run-out, Lefebvre foolishly sent back by the last man, Mallender, with four balls left and 9 runs required. Adrian's worst fears had been confirmed. 'Middlesex have an atmosphere, an attitude about them that says, "We're better than you and we'll beat you." '

Friday 11 May, Braintree

Braintree beware. Today, Nadeem left the family bosom and set up home in a two-bedroomed apartment. There was no rift with his parents, but Perth had given him a scent of freedom and he liked it. Paying the rent on a basic salary of £5,000, even with the extras that raised it to around £7,000, was impossible, so he moved in with team-mate Such. 'I know I'll be popping back to Ipswich all the time, but it will be different. Suchy and I are very unalike. For one thing he's more of the stay-at-home type, whereas I'll probably go mad at first and be out till all hours. He's a really good bloke, though, quite quiet and thoughtful, but with a dry sense of humour. Perhaps the contrast between us will be of mutual benefit?'

Two spinners under the same roof? It would be an optimistic household if nothing else.

Saturday 12 May, Hove

Sussex v. Somerset (Benson & Hedges Cup)

For a short spell during the morning, while the clouds scanned Brighton with a morose countenance, slide rules and calculators were of greater interest than events on the field. True, the equation was clear enough: the winner progressed to the Benson & Hedges quarter-finals, the loser did not. But any climatic shenanigans might lead to an abandonment, and then we would be down to decimals and scoring rates to see who joined Middlesex in the last eight. On the other hand, victory for Somerset combined with defeat for Middlesex at Derby would earn the former a home tie. The uncertainty lasted until early afternoon, by which time the heavy cumuli had dispersed and Cook was on his way to 177. Reinforced by a county record 55-over total of 321 for 5, Adrian slipped himself at his former cohorts, having David Smith caught behind for 3 and pinning Paul Parker leg-before for 1.

Their staunchest props dismantled, Sussex could seek nothing more than respectability. Colin Wells fashioned a brave 101 to clean up a mess of 40 for 4, but the eventual margin was a comprehensive 107 runs. Middlesex, meanwhile, were downed at Derby, leaving Somerset atop Group B on scoring rate. They couldn't escape Middlesex, though: the draw would pair the group rivals at Taunton.

In the ensuing twenty-four hours, Cook would top himself, racing to 132 from eighty-seven deliveries to enable Somerset to overhaul Hampshire's far from modest 246 for 3 (D. I. Gower c Tavaré b Jones 12) and so achieve their first Refuge League win of the season. 'Violent innings,' wrote Roebuck in the *Sunday Times*, 'are expected from Richards, Waugh, Lloyd, Crowe and Hick, but not from Cook. Wasn't he supposed to bat as if he were taking the top off an egg?' One over from Malcolm Marshall captured the essence of Cook that day. The first ball was drilled straight to the long-on fence, the second eased to leg, the third and fourth cut backward of point with almost feckless timing. Marshall, staggered by the cheek of it all, stood in mid-pitch, arms akimbo. The over cost 16 in all and Marshall would go to the Somerset quarters at the end to congratulate the man who had mastered him. Cook finally steered a Paul-Jan Bakker slower ball into the outfield and departed exhausted, unsure where the pavilion was. When the standing ovation had subsided there he was, lying on the bench in the dressing-room, grabbing forty winks. It was the finest limited-overs knock Roebuck, and a few others at Taunton besides, had ever witnessed.

Adrian, by his own admission 'an awful watcher' but hardly in need of proof of Cook's brilliance, spent most of the feast making business calls on his carphone. 'I see more in the nets. When he's batting there, I watch Cook in awe. If you bowl him an absolute jaffa which bounces and leaves him, he'll nick it, because he's good enough to do so. I asked Tav why he never seems capable of missing the ball. It's sad that he will have only played two years of county cricket by the end of this summer, when he intends to return to South Africa. But it is vital that he stays, as much for his influence off the field as on it. It all depends on his children's schooling. His two boys are seven and four and they are being taught here from May to

September, but I'm not sure he believes the constant upheaval is beneficial to them. I think he wants to stay.'

Wednesday 16 May, Southend

Essex II v. Northamptonshire II (2nd XI Championship)

Second XI games normally attract more canines than men, but the one between Essex and Northamptonshire has drawn at least twenty humans, plus a touch of royalty. Less than ten months after he and his colleagues on the TCCB pitches sub-committee had condemned the Southchurch Park surface, effectively depriving Essex of the 1989 Championship, Harry Brind was back at the scene of the crime to assess the improvements made to the square since Andy Atkinson was let loose on it during the winter. Stopping off in Chigwell en route, he had already received a curt reminder that his action of last July would not be forgiven in a hurry: his new car had been artistically engraved with a lengthy scratch. 'I'd love to know whether those three kids in the pub recognised me,' he said, suspecting they had.

Atkinson, a cheery, rotund groundsman in his thirties, paces up and down, outwardly mellow, inwardly wary. Should Brind turn his nose up and his thumb down, a highly profitable festival week would bite the dust. The cloudless skies, a brighter shade of pale, were on his side at least. 'I've had a lot more co-operation from the council since the points were deducted. In fact, I ripped the top of the square off four weeks afterwards,' he explains, investing the word 'ripped' with a pungent, onomatopoeic ring. 'Then I dug up two of the pitches, but there hasn't really been enough time to prepare them properly. For this game I've tried to prepare the wicket as close as possible to the one scheduled to be used in the Championship games here. It's hard on top and soft underneath, but it would have helped if we'd had Fozzie here to test it out. There's no one playing of any real pace.'

Peter Edwards deems it no coincidence that one of the umpires chosen to stand in this match is John Harris, a member of the TCCB pitches sub-committee. To the naked eye, though, the creamy hue of the pitch promises runs aplenty, and so it proves. Northants arrive early, enabling proceedings to begin at 11.15 instead of the agreed 12.00, and, while the bowlers lounge in the pavilion, taking turns to leet at *The Sport*, their batsmen soon have the scoreboard ticking jauntily along. Essex, led by Fletcher, have a useful seam battalion in Angus Fraser's brother Alastair, David Boden (both formerly with Middlesex) and Kevin Thomas, a wiry black from Mile End nearing twenty-seven but still to make his first-class debut. However, they make little headway with the prevailing tennis-ball bounce.

'Well done, Lill,' shouts Fletcher as Lilley backs up a wild throw from the deep. While the batting and bowling do not seem obviously inferior to that on offer in more senior environs, the fielding is distinctly shabbier. Long-leg lets a hook run through his fingers; cover mistimes his dive to comic effect; mid-wicket and mid-on both contrive to miss a whipped drive from Mal Loye, a slight 17-year-old who rampages on to 163. David East, whose gloves had engulfed the first eight Somerset batsmen at Taunton five years ago, displays enormous patience for someone whose career had been so rudely interrupted by a hand injury.

As play restarts after lunch, word goes round that Adam Seymour, one of the 2nd XI regulars pressed into service for the Firsts at Fenner's, had been dismissed first ball. A couple of the older fielders respond to the news with a sympathetic tut, while one or two of the younger ones convey their pity with a sheepish grin, aware that failure for one fringe player could mean opportunity for another. Later, it emerges that Seymour has made 28. Every Essex man, visibly at least, appears relieved.

Had Nadeem been in the outfield he would have papered over many of the cracks, but he is ensconced at slip until Fletcher tosses him the ball eight minutes before lunch. Plagued by run-up problems, he needs a lengthy bowl, and gets it. 'The only reason I'm playing here rather than at Fenner's is to sort out my bowling problems. I was bowling too many short balls last year, which Fletch put down to my right leg collapsing on the point of delivery. I've been trying to change my action and run-up. People talk of leg-spinners' actions in terms of the swan neck of the hand, but with me it's the fingers rather than the wrist that do the work. I used to run in too quickly, putting the ball there instead of bowling it, but now I've slowed down and reverted to my original run, still off eight paces, but with no whirling arms. Everything seems fine in the nets, but every time I bowl a bad ball I go in the head. Spin is all in the head.'

Despite a rash of full-tosses and log-hops, tea figures of 20–3–55–0 reflect improved control, if not penetration. Slower to react than in his heyday, Fletcher fails to hold on to one edge at first slip, and two more chances are floored off Nadeem before the close, leaving him mildly pissed off. The next two days are equally fallow, but innings of 43 and 33 are nevertheless sufficient to win him a place in the 1st XI at New Road on Saturday.

Thursday 17 May, Taunton

Somerset v. New Zealanders

With sponsors now striving to insert some meaning into that dormant institution known as the tourist match, Somerset fielded a stronger team against the New Zealanders than had been their recent custom. This decision, though, may have had more to do with trying to impress the returning Martin Crowe, the batsman whose glowing promise had convinced the Somerset committee that they could dispense with Richards and Joel Garner. Now among the foremost batsmen in the world, Crowe brandishes a career average second only to that of Hick. If Cook were to vacate his overseas spot, then he could well be back at Taunton in 1991.

As a man, though, Crowe does not meet with unadulterated approval from Adrian. 'The match definitely meant more because of Martin, although we were unhappy that the Kiwis didn't field a full-strength side. I can't see the point of giving them practice, but at least we did them the favour of fielding all our main bowlers who were fit. As a team man, in terms of creating an atmosphere that inspires us, Cook is better than Crowe, who became aloof in his latter years here. Admittedly, why should he care? No one talked much to him during this match. He played magnificently well in the first innings and I was pleased to see the back of him because he can make you look a very ordinary bowler. In the second innings, judging by the position he got into, he may have been expecting a short one from me, but the ball took his off-stump. I was impressed with the pace I managed to generate, but with thirty successive days' play coming up I wasn't going to knock myself out.'

Mark Greatbatch knocked Somerset out, however. Set 322 after Cook's third century inside a week, the New Zealanders scorched to victory by 5 wickets with three balls remaining, so deriving some useful practice for the following week's one-day internationals. Greatbatch, four-square and forceful, had relied on stubborn occupation for the unconquered 146 that saved his compatriots against Australia in Perth the previous November, but the natural bent of this blond, broad-shouldered left-hander lay in unbridled drives. Now he heaved two for 6 in much the same manner he employed three years ago when playing club cricket for Clevedon by the Severn estuary. In all, Greatbatch made 85 from eighty-one balls to send out a warning that England would do well to heed.

Friday 18 May, Derby

Derbyshire v. Lancashire (County Championship, 4 days)

Been a long, long time since David had rock'n'rolled quite like this. Having asked Derbyshire to emulate their 309 of the first innings, and given them a generous allocation of eighty-seven overs in which to do so, the captain took centre stage to spin Lancashire to their first Championship 16-pointer of the summer. Not since the final match of the 1982 season at Taunton, when his return was 4–22, had David produced as profitable a balance sheet as 24–12–25–4. Shame the *Guardian* had to spoil it all by linking the analysis to one S. P. Hughes, the Middlesex seamer. With Atherton having taken 5–95 in Derbyshire's first dig, this was a scorecard worth framing for fans of artful deceit.

The reluctant bowler made a reluctant dramatist. 'My plan at the start was to give Atherton and Fitton a long bowl because they are both in need of one, then to bring myself on if needed. As the match wore on it was inevitable that the pitch would take more spin and that that was the department that would win the game for us. When Derbyshire set off for that 309 on a pretty dead pitch, Fitton persuaded Barnett to drag a slower ball to square-leg and forced Morris to sweep the ball into his stumps. Atherton bowled Kuiper as he made room for a slash past point, but at 130 for 3 just before tea Adams and Bowler were beginning to settle, so I brought myself on and trapped Adams in my third over. It may have straightened. Then, in the over after tea, I had Goldsmith caught by Mendis at extra-cover so now I had 2–6 in five overs. The next three or four were quiet, so I brought Atherton off and switched ends with Fitton. I still think Derbyshire were interested. Krikken played on to me, swinging, and Jean-Jacques popped one to Jesty at short-leg. Derbyshire were nine down, but time was running out. After two or three overs at Base, I apologised to the lads after bowling the penultimate over without success and handed over to Daffy [DeFreitas], and he finally had Miller lbw with five balls to go. It was good to win.'

David's estimation of his value to the attack remains modest. 'I'm still the third spinner, although when I see Dexter struggling for rhythm, as he has been lately, I do wonder a bit. Do I carry on and say nothing, or what? He is struggling for rhythm and the only way to cure that is plenty of overs. I never lose mine. I can still drop it on a tanner. Still, Mike [Atherton] is a better and more confident bowler now, and people look at him tentatively, which is a bonus, although he's still primarily a batsman, of course. I don't think he's at his best as an opener, but I understand that the selectors have him in mind to bat there this summer. That said, a No.3 has to be a sort of opener, so I'm sure he'll do them proud. That'll be a good test for him, because he's never struggled before.'

Ah, Atherton. Apparently David's heir-apparent, talk of this quietly assertive, remarkably self-contained history graduate from Downing College, challenging Monty Bowden for the honour of being England's youngest-ever captain (and that was back in 1888) had been discernible when, before his 22nd birthday, he went with England A to Zimbabwe as Mark Nicholas's lieutenant during the winter. Personally speaking, I have never met a young interviewee with quite such a flair for deflecting questions he deems unsuitable, a crucial asset for a putative media idol. David is more circumspect. 'He exudes an air of aloofness and arrogance, but he may not be that confident underneath. He may fall down because he's got set ideas and he is very voluble in his opinions. He hasn't yet acquired the capacity to see the other view, and that's why I'd be reluctant, very reluctant, to give him total responsibility. Captaining at county level is about understanding and looking after ten other players.'

But since the captain is the buffer between management and staff, and since the very precept of authority, moreover, demands a certain distance, he must surely be at one remove much of the time. 'It does take you away from your colleagues to an extent, so I make a point of taking each of them out for dinner in turn. Thankfully, there are no cliques here, even though there are the usual set pairings when it comes to hotel rooms: Fairbrother and DeFreitas, Allott and Fowler. Everyone socialises. I've already planned a golfing tour of Scotland for myself and a number of lads for the end of the season. We always travel by bus to anywhere south of Birmingham because the players are more relaxed if they don't have to think about driving, but that also gives them a chance to chat to each other in a relaxed frame of mind.'

Saturday 19 May, Worcester

Worcestershire v. Essex (County Championship, 3 days)

If Essex eyes glinted with a steelier determination than usual this morning, then who could blame them? Here, after all, was an early opportunity to exorcise a demon or two. As far as they could see, Worcestershire, whose own square was only spared condemnation when they agreed to dig it up, were county champions merely at the behest of the TCCB and the slack-handedness of the Southend groundsman. By dusk, vindication, if not yet vengeance, was theirs.

The tenor of three ludicrously one-sided sessions was set, to no one's astonishment, by Gooch. Graham Dilley, bold, blond and brassy, and still the most resonant English paceman of his generation when at full blast, owes much of his reputation to an aptitude for the early strike. On this memorable occasion, though, Gooch curtailed his opening spell of three overs with no less than five 4s. His meticulous strokes rarely rising above the mottled turf, Gooch greeted Neal Radford and Phil Newport with similar disdain, a flurry of precise straight drives and deft glances to the short cathedral boundary seeing the 100 up at the start of the seventeeth over.

'Nothing wrong with this pitch,' asserted one New Road regular with the nervy lack of conviction of one accustomed to having his heroes' achievements denigrated by digs at the handiness of the groundsman. As Gooch's frequent gardening intimated, however, this one was not quite the batting Xanadu he was making it appear. The bounce was variable, the colour a pale green, and the home seamers suffered for their fallible line.

Stephenson had stumbled his way to 4 out of the first 37 when he prodded Radford to second slip, but that did Worcestershire no good whatsoever. Bat broadened and timing enhanced after dining so ravenously against Leicestershire, in skipped Prichard to cut anything remotely off line, he and Gooch waltzing to a stand of 98 with barely a pause for breath until the gnomic No. 3 was run out just before lunch, Gooch having rejected his call for a non-existent single to point. Botham, returning with commendable vim just two weeks after a knee operation, checked the onrush of runs for a while, but Gooch was in such omnipotent fettle that the only person capable of getting him out was himself. And so it came to pass. Having dashed to 121, his third century in four Championship knocks making him the first visiting opener to make a century at Worcester since 1988 (only three had reached 50 during that period), he sliced Newport to Steve Rhodes's waiting gloves as if weary of such easy pickings.

Gooch had established a platform and now his cohorts picked up the beat. Waugh's rattling cover-drives maintained the impetus and provided a recapitulation of sorts as he and Hardie put on 166 in forty-four overs; indeed, the polish of the New South Walian's ground strokes hinted broadly that, come Ashes time, 'Afghanistan' would be the forgotten Waugh no longer. But not until Nadeem came in in the ninety-third over did Essex's innings begin to scale the peaks of the morning. Bat frozen at a 40 degree angle, body still as stone, he allows his first delivery, from Botham, to pass harmlessly by, then strokes his second, from Dilley, square for 4. Another square clip to the boundary follows in Dilley's next over.

Confidence rising, he prances three steps down the track before propping immaculately forward to Botham, who glares at him. 'No. 57, Pilau Rice,' snaps the Greatest Living Englishman in a none-too-successful attempt to rile this young pup. 'The next one's a bouncer for sure,' muses Nadeem, who instead finds himself edging a full-length delivery for 2. Another lengthy stare from the G.L.E. The next offering is a bouncer and Nadeem employs a stroke best described as an overhead smash to glean another 2 runs. 'What do you think you're doing, playing tennis?' barks the clearly frazzled G.L.E. In the ninety-eigth over, Nadeem whips Dilley through square-leg for 4, then leaves the next delivery with a flourish befitting a man in complete harmony with his muse. Via a series of signals from the pavilion balcony Nadeem and Waugh learn that the 100th is to be the last before Gooch declares. Eschewing thoughts of a not-out,

Nadeem assails his verbal tormentor, striking three bona-fide boundaries and an edged single in the process of taking 18 from the final six balls and his personal tally to 35. Gooch settles for 447 for 4, the highest score at New Road since Surrey's 451 in 1983, then clasps Martin Weston's edge at slip in Foster's opening over.

A good day's work, rounded off on the Monday by Foster, Topley and Pringle as they swept through some half-hearted Worcestershire resistance to bring Essex within sight of a two-day win. The 10-wicket margin established the next morning supplied a sufficiently thunderous coda. 'We were disappointed about losing the Championship after our best-ever season, but we have nothing against Worcestershire,' Gooch, fresh from his Caribbean crash course in diplomacy, informed the press. 'It was not their fault we lost those 25 points.'

When the penalty was imposed, Essex accepted their ill-fortune in a temperate manner, revealing bitterness only in private. Cricketers, by and large, are too couth to utter tabloid-titillating words like vendetta. Compared to our back-biting Babel of a Football League, the county circuit is positively Utopian, although that has much to do with its lower media profile. Since its male-dominated enclave embraces a broader social spectrum, and given the oceans of time these fellows spend in each other's pockets, the lack of obvious conflict is remarkable. Nevertheless, it was difficult for an outsider to fall for the old 'it's just another game' line.

Nadeem was equally anxious to refute the grudge theory. 'People will assume we had a special team talk before we started. "Let's beat these bastards", that sort of thing. But the general feeling was that we could beat them without going mad. True, we'd all been having conversations between ourselves about the extra desire we had to beat them, but I don't think anyone went out there feeling that het up about it. In the final analysis, their batters didn't perform well, nor their bowlers. It was an ideal wicket for cricket. Not too flat and tinged with green. We thought it would do a lot even though we chose to bat, and Botham did wobble it about a bit, but it was very hard and the bounce was mostly true.'

Gooch, of course, had been the catalyst. 'He gave the whole side confidence. He usually picks on a bowler, normally their principal pace bowler, although he also seems to take particular relish in having a go at Emburey because he's his mate. He'd already smashed Agnew and Cowans this season and this time he set it up for the rest of us by smashing Dilley. I don't think he's capable of hitting an ordinary 100. Waugh strokes the ball and is generally more textbookish, but he's just as hungry for runs. Just after I came in, Gooch signalled for us to hurry along, but Waugh said he wanted his 150, so I thought, right, if he's going to play for his average, then so will I. My innings certainly didn't start like that, mind. I thought Gooch was going to send Garnham or Foster in when he called me over, but instead he said I was in next and that I should push it around, play normally. The outfield was quick, all you had to do to get a 4 was put bat to ball. After I'd played a maiden from Botham we received the message to get a move on, and, despite our initial response, we tried to do so. Botham may not be quick any more but he was difficult to get away, which prompted that charge down the wicket and the words that followed, all from him.

'When I went into the changing-rooms at the end of the day he was in the shower, so I said to someone I wasn't going in while he was there. Mind you, I don't know what I was worried about. He was hardly going to punch me. Then I was told that he'd been saying how well I'd batted. Was that his idea of a joke? He was OK in the bar, but it's hard to tell whether someone is a good bloke or not after something like that. I did feel he had been slightly racist, but whereas that sort of thing used to really get to me when I was 11 or 12, I've learned to cope.'

Tuesday 22 May, Taunton

Somerset v. Derbyshire (County Championship, 3 days)

Having a captain who holds fast to old-fashioned values, like always batting first when given the option, is proving to be something of a disadvantage for Somerset in this perfect pitch of a summer. While their batsmen are well-equipped for the chase, their bowlers are unlikely to baulk one.

Against Derbyshire, however, Tavaré changes his spots and gives the opposition first use of another belter. Adrian's bouncers and yorkers account for Barnett, Kuiper and Bruce Roberts, but he gives away runs with alacrity, 5 an over. At one stage he sends down consecutive bouncers to John Morris, who duly pulls both dismissively for 4. Undeterred, he continues with the short-pitched barrage and eventually persuades Barnett to mishook to Hayhurst. In the end, Morris bludgeons his way to a fourth successive century (also the first of his brace in the match) and Derbyshire declare at 372 for 9.

Three days later Devon Malcolm produced his first meaningful spell of the season, rounding up a precious herd in Cook (5), Tavaré (9), Rose (31) and, most critically of all, Hardy, whose 91 had given Somerset visions of a draw. Instead, they lost their last 7 for 101 and slumped to defeat by 146 runs, their first Championship reversal of the season. Coincidentally or not, Cook failed to reach double figures in either dig.

Malcolm impressed Adrian a great deal. 'He's a fine bowler. If you'd asked me a year ago about his international prospects I'd have said you must be joking, and I think a lot of people would have said the same. But he's improved beyond doubt. He's always had and always will have pace, and because of that he frightens batsmen. He has a lovely action, hits the wicket and is very aggressive, but most of all his control is vastly better than it was. He should serve England well.'

Further needled by the memory of having been thrashed for 6 by Kuiper with Derbyshire needing a single off the last ball to win the Refuge clash on the Sunday, Adrian is a tad cheesed off. 'I don't know why we put them in [in the Championship game]. It was damp, but easy for batsmen on the first day. Morris was in magnificent form, striking thirteen boundaries in his first 59. He hits through the line so well, but there is such a small margin for error when you're bowling at the moment. I'm lacking in confidence and it's because of the ball and pitches. I bowled seventeen overs in five spells in the first innings, the opening one of which was diabolical, although I did have Bowler plumb lbw only for the umpire to disagree. I was off after three and later told to space out the bouncers. Still, I ended up with 3 wickets, and wickets are like gold dust. Batsmen are able to wait and hit the ball square much as they please, knowing that the quick outfields will ensure boundaries.

'I said to Phil Frost that he could get away with putting a bit more grass on his pitches because there wouldn't be enough lateral movement to risk a Lord's report. And then there's the ball. After seven or eight overs it looks and feels like a grapefruit. A couple of the members were so concerned that they asked to see the type we used last year. The club gets a discount on those balls and, because of a surplus we're still using them in the nets and for 2nd XI matches, which doesn't seem sensible as those players will only be using this year's model if and when picked for the 1st XI. Maybe they should double the width of the bat, or force us to bowl at one stump. No, I'm not enjoying my cricket right now.'

Just to exacerbate Adrian's displeasure, Somerset have gone on an economy/health drive. The enormous communal bath so beloved of visiting teams has fallen foul of the AIDS lobby. Gone too are the orange juice machine and those delicious tea-time cakes, displaced by orange squash and fruit. 'Sometimes I don't know whether I'm bowling with a ball, a grapefruit or a Granny Smith's.'

Saturday 26 May, Colwyn Bay

Glamorgan v. Lancashire (County Championship, 3 days)

As Patrick Patterson pads in from the Penrhyn Avenue end, behind which trams once clanked so reassuringly along the sea front, a chorus of 'C'mon Patto' echoes around this intimate ground. So too does the past. S. F. Barnes practising his wizardry; Cliff Gladwin levering a 6 over Penryhn Avenue and onto a distant roof; Charlie Barnett's XI playing the West Indies during the war to raise money for the Liverpool and Bootle Air Raid Distress Fund. This, though, is only Glamorgan's sixth Championship engagement here (and the first for sixteen years) since the pavilion was built in 1924 by Wilfred Wooller senior, father to that stalwart of Welsh cricket, plain ol' Wilf. (Mind you, it's easy to see why Glamorgan have been reluctant to come here. How can you call a venue 'home' when you have had to charter a couple of tiny planes to get there from Swansea the previous evening? To Lancashire, whose journey from Old Trafford was some 100-odd miles briefer, Colwyn Bay is, comparatively speaking, round the corner.) A middle-aged fellow, presumably just back from a trip to the NASA boutique, walks by the press tent clad in a concoction best described as a pinky-bluey-purpley-grey tracksuit. More worrying is the local teenager who peers in and asks, in all innocence, 'Who won?'

By the end of the first day, however, much progress has been made towards answering the lad's strange query. Alan Butcher's recent exertions – four and a half consecutive days either at the crease or in the field – persuaded him to drop himself down the order upon winning the toss. But in the absence of the King of Antigua and Prince Regent Maynard (who, incidentally, was not only born in Oldham, but educated at the David Hughes School, Anglesey), missing on account of a split finger and a broken one respectively, poor Butcher was in the thick of it again after barely half an hour. 'Patto' bustled one through Hugh Morris, then David stood his ground as Michael Cann swished at DeFreitas, and duly pocketed a catch off inside edge and pad. Despite a resourceful spell from DeFreitas (one made all the more meritorious by his arrival in the wee small hours from one-day international duty at the Oval), Butcher soon settled into an imperturbable groove.

He could do little to contain the excitability at the other end, however. The lissom debutant Hamesh Anthony, a pacy protégé of Malcolm Marshall's, hailing, according to his registration form, from 'somewhere in Antigua', struck 39 off thirty-two balls with a controlled sonic force to bring some cheer to the sun-drenched picnickers in front of the tarpaulin sightscreen and prefab houses at the steeply inclining Embankment end. But thanks to Allott, Patterson and DeFreitas, the innings lasted no more than sixty-seven overs, the last twenty of which featured a prudent, at times impudent, ninth wicket stand of 66 between that salt-of-the-earth seamer, Steve Watkin, and Colin Metson, acclaimed by some as the handiest stumper in the country.

Now we settled back for some real batting. On an innocent surface guilty only of a smidgin of uneven bounce, Lancashire would surely spit on Glamorgan's pitiful 205. Watkin, last season's leading county wicket-taker but now suffering from a seam-induced dearth of confidence, was reduced to first change but disposed of Fowler in his opening over, courtesy of a spooned drive to extra-cover. Nigel Cowley's flattish off-break trapped Atherton at 92, but we were still only in the twentieth over. Mendis, rapacious from the off, cut Anthony to ribbons as the bowler worked up a hot pace but, in his anxiety to impress, allowed too much width. Mendis withdrew his horns in admiration, though, as Fairbrother unfurled some murderous shots. Signalling his intentions by waltzing down the wicket second ball to cream Cowley for 6, the dapper left-hander switched the turntable to 78rpm, clubbing 60 in forty-seven balls, all but four in boundaries, before Cowley clung on to a return drive that a more sensible chap would have sidestepped. For sheer premeditated bullishness, it was hard to imagine anyone matching it all summer. As he paraded around the perimeter, Viv Richards would stop and glance towards the middle every so often. What he saw during the early evening provoked a knowing, kingly smile. The ultimate accolade.

While Fairbrother and Mendis were in cahoots, David reflected on events last Tuesday, when a distinctly ungenerous declaration by Leicestershire's Nigel Briers at Old Trafford had evidently got Lancashire's goat. 'Before the start on Monday, Winston Benjamin came up to our dressing room and said "We're going to bat on – I've never made a first-class 100." The lads got really fired up by that remark, as well as the decision to bat on, and we took the last 3 wickets in no time. Benjamin didn't even add a run. Then it transpires that Benjamin had tendonitis and Chris Lewis is feeling under the weather, so they've got no intention of giving us a game anyway. We resolved to bowl them out, but the only wicket we managed on the second evening came when Peter Martin ran Tim Boon out, going for a fourth! That was it really, although we finished closer to defeat than victory at 201 for 7. The members expect us to open the game up, but I felt I'd done all I could declaring 86 behind. One bloke wrote me a letter after the Worcestershire game at the beginning of the season, complaining that I had declined a target. I can't win.'

There was one toast worth making, however, to Fairbrother, and not purely for his machine-gun scattering of the Glamorgan attack. An injury to Wayne Larkins had cleared a path for him to return to the national squad for the one-day internationals against New Zealand. (As it transpired, he did not see action at Headingley or the Oval, but no matter.) Restoration to the Test team could not be far away for the impish Warringtonian with the 204.66 average. David, naturally, was pleased as Punch. 'Neil's original omission disappointed me, however, even if I was glad that the selectors went with the players who had been in the Caribbean. Once you've gone through a tour like that, the most hostile of tours, you deserve it. Gower, whom I've always admired and got on with, did get in through the back door ahead of Neil, but he's been treated shabbily, so I was pleased for him. It'll do him a power of good to have got away from Leicestershire. But I still think there's room for him *and* Neil.'

Wednesday 30 May, Taunton

Somerset v. Middlesex (Benson & Hedges Cup quarter-final)

Just four days ago Adrian had been led from the field at Grace Road, blood seeping from the stitches inserted in his bowling arm following the removal of a growth earlier in the month. The disillusionment apparent after the game against Derbyshire is still in evidence. Yet now he is the Theseus of Taunton once more. Somerset seemed to be in a maze of their own making after being bowled out for 183 in their Benson & Hedges quarter-final against heavily-backed Middlesex. Awaiting them were those twin minotaurs, Haynes and Gatting. Tavaré talked of needing a miracle. Adrian engineered a rough approximation, cutting Haynes down in mid-flight, punching a hole in the middle by dismissing Butcher and Downton, and finally, with the fifth ball of the fifty-second over, sending Middlesex thudding permanently to the canvas. As Mike Selvey related in the *Guardian*, 'a snorting, gut-busting ruddy-faced fast bowler if ever there was one, [he] charged in one more time and, to a roar that almost removed the pavilion roof, pinned back the leg stump of Norman Cowans.'

Adrian is unsure whether to puff out his chest or split his sides at such a colourful depiction. 'Reporters have got to colour it up, haven't they? In terms of character I don't know that that's what I really am, or whether that's just the image I portray, but I do try hard. Maybe it's my asthma?'

He is rather more certain of the roots of Middlesex's unexpected demise. 'So long as we could get Haynes and Gatting early, we had a chance. Dessie played well. He struck three 4s off me during my first spell, but I think he and Gatt let the side down by going out with all guns blazing, trying to knock the runs off as quickly as possible. Maybe it was arrogance on their part, but the pitch wasn't the best at Taunton this season by any means. It was slow, and the odd ball was shooting. But there were no partnerships to speak of [the best was 34 for the first wicket], we managed two very good run-outs to get rid of Brown and Roseberry, and bowled extremely tightly. I conceded almost twice as many runs as anyone else. It was also a good toss to win. The sun came out for the first time when Middlesex batted, but it did get cloudy again later on, which I suppose helped us.'

Among the spectators was Micky Stewart, the England manager. His Somerset counterpart, Birkenshaw, is said not to see eye-to-eye with Stewart, nor communicate with him on anything other than a perfunctory level. Adrian wonders whether this is a good or bad thing for him and his aspiring co-toilers. (He would soon receive an answer of sorts when forty-three county players later received letters from the TCCB inquiring as to their availability for winter duty. Not a Somerset addressee in sight; only Sussex received such short shrift. 'I am very pleased to be still considered one of the best forty-three cricketers in England,' intoned a sarcastic Botham, who refused to reply.)

Why Stewart was in attendance was unclear. 'Maybe he wanted to see Norman [Cowans] bowl? God, he's slow nowadays, but perhaps he is becoming shrewder. Or Neil Williams? Or Mark Ramprakash? I can't think that Tav was the attraction; he's not interested and the selectors know that, I assume. I've known Micky for years through the Surrey boys, and I'm pally with Alec. He said hello to me, but I don't know about him coming specifically to watch me. Could he have? I doubt it. Who else was there? True, he's probably looking for someone to team up with Malcolm, and I am just behind the leading wicket-takers. And I did bowl well last season . . .' In Adrian's opinion, mind, those wickets would have done little to sway Stewart. 'It's more about line and length, getting the basics right, proving that you have the constituent parts of a Test bowler.'

Adrian's reward was a two-day furlough, the first of which he began at the cobblers. His left big toe is cutting up something rotten and remedial work on the boot is imperative. 'You hit the ground very hard on that foot. You're concentrating all your weight and effort into it, so it must be comfortable, not cramped.' The gaping, Bash Street Kidesque hole in the toe of that left boot is evidence of Adrian's suffering – which at 10.15 increases. The semi-final draw is broadcast on the radio. It's the one no one wanted: Lancashire, indubitably the best one-day combo in the business, at Old Trafford. 'Tough one, that.'

Wednesday 30 May, Sudbury Hill

Essex II v. Middlesex II (2nd XI Championship)

A blip. After being bowled for a duck by Marshall at Southampton, Nadeem's first dismissal in first-class play this season brings his average plummeting down to 88 from four innings. Five unthreatening overs costing 25 runs confirm that his bowling is in more urgent need of attention, but this outing to the heart of Harrow with the 2nd XI is due more to the fact that he is still not considered ready for the limited-overs lash. So, while the 1st XI subside in their Benson & Hedges quarter-final at home to Nottinghamshire, Nadeem is once again under Fletcher's microscope.

Sudbury Hill reminds one that what remains of the fastest-dwindling county on the map differs hugely from neighbouring North London. The whole of this semi-detached, surburban conurbation we call Harrow, where I spent my schooldays, is more time capsule than ambitious city offshoot, one struggling endlessly to merge a fair-to-middling outlook grounded in Attleeian austerity with the aspiring Americanisms of its newer parents. Atop Harrow Hill stands The School. Just below the peak perch cosy cottages, occupied, like those of Hampstead Village six or seven miles to the east, either by those to whom this is the only place worth inhabiting, or by career couples. Elsewhere, McDonaldses collide apologetically with chippies, a two-in-one, reasonably hi-fi ABC cinema with an ancient Granada two-screener. Sopers is now Debenhams. A shopping centre sprawls over both sides of Station Road. Thankfully, Sellanby, a record shop close to South 'Harra' tube station, was still trying to offload secondhand copies of West, Bruce and Laing LPs. Before I discovered that Anne loved me, the proudest moment in my life had been going there and taking out a permanent loan on a Genesis LP, 'Nursery Cryme' to be exact. Every lunch break, Andy Woodend, Ian Reed and myself, 'The Swot Gang' as we were dubbed by our less assiduous classmates, would bring our reject records there. The exchange rates stank, so we vowed one day to get a little bit even. Eventually the chance arose, and I slid the record into a bag containing a couple I'd purchased legitimately. I saw nothing immoral in tendering unrighteous indignation as payment.

Anyway, enough of the field trip. Nadeem is prevented from bowling by a split callous on the third finger of his right hand, the digit that ignites his leg-break. 'Sometimes I use artificial skin to protect it, or sit down in front of the TV for three hours, pickling it in vinegar, which hardens the skin. The physio usually files it down or tries balsam, but it still splits when the skin dries. It's probably a legacy of bowling twenty overs every morning for the first time in January. Last year I had a long spell against Hampshire and the finger completely stiffened up. I thought it was arthritic for a while, and so took to wearing one of those copper bracelets. The copper is supposed to get into the bloodstream, but it could just be psychological. Anyway, it cleared up.'

The wider issue, when he did bowl without discomfort, was whether Nadeem could trouble batsmen. He is beginning to doubt it. 'Fletch says I'm letting the ball go before I plant down my front foot. So why was it that I could hit an ashtray six times an over at 16, but not now? He says that because I've grown I'm dragging the ball down and bowling off the back foot.'

Nadeem certainly wasn't on the back foot when he went in to bat after that pock-faced maestro, Clive Radley, had helped guide his Middlesex cherubs to 373, the Reading-born Aftab Habib contributing 96 of them. After a few rousing blows he is caught in the deep trying to whoosh Paul Weekes, an off-spinner on the fringes of a senior breakthrough, over the top. 'It was a silly shot. When I came back to the dressing-room I threw down my bat and waited for a bollocking from Fletch. In he came, but all he said was that I shouldn't worry. He added that I was right to be positive, which is something he always encourages me to be, but perhaps I should have held on a bit because we'd lost a wicket in the previous over. We then lost 6 for 8 and it all came back to me. Then we followed-on and lost 2 quick wickets, so I spent most of the final afternoon making 21 before I went for a fine sweep, again off Weekes. I'd completed the shot when the ball bobbled off the back of my wrist, someone shouted "Catch it" and the wicket-keeper duly did so. When I got back to the dressing-room Fletch was waiting for me. But all he said was, "Just as well you've got all your bad luck out of the way early." '

Fletcher's judicious man-management was again in evidence

when Nadeem rolled up at Ilford ready to do battle with the Middlesex seniors on the Saturday. 'I got up expecting to play and there I was, in at 9.30, doing some TDs [throw-downs, throwing balls at a batsman from short range] with Nasser. An hour later the team was announced and I wasn't in. I was disappointed, naturally. Fletch told me that they thought the pitch was going to turn and so they wanted two specialist spinners, Charlie Childs and Suchy. I asked him whether I would have been picked had I been bowling better, and he said no. A little later he said that if I'd been bowling brilliantly I would have played instead of Suchy. He's a clever guy. I did get on, mind, when Foster had to pop off to the toilet for a couple of overs. I'd just been settling down for a snooze and I was half asleep. I took his place at slip and, what do you know, Roseberry has a dart at Pring and edges the fourth ball of the over a yard and a half to my left. Gooch kept saying "Nad", but all I did was follow it with my eyes. For the rest of the day people kept saying "Don't worry about losing us the Championship and the £40,000 that goes with it." Fletch said I should have gone for it but that it was wrong to blame me.

'I can't believe I ever felt that way, but when I first met Fletch I was a bit scared of him. He came down to the nets in a blazer and tie, and I'd been told that whatever he says goes. But he susses people out quickly and treats you as an individual. I've never seen him slag anyone off.'

Later, following a two-hour net with Fletcher, Nadeem found himself deep in conversation with Doug Insole, county chairman, and Graham Saville, county cricket chairman. 'Saville wasn't sure whether I should stop bowling for the rest of the season and go back to basics with Fred Titmus's help, as Childs did a couple of years back, or with Don Wilson at Lord's. I agreed to have tuition with someone for two weeks at the end of the summer and then go back to Perth in the winter. Yet Fletch reckons that if I could carry on bowling and make some progress, I could go on a winter tour as a batsman who can bowl. He keeps telling me that he's not looking for five-fers from me, just that I should develop over the next two years and succeed Childs as the main spinner. It's wonderful to have someone show such faith in you, but I don't imagine I'll be doing much more bowling for the 1st XI this summer.'

A turbulent day ended in discomfiting fashion, Hussain discovering that his car had been vandalised. Word had it that this was the work of a local redneck. Nadeem took it in his stride. 'They don't really know about me yet, but when they do someone will probably take their prejudices out on me. You just have to grin and bear it, because there's nothing you can do to change people like that.'

The following afternoon a visit by Glamorgan provided the cue for a few racist jibes to be flung at Viv Richards. During the Essex-New Zealand game at the end of the month, Kevin Thomas, the coloured East End quick, would be showered with apple cores on his first-class debut. The cancer of jaundiced nationalism is far from being wholly confined to Headingley.

Old, new, borrowed, black and blue. David, wearing a pair of oversized boots lent to him by the Essex batsman Bob Cooke, slips and falls heavily to earth at Old Trafford in attempting to deliver his inaugural ball in first-class cricket. By way of consolation, Donald Toft, the statuesque Oxford batsman at the striker's end, holed out two balls later.

His cup bubbleth over. David poses for the papparazzi after his Gillette Cup assault on Gloucestershire's John Mortimore in the Old Trafford gloom had spirited Lancashire to their first Lord's final in July 1971.

Young gun.
Adrian charges in
for Sussex against
Middlesex at
Hove in 1984.

Same opposition
six years on
as Adrian leaps
into his delivery
stride at Uxbridge.

Jumpin' Jive.
Gloucestershire's
Jeremy Lloyds
edges clear of
the leaping Graham
Rose at Taunton,
where Somerset,
and Adrian,
began their
Championship
campaign with
such deceptive
promise.

Where did I go wrong, man?
Patrick Patterson, whose dismissal has just
ended Lancashire's Oval orgy, asks David how he managed
to contribute precisely nothing to a total of 863.

Left Another brick in the wall. Nadeem eases towards his hundred against Lancashire at Colchester with a deft glance. *Right* Nothing to it. Dispensing with his customary lemonade and lime, Nadeem takes to the hard stuff after scoring his maiden first-class century in the familiar environment of Castle Park.

Rather you than us, son. Nadeem evades a short-pitched ball from Waqar Younis during his gritty innings of 27 against Surrey on a testing pitch at Chelmsford. Graham Thorpe (left) and Monte Lynch seem relieved that the game's outstanding young bowler is on their side.

Look, no strings!

I still know how to use this thing, y'know. David, rarely called upon to supplement the powerful Lancashire batting order, helps stem the tide during his rollicking 57 against Essex at Colchester.

Cock o' the North. David relaxes with the author at Blackpool during the game against Surrey. Twenty-four hours later Lancashire's NatWest Trophy triumph at Lord's cemented their claims as the pre-eminent northern county.

300 for 2 and another long afternoon in prospect.

How do you bowl to this man? Adrian ruminates as the insatiable Desmond Haynes, whose century kick-started the thrilling Middlesex run chase at Uxbridge, awaits another opportunity to pepper the perimeter.

Have a spell, lad. David in consultation
with Wasim Akram during the NatWest Trophy final.

Preying or praying?
Nadeem in the dead man's shoes on Boot Hill.

The boys of summer:
Graham Gooch, Jimmy Cook, Nasser Hussain and Neil Fairbrother.

8 June

Saturday 2 June, Horsham

Sussex v. Lancashire (County Championship, 3 days)

Beneath the twisted spire of St Mary's Church, at the oldest Sussex ground still in first-class employ, things remain much as they were. In 1855, all 10 MCC wickets fell to catches; on this Saturday, Sussex were caught out with similar uniformity.

The opening offering, appropriately enough, was accepted by Mendis, who fastened on when Neil Lenham sliced Watkinson's very first ball to gully. As a Sussex old boy (chosen, incidentally, by the incumbent captain, Paul Parker, in his all-time county XI), Mendis did his damndest to mute his celebrations. Allott, Patterson and Watkinson did most of the damage as Tony Dodemaide manned the burning deck with gritty resolve, but Atherton dealt two late blows for spin in a spell of tight top-spin and googlies before Sussex finally subsided for 235. Fitton chimed in by snaring Alan Wells, but was generally off-key. True to his word, however, David gave both young 'uns a longish stint. Fitton was in by the close, though that did not indicate a Lancashire collapse in the nine overs that remained: Fowler had been indisposed since a deflection off Hegg's gloves thudded into his top lip in the second over of the day. Fifteen stitches were required to disguise the casualty as Eva Braun's lover, and instead it was Atherton who walked out with Mendis, who quickly fell leg-before to Dodemaide, bringing in the nightwatchman, Fitton.

The day's play, unlike Wednesday's Benson & Hedges quarter-final at Old Trafford, finished at a respectable time. The opposition that day had been Surrey who, along with Warwickshire, had once approached Lancashire in the hope of signing David during his dissatisfied days at Old Trafford; naturally, the then-chairman,

Cedric Rhoades, emphasised his autocratic reputation by omitting to inform David until much later. Not that David would have considered any offers with anything more than passing curiosity: 'Lancashire are the only county I could ever play for.'

Surrey had finally caved in at the ungodly hour of 8.20. At 185 for 2 the threat flickered, but the visitors had faced an uphill slog of 6 runs an over with thirty overs to go and ultimately fell 46 short of Lancashire's 279, to which Fowler and Atherton supplied the straight lines, Fairbrother the frippery with 61 not out from thirty-six balls, including his 1,000th run of the season in all formats. To Lancastrian eyes, any match concluding after 8 p.m. kindled memories of that Gillette semi-final. The papers were full of it on the Thursday, though David scoffed at any comparison. 'We only carried on *that* late because, having had only six non-playing days out of the last thirty-five, we just wanted to get it over with. The papers harked back to '71, of course, referring to all that "if I can see 'em I'll hit 'em" guff. I don't remember saying that, and I don't recall Arthur Jepson saying anything like "You can see the moon – how far do you want to see?". Then again, sometimes I can't remember what happened twenty-four hours ago.

'Wednesday did make me remember one thing about that day, mind. After play was over, I offered John Mortimore a glass of champagne, and he rejected it. He must have been bitterly disappointed, having bowled Gloucestershire into a winning position. Then a few years later I wrote asking him to contribute to a benefit brochure. I never received an answer. I like to think he never got the letter.' For some, nevertheless, failure hurts almost as much as love.

David was able to brush off that little slight without too much trouble, just as he had risen above those sharp darts in the press last season from Frank Hayes, who described him as an embarrassment to Lancashire. 'It was quite sad really. Hayes has had his opportunity as captain. It isn't a six-month job, it's about man-management, communication. You have to take an interest in each player, treat them all as individuals, in order to get the best out of them. That sort of attack doesn't bother me. I'm sensitive to things around me, but not to journalists or ex-players bawling at me. I'm the type to blow up and then forget very quickly. I certainly don't bear grudges. Of course there's always the odd disgruntled supporter. I try not to have favourites among the players, so along the way you upset people who watch and do have favourite players. There's this chap who writes to me from Levenshulme. He signs the envelope "OHMS", doesn't put on a stamp, and just writes obscenities. It causes great amusement. He's currently criticising me for not playing Mendis on Sundays. So I can absorb a fair amount of criticism, but if it was on the level of what Bobby Robson has had to put up with . . .' The voice trails off, unable to convey the requisite disbelief at the treatment meted out to the English media's favourite sporting pin cushion.

By early Tuesday afternoon at Horsham, Lancashire had completed a 9-wicket victory to move up to the fourth rung in a deceptive Championship ladder that had Nottinghamshire at the top with 89 points from seven games, and Surrey in the cellar with 19 from four. That meant that if the Ovalteenies were to win all three of their games in hand, and garner a further 23 bonus points, they would be top. So much for the relevance of early season tables. Even so, the inevitability with which Lancashire, and DeFreitas in particular, strolled past a brittle Sussex, provided evidence of a durable contender. And to think Monsieur Akram had yet to enter the starting stalls.

After Atherton, Watkinson and the stitched-up Fowler (54 not out at No. 9) had built a lead of 89, the day saw a demolition job not dissimilar to that achieved at Lord's last July, when DeFreitas and Patterson had shoved Middlesex over the edge for 43. This time the same pair sent Sussex spinning from an overnight 57 for 1 to 108 all out, DeFreitas pitching the ball up for once (Ormrod later spoke of his tendency to bowl a 'West Indian length', i.e. one or two yards short of a good one) and deriving swing in both directions to take the first 6 wickets of the day and walk off with 6–39. Not a bad prelude to the first Test against New Zealand forty-eight hours hence.

Compensation, then, for the frustrations of Colwyn Bay, where rain and the Glamorgan third-wicket pair of Ian Smith and Alan Butcher had linked arms to foil Lancashire. For David the final day at Horsham had been a case of sitting back and watching from short-leg as his quickest available bowlers competed against each other. 'Daffy was bowling into a strong wind, but he still matched

Patto for pace. The previous evening he'd been unlucky, but this morning I put him on straightaway and from his fifth ball I caught Dodemaide, then, with the next, he had Alan Wells leg-before. If it hadn't been for the doubts over Chris Lewis I'm sure Daffy wouldn't have had a chance of playing in the Test, and he feels the same. If he does play, he pointed out to me, it will be the first time he has ever played three Tests running. The great thing is, we're now starting to bat other counties out of the game, which is what the Aussies did to England last summer.'

One fascinating sidelight of the Sussex game had been the continuation of David's ill-luck with the toss. In sixteen games he had now won just four, compared with a 1989 success rate of 66 per cent. So much for the laws of probability. On these pitches it all meant little, of course, except that winning the toss means accepting the greater share of responsibility for engineering a result. 'The popular conception at one time was that if I didn't win the toss in a one-day game we were staring at defeat. What rot. How can you depend on the toss of a coin?'

Monday 4 June, Woolwich

The Army v. Essex II

A peculiar setting. Woolwich Barracks, with its Crimean guns to the fore, security paranoia at the core and tower blocks to the rear. In the middle distance sit the dockyards and a posy of gargantuan British Telecom satellite dishes. 'Socialist Revolution Is The Only Revolution' is chalked on a nearby wall. Down the road lurks Silvertown, all industrial flues and no soul. Next to the ferry stands the rail museum, homage to a cleaner age.

The Army cricket ground is sited in Haha Road, and much of the first day's play, fittingly, is laughable. On a pitch with such spiteful traditions that Fletcher had requested, unavailingly, that the fixture be cancelled, Nadeem makes 11 for the 2nd XI. The home team are duly disposed of for 63 that same afternoon as six slips ring the bat. Following the game's progress on the neon-lit electronic scoreboard is of limited use: even in such grisly light it is virtually impossible to distinguish between 33 for 3 and 88 for 8. The follow-on enforced, Nadeem is entrusted with the final over of the day. As distinct from previous sightings, his approach to the stumps, longer than hitherto, is more a quickstep than a spring, while the knees pump up almost apologetically prior to delivery. A degree of hesitation about the follow-through reaffirms a certain wrong-footedness. The penultimate ball is driven square towards the parade ground; the last is nicked a whisper past first slip's left hand, lax work in the field turning an iffy single into a comfortable 2.

Lilley promptly summons the other Essex fielders into a huddle. As umpires and batsmen reach the prefab pavilion, his right forefinger is still jabbing the cool evening air. That slovenly piece of fielding had angered the captain, but this was essentially Lilley's way of demonstrating that being led by him, rather than the absent Fletcher, should not be the cue for any lapses in discipline. 'Seven-thirty dinner sharp,' one military minion advises a suitably chastened Nadeem when he is finally allowed to return to the pavilion. Then it was time for bed, in the officers' quarters, where else?

Tuesday 12 June, Edgbaston

Warwickshire v. Essex (County Championship, 3 days)

Not only has Gooch's preoccupation with the national interest at Trent Bridge allowed Nadeem to retain his place in the Championship side (a score of 15 had been his main contribution to a rain-ruined game against Gloucestershire), but now he was in the Refuge side too, if principally for his energetic fielding in the deep. He catches the Warwickshire top-scorer Tom Moody off Childs; listed to come in at No.7, he never even gets to pad up, Pringle and Lilley adding the final embellishments to a 7-wicket win that lifts Essex, now on a roll of three consecutive victories, to eighth in the table.

Ever more intent on doing something to earn his keep, Nadeem has to wait awhile on the next day, Monday. The one-for-all, all-for-one delight in the visitors' dressing-room is considerable as John Stephenson, without a first-class 50 since Lord's in April, withstands blows to fingers, elbow and head (by a throw, of all things) and girds his loins to fashion 85 in five and a half hours. Waugh, at the other end for much of the duration, is altogether more assertive, acquiring his fourth first-class century of the season. Rarely can two batsmen have simultaneously played such differing knocks against the same attack. After Stephenson had been caught behind off a top-edged cut and Allan Donald had sent back Lilley for a single, Nadeem enters in imperfect light. Visibility proves no obstacle, however, as he surges to 75 not out with eleven assorted boundaries, dominating an unfinished stand of 87 with Garnham. In preparation for his report in the *Independent*, Mike Carey, one of the most respected judges in the press pack, jotted down the word 'elegant'. That was better.

'I've a feeling things might change for me now,' a flushed Nadeem said that evening. 'If I fail, I get so depressed, but now I've made my first 50 of the season. Knowing me I'll probably expect a big score every time now. I had to get a move on because we'd already lost nearly 100 overs to rain, but I didn't slog by any means. It was very dark when I came in, and after three balls from Donald, two of which were bouncers, we came off. Before we came back Pringle said the target was 300, but Stevo, who'd made 60 in seventy-odd overs, decided 250 was more realistic, so I thought, why should I throw my wicket away?

'All I got from Donald were bouncers, five in one over. I had a dart at a hook, which is unusual for me, but I couldn't reach. We were off again after another seven overs, and when we returned I thought that if I gave my wicket away now it wouldn't matter. Last year a 50 would have taken me two and a half hours, but this one came in half the time [the innings in toto occupied 128 balls]. Towards the end I was even punching balls pitched outside off-stump off the back foot. Normally I'd leave those alone.'

The fact that Nadeem did not seem quite as elated as one might have expected suggests he is acquiring a sense of the reality of professional cricket. 'I should be over the moon, but playing every day detracts from your enjoyment. It all came home to me after playing for Copdock three weeks ago, my first taste of club cricket for a year. If you just play at weekends you have a whole week to dwell on and relive a good innings, but when you're playing daily you're only as good as your last innings. I'll probably have forgotten most of this one within a couple of days. Mind you, the county feel that the more I play the better because they don't want me to get bored. So instead of hanging around as 12th man – which means getting the lemon and lime ready, ensuring everyone has the food they need, fetching the physio for anyone who needs treatment, and having a kip – I've usually ended up playing for the 2nd XI. The only trouble there is that I may have become over-confident by playing too much for them.'

If that innings did little to dent Nadeem's confidence, it has little effect on Essex's flagging fortunes in the Championship. The obligatory mathematical sleight of hand ensued the next day, Warwickshire declaring their first innings at 41 without loss, 290 behind, then, after Pringle had forfeited the Essex second innings, snapping up a somewhat free-spirited offer of 291 in eighty-five overs with 5 wickets and more than eight overs up their sleeve. There were some chortles along the way. Despite the leniency of the target, three batsmen were run-out; Humpage survived an lbw appeal only to find himself stranded down the wicket.

Not that Essex faces were exactly bursting with mirth by the end. Waugh, Hardie and Gooch might be in the top seven of the batting lists, but one win in seven games is hardly the breakfast of champions. Significantly, only Kent have fewer bowling bonus points, seven to Essex's nine. The key to any sort of volte-face is the standard bearer of the attack, Foster. Returning for a token over as the Edgbaston contest edged to its predictable conclusion, he had ambled in off a run even briefer than his Sabbath effort, yet still donated a wide and a no-ball.

Although his early encounters in the Essex sixth-form common room were proving most amenable, Nadeem is also finding himself perplexed by Foster. 'There's even more humour in this dressing-room than I thought there would be, enough to get us over games like this. There are no factions or enemies, and everyone takes the mickey, but it's all so friendly. Win or lose, we have a laugh. Hardie's always cracking jokes, Lilley too, but there are quite a few of us who represent a new generation who have all been coming through around the same time, so although it's a big step up to the 1st XI, all the 2nd XI players know the first teamers and so we all muck in together. You're not made to feel like a junior. A couple of Sundays ago I was sleeping on the bench and Mark Ilott kept chucking tennis balls at my nose to wake me up. If I say something stupid the punches rain down on me from all quarters, particularly from Foster. I take that to mean I'm gradually becoming accepted.

But the other night we were having an Indian meal and Foster asked me why I, as a young player, couldn't keep quiet. After all, he said, he was quiet when he started out. But I'm not like that, and no one else has made me feel as if I should be. Neil will always help me in the field, but he can be moody and sometimes bowls accordingly. He's still one of the best bowlers in the country, though, and being banned by England has only seemed to make him that bit more determined for Essex. He doesn't complain about the seam as some of the seamers do, but I'm sure he must be dying to get on a pitch that isn't flatter than a pancake.'

Although Pringle's forfeiture might have baffled some, Nadeem felt his captaincy had much to commend it. 'The mood under Pring is more relaxed than it is under Gooch, which may or may not be a good thing in terms of achieving results. I suppose it's because of his age, but Pring is closer to the players and he asks for help from the senior members of the team, whereas Gooch is more sure of himself. With him, there's a definite reason for that fourth slip.'

Wednesday 13 June, Old Trafford

Lancashire v. Somerset (Benson & Hedges Cup semi-final)

As overtures go, it was not propitious. At least not so far as the prospects for a riveting semi-final were concerned. Since ousting Surrey in their Benson & Hedges quarter-final a fortnight previously, Lancashire had risen to the Championship summit on the back of successive, wholly comprehensive victories. Fairbrother led the batting averages with 120.83 and the one minor blip, a Refuge League defeat against Gloucestershire at Old Trafford, had merely widened the gap between themselves and the leaders to 6 points. Since mugging Middlesex, on the other hand, Somerset had retreated. In the Championship they had had by no means the better of a draw with Gloucestershire, followed by a rain-out at Basingstoke (though there was time enough for Cook to become the first batsman to reach 1,000 runs, a week behind schedule). Then, at Canterbury over the last few days, Kent had consumed 117.5 of the final 151.5 overs of the match to ward off defeat, 2 wickets standing groggily at the end. That left Somerset an illusory ninth in the table, having played more games than the other counties. Sunday surrenders at Bristol and Canterbury found them fourteenth in the League. There were better ways to approach one's hottest date of the season.

For Adrian, moreover, spirit and flesh were weak. The body of a fast bowler is a finely-tuned instrument, prone to atonality should so much as one string be off-key. This susceptibility gives rise, of course, to a degree of paranoia and hypochondria. Chris Old, to whom a broken fingernail was as debilitating as an ice pick in the back of the head, is but one example of talent being squandered in such fashion. Then again, illness or injury tends to provoke an equivocal reaction in most people. Annoyance that you are experiencing physical distress and cannot do certain things you like or have to do, delight that you can slob around for a while. Any excuse will do. Despite appearances, Adrian falls into the former category. His chief source of pride in the 1989 season was neither wickets nor runs, but the fact that he was ever-present, even though there were times when mind persuaded matter to do what it clearly did not feel up to.

Now, though, mind was making promises that body could not keep. The ankle was still giving him gyp, the remnants of a cold were stifling him, and then there was this damned left knee. On the second day at Canterbury he bowled Mark Benson for a duck before being forced off the field for the remainder of the match. As if to rub it in, Benson proceeded to a match-saving 116 in the second innings while Adrian sat impotently in the pavilion, arranging to consult a knee specialist. He had time to ponder his output so far. Since pulling the rug from under Gloucestershire at the end of April, he had added 12 first-class wickets to his carpet bag when he might have expected 25. In all formats, he had taken more than 2 wickets in an innings just the once. Still, 20 first-class victims in toto wasn't bad in the circumstances; no prominent seam bowler had yet nailed 30 with this mushy pea they called a ball. More pertinently, of Adrian's 8 one-day victims during those six weeks, half had come in that Taunton quarter-final.

'I was desperate to play, and they were keen for me to play. I had a long bowl in the nets after the match at Canterbury, wearing a brace, but I still collapsed on the knee. Then I did the same at the hotel in Manchester. I took an inflammatory tablet, then spent fifteen minutes this morning in the nets here with Tav. I told him it could go at any time, but I think he felt that, with Robey still struggling with a virus, he needed the experience. Maybe he thought that five overs from me would be better than eleven from a youngster like Jeremy Hallett. I told Tav and Birky that I didn't want to carry the can if I bowled badly, but they told me not to worry. The hardest thing will be standing at long-leg, feeling it stiffen. I'm not sure what it is. It may be something floating around that sometimes locks in the joint, or else it could be a deep tendon pull that has inflamed the joint. I hate all this. The last time I missed a game through injury was two years ago. I pulled some ankle tendons, but fortunately it happened just before the last game of the season.'

Somerset, who had bused in from Canterbury the previous evening, arriving in Manchester well after midnight, were not in the best of shape. The virus besetting Roebuck was circulating the dressing-room and fifteen days on the road were beginning to take their toll. Lancashire, in direct contrast, were thirsting to get cracking on their first knockout semi-final at home for fifteen years. One-step-from-Lord's tension? Not according to David. 'We're brimful of confidence. We really fancy our chances. And, as a Lancastrian, there's no finer place to be than in front of a packed house at Old Trafford.'

If the official gate of around 12,000 paled by comparison with the pre-match marketing bluster about a 20,000 sell-out, David did not see the turnout as a slight. 'It has taken a while to get the crowds back here in numbers comparable with the early 1970s. Back then, they flocked here, but whereas most of them had played cricket at school, many of today's generation of cricket watchers have never held a bat. The cost is another factor. Nowadays a smaller percentage of people have more money and a greater percentage less, so £13 is a lot to pay for admission. I know you cxpcct those prices in London, but up here it's different.'

Yet to an English cricketer brought up on a dribble of members during the week and the odd Sunday swell, a 12,000-strong audience of critics can be unnerving. Adrian certainly felt it. 'When we got to the ground we came face-to-face with this massive Lancashire crowd. Imagine, 20,000 Lankys? They're the worst, but they seem to know their cricket. Make a misfield in front of the bar, or bowl a bad over, and they really get stuck in. There were quite a few of our supporters there, but it still felt as if we were on our own.'

David recognised the advantage such a partisan populace gave his team. 'Just as it does at Anfield, say, a large crowd can intimidate the away team and I think Somerset were probably affected by ours.'

The outcome, however, turned on individual heroics rather than the pressure imposed by the vociferous Old Trafford chorus. No contribution was more critical than Akram's. DeFreitas took the new ball with the niggardly Allott, but failed to locate line or length in his opening four overs, so David tossed it to the raggle-haired left-armer from Lahore. At 50 he ripped through Hardy's drive, inducing a skyer to Allott, running back from slip. At 55 he had Hayhurst caught behind and Somerset were crumbling. Cook had taken root, but Tavaré soon went, caught by David off Austin, and, on the brink of lunch, Harden went to pull a long-hop from DeFreitas, mistimed it horribly and swivelled to see Hegg fling himself horizontally and bring off a stunning catch. While Cook remained, hope flickered. However, in the first over after the interval he went to steer Austin behind point for the single that would signal his 50 but succeeded only in getting a thickish edge for Hegg to pouch a straightforward chance with minimal fuss and maximum joy.

That made it half out for 113 and the Somerset totter had assumed a dismal droop. Rose, Lefebvre and Burns (another caught by David) threw the bat to useful effect, but 212 for 9 was nothing like sufficient and the rest of the contest was nothing of the sort. Adrian bowled Fowler at 34, Swallow swallowed a return catch from Mendis at 74, but that only left Atherton and Fairbrother in the saddle: ice and fire, a doubly destructive combination. Fairbrother peppered the perimeter as he careered to 78 off fifty-three balls, sashaying three paces down the wicket at one point to smite Lefebvre for one of his three 6s. Atherton, cooler than a cucumber, warded off any further cracks in the superstructure with his unbowed 56, and Lancashire swanned home by 6 wickets with sixty-one balls left unused. A huge margin.

In Adrian's view, the spin of the coin had exerted a significant influence. 'The wicket was a bit damp, Hughes won the toss and that was it. The ball did a bit early on. Allott bounced one full-length delivery over Cook's head, over Hegg and over the boundary for 4 byes. Maybe it skidded on the slight ridge at that end? Losing our fourth wicket when we did, and in the way we did, also played a part. Harden had been going really well, but Hegg made a great catch to get rid of him. It makes a difference when you've got a good wicket-keeper.

'Over lunch, Tav said we should play sensibly, take advantage of our wickets in hand and make sure we used the overs up. That's the thing about 55- and 60-over games: unlike that Sunday rubbish it's a proper game where you need wickets in hand. But although the pitch gradually got easier, Akram bowled quick and well, Hegg caught everything and the best team in the country simply put on a very polished all-round performance. Their only weakness is their dependence on Fowler, Mendis, Atherton and Fairbrother. If you can get rid of them there's not much to come. Fairbrother is very flamboyant, so he gives you a chance, but he's got so much confidence right now that it doesn't seem to matter and he rode his luck well today. Atherton played a magnificent anchor role and while he was there Lancashire were always going to win. I've heard people suggest he may be a bit arrogant, but then again many people who have success early on are arrogant. They have reason to be.

'But I'm sure they keep him in his place, because every county has a pecking order. It's no bad thing that a player who has done his best for his county for ten years should feel he has precedence over some young Turk who's been around barely a couple of years but is already being talked about by everyone. It gives the older man respect and keeps a youngster's feet on the ground. That said, you're never reminded that that order exists until someone oversteps the mark.'

David tilted his titfer towards Akram. 'We batted well, but Cook looked tentative, possibly as a result of the pressure on him to bear the hopes of his team, but also, I suspect, because of the crowd. And then there was Akram, who bowled beautifully, with plenty of pace, so much so that he beat Cook five times in one over. He certainly adds a new dimension to the side. He's the best all-rounder in the world and there have naturally been tremendous demands on his time. He hasn't been fit, either, but now he's come through for us in two vital one-dayers.' As one of the counties making the most of the last season in which it would be permissible to register two players not qualified to represent England, Lancashire – unlike

Northamptonshire, say – were fortunate in that their twosome, although both top-ranking Test fast bowlers, had no grounds for conflict. Patterson was assigned to the majority of Championship fixtures, Akram almost exclusively to limited-overs responsibilities. 'Pat generates his pace from his run-up and footholds, but when you are limited to bowling off fifteen yards in the Refuge, that's no use to him or us. In any case, he doesn't like Sundays much. Too much of a rush.'

Despite guiding Lancashire to their ninth Lord's final, one shy of the record held by Kent, David's own limited incursions into the fray were not allowed to pass into oblivion without a few crass jibes from a hypercritical few. Adrian caught the feeling. 'People say he's under pressure because he doesn't do much bar toss up, make bowling changes, set fields and arrange the batting order, although none of the Lancashire lads griped to me when we went for a drink with them after the game. They belong to a very powerful club and perhaps no one wants to upset the politburo. We had the same situation at Sussex in John Barclay's latter years as captain, when he was clearly keeping out a younger player. Hayhoe [Hayhurst] is a very talented player who would have been guaranteed a place but for Hughes's presence. But who else could captain Lancashire so well?'

Despite his lack of tangible reward, Adrian impressed David. 'He could be knocking on the door for Test selection, you know. He has the ability to be really quick, but his run-up is all a-cock. He takes short steps rather than increasing stride towards the end of his run. He may feel that what he does is adequate, but from sideways on it doesn't look right to me. He could have a word with Hadlee.'

Given the import of the occasion, this match also afforded an opportunity to compare styles of appealing. Not that today's cricketers need much incentive to appeal, nor to go batty when their cries are heeded. Every wicket triggers an explosion, usually a bit of a cavort followed by a jocular huddle around the bowler and/or catcher.

The high-fiving first practised by the West Indies, obviating the need for any verbal communication, can be exhilarating, though if we must continue to ape American sporting mannerisms, heaven help us. Whenever the Oakland A's score a home run, their players bash each other's forearms, surely the ultimate in showy machismo. Even kissing is preferable to that, though better still the Essex Variation: finger-pressing. Minimalist and sardonic, something that only those who have made a friend of fortune have an excuse to dream up. For the rest, the scent of success is too heady to prevent a bit of nuttiness. And, as that self-confessed cricket nut Barry Norman would doubtless put it, why not?

A Lancashire slip chorus is something to see. With harmony the key, it takes its cue from the effusive, combative Allott and the chirpy Fowler, gaining its resonance from the bouncy Hegg. The resultant enthusiasm for any possibility of a favourable decision smacks more of fun than fiddling, but there are certain stuffy citizens who remain unconvinced. If we accept that concerted, machiavellian imprecations are the norm, is there really any sense in po-faced blabber about morality? Perhaps. Lbw claims have been known, after all, to filter through from fine-leg and backward point. Convention, though not the laws, stipulates that if a fielder sincerely believes he has made a clean catch at the instant the ball thwacks into his palms, then his mates are entitled to support his entreaty. This mostly takes the form of an abbreviated query, 'Howzat?', loosely translated in its original context as 'How was that ball, Mister Umpire, sir?' but later reinterpreted as 'Here, you in the silly-looking grocer's jacket, was that bugger out or what?' As the stakes have climbed, so the pleading has evolved into a demand. Still, as the old saying goes, if you don't ask, you don't get.

Although Rose was now apeing Adrian's rendition of Lillee's pushy appeal, an impassioned outpouring defying the recipient to demur, Somerset were not in Lancashire's league as a whole. A case of lower expectations? Adrian for one is torn between ethics and pragmatism. 'You shouldn't put pressure on an umpire, but it is an advantage to be known as a good appealer. However, if I don't think the guy was out, even if the slips go up in unison, I won't make a murmur. If I think there's a chance, mind, I give it everything, which is something I think the Taunton crowd, and crowds in general, quite take to. It excites them, and lets them know how much you care and want to win. I don't think they see it as cheating. I certainly don't. I've beaten batsmen and been the only one to appeal for a click I might have seen and heard when coming down low in my follow-through. A lot happens in that follow-through, all that snorting and dust flying, so much so that it can be difficult to see what precisely has gone on in those split seconds after delivery.

'The louder and more impressive the appeal the better. It has to affect the umpire. If I was playing in club cricket and I roared an appeal, I may get a wicket. So many umpires don't make decisions that it's good for them to be jerked into a response, but if you keep on appealing, you lose credibility. It's more difficult to give someone out than not. Still, the common theory in this country is that if you are an overseas bowler you get away with one or two, but not if you're me.'

After a drink with their vanquishers in the committee room, and a brief snifter with David, who spent the evening hopping from hospitality room to hospitality tent, the Somerset contingent wended back to the coach. Victory would have made it all bearable, of course, but defeat just made it less so. There were no recriminations, merely recognition that, even with rested limbs and refreshed spirits, Somerset would have been unlikely victors. Sit bolt upright for four and a half hours, play a couple of hands of bridge and watch some videos, in this case John Arlott's *Vintage Cricket* and a couple of *Match of the Day* highlights from the good ol' 1960s and 1970s. Best, Charlton, Law and Greaves. Fab gear, eh what? Adrian remembers how rare it is for him not to be driving. He and Mallender were in charge of organising the usual fleet of six sponsored Mazda Estates (two passengers per vehicle), taking care to interchange partners on a regular basis and so avoid cliques. Now, though, he could gaze into the middle distance. 'I still don't know whether Amy knows who I am. She's probably thinking to herself, "Who is this guy who comes into my life every couple of weeks?" '

Lancashire had never looked anything but victors. With an opening quartet making forceful overtures against impossibly broad blades, an attack coming to grips with the accursed new seam and an urgent, canny captain infusing self-belief and making all the right moves, they seemed to have reached a peak. The next few days spelt R and R, and about time too. Just because winning has a habit of making aches and strains more tolerable, and disguising tiredness, doesn't mean that it eliminates them. Time now for a few rounds with Allott and the others at Warrington Golf

Club while the England trio knocked up in The Parks. This was not David's idea of a punishment for DeFreitas, Fairbrother and Atherton, however. 'They have to play against Oxford because otherwise they wouldn't have had a first-class game in between the first and second Tests – and they need one.'

For the rest of the regulars, the hiatus between now and the following Wednesday, interrupted only by the merriment of a benefit match for Allott, represented the midway point of the season. David is already thinking about the final whistle. 'I wish it was 22 September because that way I'd know it couldn't all end in anti-climax. We've reached half-time in good health. We're in the position I'd hoped we would be in by now, despite the fact that we haven't always played well. God knows what might happen if we're ever consistent! What's nice is that so many people have told me not only how much they are enjoying watching us, but how much we appear to be enjoying ourselves. You have to. Otherwise it gets to be hard work.'

Friday 22 June, Old Trafford

Lancashire v. Middlesex (County Championship, 3 days)

As the spirit of the Manchester Starship Enterprise, David is beginning to evoke Captain Kirk in his idealism. After Lancashire had expended ninety-seven overs spread over two days to reach 222 for 5 against fellow aspirants Middlesex, David's distaste for mundanity resulted in him setting 302 in seventy-three overs following the obligatory forfeitures. Even if Patterson (who yielded 59 from his first nine overs) had not sprayed the ball around with the benevolence of a registered charity, the task was far from impossible. Haynes and Roseberry began with precisely 100, Gatting, still waiting for his first 'proper' 100 of the season, waded in with an unbeaten 95 from 121 balls and Middlesex romped home with 13.5 overs remaining to move above their victims into second place. A galling and possibly critical loss.

To David there had been no option but to open up the game and give Middlesex enough rope to string themselves up with. 'There was no other way out. And, in any case, this is the time of the season when both sides generally want to play a game, whereas if you are in the contending three or four in August people know you'll do silly things anyway so they don't really feel the onus is on them to make a contest of it.

'I thought we might bowl Middlesex out if we gave ourselves enough overs, but I was misled a bit by the batsmen's interpretation of the wicket. They had said it was turning and seaming, and Mendis spent 108 overs over his 114. But we bowled badly, and once they'd reached 80-odd after eleven overs they were always going to walk it. If they had been 80 for 2 it might have been different, but Roseberry has been having a great time lately and he and Haynes gave them a perfect start.' Regrets? 'I never regret a game of cricket, never. I became a bit impatient at times, and had the odd shout, but I like to think the lads understood me.'

Friday, 22 June, Bath

Somerset v. Glamorgan (County Championship, 3 days)

Lying deep in the heart of a bowl on the banks of the Avon, the natural amphitheatre known as the Recreation Ground (more renowned these days as the home of the all-conquering Bath RFC) has been a wayward mistress to Somerset since their first performance here in 1880. In 1906, George Hirst became the first, and so far only, man to make a century and take 5 wickets in each innings as Yorkshire won by 389 runs. Four years later Lancashire declared at 286 for 2 and won by an innings. Later that same summer, Somerset benefited from an erroneous decision to give George Cox out stumped off a no-ball, but Sussex still romped in with an innings to spare. The pits came in 1914: Somerset caught on a rain-ravaged pitch and summarily dismissed for 83 and 38 by Hampshire, their second innings over in fifty minutes. But for two dropped catches they would have been pushed to last half-an-hour.

The immediate post-war years brought a change in fortune for Somerset. In 1919 Jack 'Farmer' White, an artful slow left-armer acclaimed by the former Australian captain Monty Noble for being 'always able to call the tune and compel the batsmen to dance to it', lured sixteen Worcestershire batsmen to their doom in a single day. The Hampshire humbling was avenged in 1924, Somerset routing the visiting bowlers to the tune of 675 for 9 declared, still their loftiest total. Another thirteen years and there were Bill Andrews and Arthur Wellard, bowling virtually unchanged throughout the match to sew up victory by 419 runs over the Kent of Woolley and Ames. Andrews, 'The Hand That Bowled Bradman', completed a notable double by lassoing both legends with successive balls in each innings. On to 1956 and Brian Langford, an off-breaker who took 28 wickets for 267 runs during the three Festival games. The hallelujah day, though, came in 1977, Richards, Garner and Botham conspiring with lesser lights such as Phil Slocombe and Graham Burgess to defeat Greg Chappell's Australians by 7 wickets, Somerset's first such victory in twenty-two attempts since 1893.

Although jaunts to Bath provide an excuse to wallow in the Georgian splendours of Queen's Crescent, those entrusted with fashioning a worthwhile game of cricket there are frequently confounded either by sweltering heat (temperatures at the base of that bowl can be terribly oppressive) or mud. The pitch, meanwhile, often renders proceedings annoyingly one-sided in favour of the bowlers, as the aforementioned scores amplify.

This year it behaved impeccably, too impeccably to facilitate a decisive result, still less any vestige of festive fare. Against Essex last Saturday, Adrian bowled seventeen uneventful overs for 59 on the first day as John Stephenson ground to a maiden double century out of 431 for 3, the seventh knock of such magnitude at the Recreation Ground. The elements dictated matters thereafter, just 4 more wickets falling before a ferocious thunderstorm at lunch on the third day necessitated an abandonment.

The Glamorgan game that followed was even more of a fiasco: 41.3 overs on the first day, 3.4 on the second, then a one-innings bunfight on the last. Rose gave a solemn commentary on the depths to which the teams were prepared to sink to contrive a result, blocking the last three balls of the Somerset innings when 3 short of his maiden century. Set 302, Glamorgan immediately struck a reef when Adrian had Morris held by Harden, Mallender trapping Holmes shortly after, but Somerset's momentum was slowed, first by the indomitable Butcher, then by the loss of fourteen overs through rain in mid-afternoon. Swallow sent back the Bash Brothers, Maynard and Richards, in quick succession, Glamorgan sliding to 113 for 4, but Butcher refused to budge, so consigning a half-match to a tame conclusion.

For the organisers and sponsors there was some consolation for a vapid Festival Week: not too far away, at Iffley Park, Gloucester, the game between Hampshire and Gloucestershire spanned 20.1 overs. On the second day, the grand total of £4 was taken at the gate. One customer, in other words.

Adrian, needless to say, could barely wait to leave town by the end. 'I hate Bath. It's a home game that's really an away fixture for us. Taunton is sixty miles away, but you generally get stuck behind a tractor or some cows and it ends up taking 1½ hours to reach the place, so I have to stay at a hotel rather than go home. Sponsoring and catering provide enough revenue to compensate for the weather, but the pavilion is not very comfortable and the showers are not particularly good. The outfield is so uneven you could mistake it for a cowfield, so when you're fielding out there you get hit in the chops, wrist, legs, you name it.

'I felt I bowled with good rhythm, but there was no point. It's always the same here. The wickets are so bloody slow that once you're in you're in for life, and very rarely do we get results. What, then, is the point of playing on a festival ground? The wickets they offer are not normally as well prepared as those at the regular venues, which can make for exciting games, but not at Bath. It's not fit for first-class cricket, at least not entertaining cricket, and I don't think any of our players enjoy going there. One of the problems is that we've been spoilt by playing at Taunton where the pitches are faultless for batting, so it's a shock when batsmen come up against one that affects their timing like the one we had here. Essex adjusted by looking for singles, whereas we rely on Cook and Tav, who tend to score in fours. The joke is that the club were considering holding a NatWest tie here next summer, but they've since knocked the idea on the head. The council won't do anything about the wicket, but if we stopped going there Gloucestershire would nip in, and that wouldn't do, would it?'

During the Essex game Adrian took the opportunity to share his grumbles with Foster, who had been carrying the Essex attack up to that point. 'We both feel we've been putting in a lot of effort, but he's only got 21 wickets and I've got 27. Like me, he feels that we're simply there to provide the batsmen with runs, then we score some more, then we give them a few more so they can declare, and we chase. The main problem with Somerset is that we always seem to be doing the declaring.

'But maybe Fozzie and I feel this way because we both play most of our cricket in the south, where the groundsmen are obeying the new rules on preparation, while in the north and Midlands they seem to be bending them. The results are coming at all the usual result venues, such as New Road and Grace Road. In the north and Midlands there has been a slight tinge of green and a bit of damp in the pitches, and that's where we've been taking most of our wickets. At Leicester the pitch was green at the start. How do they get away with it?'

The figures bear out Adrian's suspicions. Of the top nine county batsmen in the latest averages, eight represent southern counties, while nine of the leading ten bowlers are based to the north. In four-day games, bowlers exerted the decisive influence in the eight conclusive finishes north of the Watford Gap where the elements did not compel contrivance. Three games ended in three days, one in two, while of the seven counties currently boasting more than 20 bowling points, only Surrey do not hail from north of the invisible border stretching from Gloucester to Colchester. South of that border, where Messrs Fairbrother, Cook, Greig and Prichard all passed 240 on Slumberdowns, there were half as many definite results in uninterrupted four-day contests. The TCCB pitch doctor, Harry Brind, an Essex man, appears reasonably content. 'By and large I'm happy. It could be possible that not all pitches have conformed to the guidelines. They might be a little greener towards the north, a bit harder in the south, but it's wetter up north too, don't forget. And some wickets have looked green and haven't done anything.'

Though not speaking for himself, the Lancashire groundsman, Peter Marron, whose own creations have been above reproach, believes that some of his neighbours may have been cocking a snook at Lord's. 'Some groundsmen up here don't like being told what to do and they can take exception to orders from down there. There is also a bit of jealousy towards Brind, naturally enough, and that might have provoked a few.'

The Essex match at Bath also threw up one particularly unsavoury and unfortunate incident, one that would add lustre to Adrian's reputation. 'On the second afternoon, just after the umpires had told us play would resume, we came out for a knock-up. I bowled one to Hallett and it jumped a bit, forcing him to hit it high up on the bat. The ball went past me, over the boundary board, hit the top of a chair and flew straight into the face of a lady who was busy eating her lunch. We ran over to see if she was OK, I called the physio over and eventually she was taken off to hospital with Hallett by her side. So naturally, when Burns comes across and asks me to chuck up a few catches, I suggest we move away from in front of the tents to an expanse of about twenty yards. It was good enough for our purposes and I was only tapping the ball to him from five yards, so there was no danger to anyone.

'Then suddenly this chap comes running out and starts shouting and demanding that we move. He was very irate and very rude. I asked him what authority he had to demand anything, so he gets all upset and goes charging off to Tav, who says it's nothing to do with him. Then over comes a lady who had apparently had a few drinks, and she starts swearing and shouting. I think she thought I was the one who'd hit the ball into her friend's face. I explained once again that there was no danger, but she got very uptight and upset, and kept telling me that her friend had been taken to hospital with a broken cheekbone. At that stage we didn't know anything for sure, so I said I was awfully sorry. As I did so, she sort of hit me with the back of her hand across my cheek. I was quite stunned. I told her there was no need for that, so she said that was as hard as I had hit the ball into her friend's face. I said I wasn't the one who hit it and then some chap came across and took her away, thank goodness. I don't know what's happening now. It turned out that this other lady had sustained a hairline fracture. I don't know whether they're going to sue for damages or what.'

Wednesday 27 June, Torquay

Devon v. Somerset (NatWest Trophy first round)

For the common or garden county pro, NatWest first round day is possibly the least appetising date in the calendar. For fifteen Minor Counties, by contrast, it represents a few precious hours in the limelight, a chance to ruffle a feather or two and, who knows, if the pitch is dodgy, maybe even carve a notch on the bedpost.

Since 1963, seven notches had been carved, two of them by Durham, the first underlings to beat first-class opposition and now

Lancashire's opponents. David's philosophy is straightforward enough. 'I go out to crush them as hard as I can. Durham are joining the Championship in a couple of years and they have to be shown what being first-class means. We lost to Scotland in a B&H game at Perth in 1986 and I never want that to happen again. The wicket was soaked, pieces of it were pushed up and they just slogged. We needed 33 from the last three overs and lost by 2 runs. It was a lesson to everyone. Losing to a side like that means having to endure their shouting about it afterwards. We shared a few drinks with them but we were glad to get away.'

For Adrian, the incentive to go in with guns blazing against Devon, though less fiercely motivated, was equally apparent. 'We need to impress, particularly me. I hate this "take it easy" approach that some have. It's a bloody long day too, and you want to get it over with a.s.a.p.' Adrian, too, had sampled degradation under such circumstances, in 1987, when Somerset traipsed to true-blue High Wycombe to tackle Buckinghamshire. So steeply did the ground slope that Roebuck had to yell his instructions as if bellowing down a mineshaft. The vicissitudes of a spiteful wicket were mainly responsible for Somerset's failure to pass 154 and the young-and-old Bucks squeezed home by 7 runs.

Before arriving at Torquay Rugby Club for the off, Somerset spent the night on the English Riviera, a soubriquet that says little for the French or Italian versions. Most of the players sat glued to the TV, urging Bobby Robson's lacklustre England team to beat Belgium. Hayhurst and Swallow whooped it up when David Platt stole in for the last-minute clincher, and even Cook, at one time a professional footballer in Transvaal, forgot he was supposed to be impassive. Adrian was more concerned with trying to shake off a cold, fruitlessly as it transpired. 'As a kid, I never even liked soccer, still less played it. It was always cricket, rugby and hockey for me.'

Just outside the centre of Torquay is a bed and breakfast named 'Fawlty Towers', next to it a house called 'EastEnders'. Talk about life imitating soap suds. At the ground itself, a couple of enormous blue-and-white striped tents house a teeming mass of bank managers from Taunton to Totnes. Behind them sits a van advertising those perennial patriarchs of the seaside smirk, the Barron Knights and Rod Hull (plus anonymous emu). The outfield is worn and undulating. Bright crimson bucket seats adorn the musty, rickety stands. Ruddy-faced Devonians perambulate the perimeter, frequently straying on to the playing area or in front of the sightscreen while play is in progress, blissfully ignorant of protocol. Bubbly ladies in floral and gingham dollop clotted cream on scones, each one a Henry Moore. No one, but no one, hurries. The seafront in the near distance completes a quintessentially Anglo-Saxon scene. All that is missing (surprise, surprise) is the sun.

Among their enthusiastic crew of whippersnappers and wonky knees, Devon include a stumper called Ricky Turpin ('It's never Dick,' one local reporter asserted; unlike their plebby footballing counterparts, cricketers at least try to be inventive with their nicknaming). Hotfoot from the Oval, where he had been playing for Middlesex 2nd XI, came a fully-fledged Richard, the 16-year-old son of a Minor Counties legend, Doug Yeabsley, who had driven his offspring westward ho! late the previous evening. Doug it was who had sent down the solitary maiden over at New Road when Worcestershire pummelled the Devon attack to set the competition record of 404 for 3 on the same day that Buckinghamshire bucked the trend against Somerset. Then there's Mark Woodman, 90 per cent deaf and 50 per cent dumb, a young man for whom fielding constitutes a daunting venture down a dark alley. Whereas the player with a full hand of senses can gauge the pace and direction of a shot by listening to the degree of contact between bat and ball, or, if unsighted, await vocal clues from his fellows, for Mark the process is something of a lottery. Appealing is another awkward manoeuvre.

Tradition and commercial sense dictate that when the minnows win the toss, they put their opponents in. That way the match is extended to tea at worst, bar (and on this occasion, beverage) takings tot up, and everyone feels as if they've had a proper day out. Batting first runs the risk of being tumbled out by lunch, beaten by 3.30 and out of customers by 4. Devon duly insert and Somerset plunder. Adrian settles down to trim his toenails, whiten his boots, do a couple of crosswords and find out where the nearest Mr Whippy van is. 'One loo for all. This place has a festival ground feel to it. Temporary stands and bad facilities.' He does not expect to bat.

Cook and Roebuck raise 79 in no time before the teacher summons the graduate for a single. Graduate refuses and teacher is run out by a matter of feet. Cook's walk back to the pavilion is as near to a stomp as this scholarly gentleman can ever have managed. His chagrin soon dissolves, however. Unbuckled and unpadded, he glides over to a bench and cuddles two small boys in matching sweaters: his sons. Meanwhile, Roebuck has gone, caught and bowled by none other than our friend Mr Woodman. When not sending down his military medium seamers, Mark has been pointedly positioned in the invisible shadow of the square-leg umpire, whose evasive action would give him a pretty good idea of the pace and whereabouts of the ball. Now, though, there is no guide, other than the fact that Roebuck's mistimed drive pops straight at him. Hayhurst and the captain now; hell is beginning to break loose. First, though, a couple of hiccups. On 45, Tavaré is floored by Yeabsley Jnr at mid-wicket off Kevin Rice, formerly an incidental off-spinner for Gloucestershire 2nd XI. Rice doesn't do himself any favours, dropping Tavaré's return drive when his score reaches 54.

Hayhurst promptly splinters the top of the sightscreen with a witheringly struck five-iron, but soon vacates the stage in favour of Rose and some right old roistering ensues. 'It's not really fair, is it?' one besuited, de-tied NatWest nabob moans as Rose sends a pulverising drive over the sightscreen and smiles with just a tinge of embarrassment. Somerset go from 200 to 300 in less than eight overs. Dot balls receive a round of applause. A boy in a Johnny Rotten T-shirt strolls by, turning heads. Anarchy in the UK? More like Torture in Torquay. Adrian wanders around the boundary edge, marvelling discreetly at his chum's onslaught. 'Rosey's got a lot of strength, but until this season he hadn't used it much. Last year he couldn't do a single press-up.'

In the penultimate over the overworked soul on the mid-wicket boundary palms a Rose drive for 6 with Shiltonian panache, bringing up the 400. In the final over an extra-cover drive for two spirits Rose to 101, a maiden century. Off thirty-six balls, the fewest in the competition's history. Quite why he feels demolishing Devon is more valid than mashing Maynard, Cottey and Butcher is a moot point. The next ball goes for 4 to ease Worcestershire's record from the 60-over annals. Rose signs off in style, caught on the cover boundary off the 365th and last ball of the innings. In seventy-one deliveries, Tavaré and Rose have cut, driven, hooked, pulled and basically murdered some very ordinary bowlers to earn 189 runs. Pretty much keeping pace with Rose, Tavaré has taken twenty-three balls to go from

100 to 162. As the pair approach the dressing-room, a lad in a leather jacket walks over to embrace Rose, punching the air with his free hand. His chum snaps the happy scene.

One-day statistics have yet to stimulate the religious fervour attached to those pertaining to first-class figures, so no one could say without fear of contradiction that a side had never made as many as 413 in a limited-overs contest. Then again, no one could seriously imagine that they had. It was certainly the most an English audience had witnessed. Amid a season devalued by torrents of cheap runs, this was inflation at its peak. Still, the punters seemed satisfied enough. What followed was cheaper still. Watched by a prambound Amy, Adrian bowled the opening over of the Devon reply, pinning captain John Edwards leg-before with his fourth ball. As his six-over spell progressed, however, determination to do his bit, plus that perpetual sniffling, combined to dull his threat. In between overs he retreated to fine-leg, patrolling the rim with diminishing enthusiasm and at one point asking a young boy to bring him a glass of water.

Fortunately, predictably, his services were no longer required. Lefebvre's pronounced swing so bemused the local batsmen that he wound up with 7–15. Before those clotted cream scones had had a chance to go down, it was over, Devon all out 67. The record winning margin, 346 runs, was Somerset's; so too was a plum home tie against Botham and Worcestershire.

At the end Adrian realises that his season is almost half-over. Time for some self-assertiveness. 'I know I've been whingeing a lot, but when I've been fit I think I've been bowling well. I mustn't look at my aggregate of wickets and think I should have done better. Flat pitches and constant sunshine, and balls that don't have enough stitches in the seam to deviate off the wicket, mean we've all got to reduce our targets. I've bowled quickly at times. I've been working on moving out rather than in in my delivery stride, and that seems to be making a difference with my accuracy.'

For once, a relatively short trip home from an away game. 'What happened to Lancashire?' Hayhurst asks someone, anyone. 'They doddled it,' chirps a man in a lurid pink tracksuit. 'Bowled 'em out for 164 and won by 8 wickets. Fairbrother 50 not.' The only real comers were Berkshire (206 for 4 at Lord's and beaten by the relatively narrow margin of six wickets) and Hertfordshire (208 at St Albans in response to Warwickshire's 336 for 7). No notching this year.

9 July

Tuesday 3 July, Maidstone

Kent v. Lancashire (County Championship, 3 days)

Amid the mellow expanses of Mote Park, a melodic send-off as Lancashire adjourned for a welcome three-day break. After thrice letting Kent off an amply baited hook, they nailed down the victory that had had their monicker on it ever since they had trimmed the home order to 76 for 6 on Saturday morning. It was more shrink and grow than ebb and flow. In response to Kent's eventual 237, Lancashire stuttered to 6 for 2, recovered to 174 for 2 (Atherton 101, and Jesty 98), than sank to 249 all out. The collapse nevertheless facilitated a breakthrough for David, who had not scored a Championship run since his 33 at Colwyn Bay on 28 May (his only innings since had been a duck at Horsham; since his Derby day, moreover, he had sent down a piffling 137 deliveries in three-day cricket). A single scarcely bust the dam, mind: he fell without addition to Richard Davis's ripening left-arm spin. Kent then reached 89 for 2, slithered to 154 for 8 and beached at 201, Atherton securing 4 wickets for 23. Four of the others had come in a six-over spurt first thing from DeFreitas, suitably energised by a Test-best 5–53 against New Zealand at Trent Bridge, and Patterson. Davis, meanwhile, added 19 to his first-time 59 to become Kent's heaviest scorer in the match. Needing 190 from a minimum of sixty-five overs, Lancashire maintained the staccato rhythm. They lost Fowler and Jesty for 37, recovered to 151 for 3 through Atherton, Fairbrother and Watkinson (who biffed 66 off sixty balls), then shed another 4 wickets for 38 before DeFreitas hit the winning runs. David marched in with him, weary-eyed and runless at the end of a taxing match that removed some of the glister from a surprising statistic: for only the fifth time in thirty-six Championship clashes since 1965 Lancashire had beaten Kent.

David seemed more peeved than relieved. 'It was a very slow pitch, one where you needed that extra yard of pace, but we should have wrapped this one up long ago. We had them by the balls in both their innings but squandered our chances. I'm happy with the batting and bowling, but we're a bit inconsistent in the field, occasionally a bit sloppy.' In the wake of recent misfortunes, though, this represented a much-needed about-turn. As with the Middlesex match, Lancashire's previous Championship fixture against Hampshire, again at their watery Old Trafford grave, had been sorely affected by rain. This time a draw resulted, but the 40-over washout, their second of the season, was possibly even more disruptive. David missed both with a cold chockful of catarrh, rising from his bed to pick up the team's Benson & Hedges Cup Final suits from Coventry. 'I felt awful. It's not like having an injury: you just have to wait and get through it. A virus has been going around Old Trafford for a few weeks now: Fowler, Hegg, Jesty, Watkinson, Ormrod's wife and my son James have all had it. I can't remember missing many games through illness in the past. Most of the ones I have missed have been because I was dropped.'

Yet despite these interruptions, Lancashire had now risen to second in the Championship – 18 points behind Middlesex – and fourth in the Refuge order, Graham Lloyd commemorating his 21st birthday here on Sunday with an undefeated century against the long-time if fading leaders. Given the chance to establish a consistent rhythm, the possibilities seemed endless.

Tuesday 3 July, Taunton

Somerset v. Northamptonshire (County Championship, 3 days)

Another third day, another pristine pitch, another pre-planned spectacle. Leading Northamptonshire by 247 after the first six sessions had yielded 749 runs and 10 dismissals, Somerset carried on clubbing throughout the seventh. Cook totted up his fourth first-class 100 and then, much like Rose in the Glamorgan game, became a trifle bored. To his credit, Allan Lamb had resisted feeding runs for most of the morning, but the introduction of Rob Bailey's presentable if rarely-used off-breaks proved too much for Cook's pride. During Ray Illingworth's tour of Australia in 1970–71, an unwilling Geoff Boycott was convinced by his colleagues that it would be in the best interests of the side to declare himself 'retired hurt' against Queensland; he had already made 124 and the first Test was but days away. Cook, a considerably more selfless character, needed no such persuading, although, unlike Rose, he made sure he posted that third figure before washing his hands of the stage-managed silliness of it all.

Tavaré eventually asked Northants, a temperamental ticking bomb of a batting side prone to two or three explosions a summer, to pursue 329 at nearly 5 an over. Trying, but, in the present environment, far from impossible. Lefebvre took no time to remove the rejuvenated Somerset old boy, Nigel Felton, but that was Somerset's last slice of encouragement. Alan Fordham, Geoff Cook's successor, was joined by Bailey and the two put on 185 to settle the matter. Adrian skittled Bailey for 101, but that only brought in Lamb, whose gung-ho style and blatant disregard for textbook protocol make him desperately difficult to keep quiet in this sort of situation. Somerset failed to do so, and Northants skated in by 7 wickets.

'The trouble is,' reasoned Adrian, 'that it's so hard to judge what a good score is here. Declarations are therefore really tricky, and I sympathise with Tav on that. Maybe we just aren't scoring quickly enough, although we've got more batting points than anyone else, which certainly suggests that's not the case. The batsmen just wish they could chase for a change, and who can blame them?' Who indeed?

Friday 6 July, Maidstone

Kent v. Essex (County Championship, 3 days)

Until today, that three-quarter century of Nadeem's at Edgbaston had been fading into the recesses of the public memory. Left out at Bath in favour of his Braintree co-habitee due to futile expectations of a turning wicket, he was omitted from the next 1st XI fixture against New Zealand some two weeks later, though only because the TCCB had insisted that the counties field their strongest sides against the tourists. Now, though, came a chance to make up for lost time, in more ways than one.

After the parched expanses of Mote Park had been given a severe watering over the first two days, Chris Cowdrey asks Essex whether they would mind having a stab at making 309 in eighty-five overs. A second-wicket partnership of 106 between Prichard and Stephenson is succeeded by the loss of 3 wickets for 16, Richard Davis accounting for Stephenson and Waugh with successive balls either side of tea, bringing together the so-called Biryani Brothers: Hussain, taking guard in the Championship for the first time in 1990, and Nadeem. Resisting any verbal response to some choice words from the Kent seamer, Chris Penn, rich expressions pertaining unequivocally to their origins, the two friends add 98 to lead Essex beyond the cusp separating victory and defeat. Hussain departs for 41, Nadeem soon after, run out in a mix-up with Pringle for a 63 encompassing eighty-five balls, but Pringle knows the hard work is done. He follows up two reverse sweeps with a sliced drive, and Essex have that inordinately delayed second Championship victory with 4 wickets and a dozen balls remaining.

During the celebrations, Nadeem stresses how much Hussain's presence meant to him. 'It's great having him back again. I tend to look to him for a bit of guidance and he does more than anyone else to make me feel at home, introducing me to players from other counties and ensuring that I'm never left out. Because of the success he's had, he has this glow of assurance about him, an inner ring of confidence if you like. Gooch has already told him that although his wrist injury means that he is unlikely to recover enough ground to tour Australia, he would probably attain a place on the A tour to Pakistan no matter what he does for the rest of the summer. I'm sure knowing that will help him get back in the swing of things quickly. We both had a bit of a laugh about Penn's comments. If he thought saying silly things about us being Pakis was going to disrupt our concentration he was mistaken.'

Even though Nadeem was now tapping a rich vein at No. 6, it is not a position he especially favours. 'Every time I bat there I have to play the way the game dictates. I can't play my natural game. If the slog's on, which it has tended to be this summer, I just have to go out and slog. I opened throughout my schooldays, but that doesn't seem right for me now. Do I go out and play my normal game, do I grind it out, or what? And you have to concentrate on every ball that bit more carefully. But if I bat at No. 3, 4, or 5, which Fletch thinks is my niche, it's a nice sort of jigsaw. You can put your pads on, relax for a while, then slip in knowing that there's good batting around you. I've usually gone in at No. 4 or 5 in recent years, but I've been going in at No. 3 for the 2nd XI since the start of the season because Keith Butler hates that role, so I swapped with him. With JJ [Jonathan Lewis] and Nick Knight at college until July we've only got one opener, Adam Seymour, so batting at No. 3 means you can be in at any moment. Ideally, I think I'd prefer a brief rest first.'

Fletcher seems unconcerned where Nadeem bats, just so long as he keeps playing. 'His ideal place is No. 3 to 5, but with Nasser back now and Gooch away with England, opening might be his best bet. Not only is he extremely mature, his temperament is excellent and his technique is very sound, and he also plays fast bowling very well. By next year he could be knocking on the door so far as Test cricket is concerned. Both he and Nasser have flair, though Nasser more so. When he is going he is very difficult to bowl to. He could get 100 in two hours. Nadeem couldn't.'

Wednesday 11 July, Taunton

Somerset v. Worcestershire (NatWest Trophy, second round)

'The first thing we knew about it was when we turned up at the ground on the morning of the match. We all thought it was a good idea. Cricket needs to attract more revenue and it seems as good a way as any.' As far as Adrian, the rest of the Somerset team and the Worcestershire players were concerned, there was nothing untoward in it, but reactionary buffers the breadth of the country could be heard spluttering into their teacups. There it was for all 5,000 of the sellout crowd to see, plus a million or so TV viewers. On the playing area at Taunton. About fifty yards from the stumps, marked out in hydrated lime: a vast NatWest logo.

True, Reliance had managed to get their imprint emblazoned over the outfield in Calcutta for the 1987 World Cup final, but such heresy was totally new to the home of the game. In their insatiable hunger for exposure, cricket and its sponsors had made it inevitable. Surrey and the TCCB, so the grapevine had it, are at this very moment holding negotiations with Cornhill to parade their sugar daddy's insignia during the Oval Test against India in late August. Another brick from the wall.

According to Adrian, however, commercial sensibilities are not what they could be. 'It's pathetic. The local ads at the top of the scoreboard today are covered up by a BBC tarpaulin. Bloody BBC! If they lightened up we would attract more revenue and therefore we wouldn't need Sky. There are so many more avenues to explore. For example, we should be allowed to wear larger manufacturers' logos on our shirts. The maximum size permitted is a quarter inch, but would it really make so much difference to the game if they were three-quarters, say? As for sponsors' logos, we have to cover them over with Elastoplast when we play in front of the cameras. Ridiculous.'

And so to the main business of the day. Somerset versus Worcestershire in the second round of the NatWest. Roebuck meets Botham, The Sequel. Recently asked if he would be prepared to go on tour for England with his apparent nemesis (how the pair had ever co-authored a book is beyond the ken of most), Botham had responded with an acute understanding of tabloidology: 'I would love to sit in a deck chair and watch Malcolm Marshall knock his block off.'

Both men had experienced variable seasons so far. Roebuck began sketchily, dropped out through illness and lost his place on merit during Bath Week, before returning with 60, 44, 114 not out and 90 not out in Somerset's last two Championship games. Acknowledging that his days with the new ball were over, Botham ushered in the season by stating his determination to nail down a place in the Test team at No. 4. He certainly started splendidly, winning a Benson & Hedges tie at Bristol with a massively authoritative 138 not out that even made an impression on Gilbert Jessop, one of his six 6s bouncing off the top of the pavilion steps, bounding on through the door and shattering the glass frame of the great Edwardian's photograph. Setting his stall out to redefine a reputation for frippery, Botham was the personification of thrifty solidity in compiling his first Championship century for three years in the match against Surrey. Consistency, though, was elusive, and places in the rampant England middle-order were in short supply. Described somewhat ungraciously as 'a fat has-been' by Warwickshire's Dermot Reeve, a never-will-be, he at least had the consolation of knowing that the world would not be free of Bothams for a good while yet; playing for Cundall Manor Prep

School against Red House of York, Liam Botham slugged 161 out of a total of 208, then took all 10 wickets at the outrageous cost of 3 runs.

Of the two sparring partners, Botham had by far the greater say in proceedings, and without scoring a run. Initially held in check by Stuart Lampitt, a clever young seamer who bowled Roebuck and had Cook leg-before before the total had hit 75, Somerset were prevented from slipping the leash by their erstwhile colleague. In the absence of the injured Graham Dilley, Botham did indeed take the new ball and, in the midst of a charitable spell, he ejected Rose and Harden to neutralise the middle order. The upshot was that despite Tavaré's unbeaten 99, a noteworthy effort that might have accrued rather more than four boundaries but for Phil Neale's astute field placing, Somerset acquired 283, approximately 40 under par for this abundant course.

Bowling twelve overs in an innings for the first time since 16 June, Adrian was rusty and it showed. Nowt wrong with the old aggression and pace, mind. One delivery rammed into Martin Weston's ribs just below the heart, causing him to stagger and call for a runner. But by then Weston had already passed 50 and Worcestershire were almost halfway home without a wicket down. Curtis's second atypically rapid 100 of the summer against Somerset dominated the scorebook and won the match award, but it was Weston, the only Worcester-born player in the side, who stole hearts, carrying on like the proverbial trouper to make 98 as the first-wicket pair posted 188. Weston, a pro if ever there was, highly competent with bat and ball, steadfast and true, but never likely to tickle a selector's fancy. Botham, who else, had the final word, nudging the winning leg-bye off the second ball of the fifty-eighth over.

To all intents and purposes, Somerset's season was over, and Adrian knew. 'We all feel down after that. We're not in the running for anything now. There is plenty of motivation left, of course. We have to lift our position in the Championship and look at our personal targets. If you've got little targets, that helps see you through at times like these. Meeting them gives you a sense of self-satisfaction and it helps the team, so I don't really see that as being self-centred. The point is that we don't seem to be getting any breaks, yet we're certainly better than average. We didn't get enough runs today, simple as that, but Cook did get one that didn't bounce. Had that not happened perhaps we would have made 330 or 340 as we should have done. Losing him and Robey relatively early set us back, but Hayhurst didn't get on with it and Tav should have gone in ahead of him. Fancy being not out 99 in a one-day match.

'The wicket got even better as the match wore on, and we probably bowled too many four-balls. We certainly didn't get any early wickets, which was partly thanks to Weston, who surprised me. A lot of guts that man's got. I'm sure I wouldn't have batted on after a blow like that.'

The next day Harry Brind schlepped down to Taunton to authorise and oversee the removal of the hydrated lime. Had he been so disposed, he might have sneaked a look at Phil Frost's latest toy: a contraption that knits grass tighter together and so makes pitches flatter. Sounds exactly what the Somerset bowlers need to boost their sagging confidence.

Saturday 14 July, Lord's

Lancashire v. Worcestershire (Benson & Hedges Cup final)

Despite being a salty old warrior with seven previous Lord's medals (five wins and two defeats), David is as enthusiastic as he had been that September morning in 1970 when he rolled up here for his first Gillette final. The only one he had missed had been the 1986 NatWest loss to Sussex, perhaps in hindsight fortuitously so. Before Chairman Rhoades was effectively turfed out of his imperial throne, he issued a final decree, dispensing with Jack Bond, the manager, and Peter Lever, the coach, whose personal differences reflected a divided, ineffectual dressing-room. That David was not associated with the defeat that broke the emperor's patience no doubt helped his cause when Rhoades named Clive Lloyd's successor as captain. But that was then and this is now.

'This is a special match for me, going in as captain for the first time. In the 1970s I was young and it was all very exciting, but this is the most important one for me. It's now, it's in the present. To play in Jack Bond's teams was a pleasurable experience, but it's gone. So have the early 1980s, when we didn't really have what it takes to get to a Final. There were lots of players in the side then who never appeared in a Lord's Final, and they didn't want to know about what happened ten years earlier. These youngsters I have now wanted to know what it was like. I told them that I enjoyed the traditions and the history at first, but that I was never overawed, and that playing at Old Trafford in front of a packed house was just as exhilarating. In many ways this is just another game. The sad thing is that events like this tend to merge with other days. Tomorrow should be a rest day, but we've got to be back at Old Trafford by the morning for a Refuge game, against Worcestershire!'

Fearnleyshire had limbered up for their sixth stab at winning a Lord's Final by steamrollering Somerset whilst fretting over Dilley's knee and Neal Radford's tummy. Lancashire had had the benefit of a more arduous NatWest engagement at Derby. Before the thickest gathering at the County Ground for three years, Barnett and Morris skipped along gaily, adding 105 in twenty-four overs for the second wicket before the captain played on to Akram at 123. Morris, now less Gattingesque in shape but ever more so in his disdain for bowlers, had his push for promotion to the Texaco squad interrupted by Atherton, depicted as a purveyor of leg-spin for Volvo owners by David Hopps of the *Guardian*. Soon 180 for 3 whimpered to 241 all out from 56.5 overs, DeFreitas and Akram snuffing out the last five candles for 2 runs in ten balls as the clouds congregated. The generosity of Watkinson and Peter Martin (the former Doncaster schoolboy whose fast-medium promise had tempted Yorkshire until he informed them he was from the other side of the border, in Accrington) forced David to do the unthinkable, i.e. put himself on. Three overs for 19 neither lost nor saved the day, but at least that stiff left arm was doing something other than pointing for once.

It certainly got no further exercise that day, although David was next man in when the spoils were secured. With Fowler bedevilled by a back complaint, Atherton did as he had been doing for England and went in first, with Mendis. The two of them took two overs to see off Devon Malcolm, Derbyshire's only real bowling weapon following the substitution of Adrian Kuiper for Ian Bishop, and, with Fairbrother and Lloyd, Fowler's deputy, chipping in to sound effect, Lancashire were 184 for 2 when a minor tremor saw 5 wickets ebb away for 31 as Malcolm stormed back for a second spell.

Hegg and Austin, though, soothed the palpitations and tied up victory with four balls to spare.

Lancashire convened at the Lord's nets yesterday afternoon, David's theory being that with Akram, DeFreitas, Hegg, Austin and Atherton new to a Lord's Final, it made sense for them to 'soak up the general atmosphere, be there, settle down, instead of coming in cold on the day'. They talked about Worcestershire only briefly. 'In that kind of situation I normally try and tell the younger players their opponents' weaknesses, such as whether he's a cutter, or he's a hooker, or who plays off the back foot. But everyone knows all about Worcestershire. The danger is in going over the top, of over-psyching. I don't think there's much chance of that, though. Everyone is keyed up, but there are few apparent nerves, although I was surprised to hear Mike [Watkinson] admitting to some. Still, you can't give of your best without a few butterflies, can you?'

A leisurely net reminded David of one of his bugbears. 'The decline of net facilities in the past twenty years has been terrible. Only here and at the Oval can you have a net without having to erect one in the middle. I appreciate the lack of space, but nets should be available all the time, making "knocking up" in the outfield unnecessary. I used to have a proper net in the Old Trafford practice grounds when I started, but now those practice grounds have been diminished by the office blocks on the Chester Road side of the ground. The nets have been very poor for a long time anyway, but the quick bowlers need to run in, so we use the square on the practice ground as often as possible. However, the ground staff have been spending time laying new nets on the "back field", as we call it, so I'm hopeful that things will improve.'

After feeding time, David had an early night. Did he have any specific plans for the toss? 'If I win it I'll field because we've won games that way and we prefer the chase. Whenever we're fielding members say, "You've won it, then". The only time I've inserted and lost this season was against Gloucestershire in the Refuge, when we played badly. Still, I don't regard the toss as being of vital importance in one-day games unless the pitch is green or damp. Bob Willis did complain in 1984 when Warwickshire slid to 139 all out against us, but they collapsed from 100 for 2 at lunch, so he couldn't legitimately blame dampness. However, there have been a number of damp wickets at Lord's in recent years.' Those who paid good money to see Middlesex and Worcestershire contest the 1988 NatWest final, a game containing two half-centuries and decided by the toss, would certainly subscribe to that.

A year ago, with Dilley, Radford, Hick and Botham in the saddle, Worcestershire would have been narrow favourites, but they currently languish in the lower reaches of both Championship (two wins in nine) and League (four in ten). Dilley's knee, not half as attractive as Claire's but almost as bothersome as Jenkins's ear, prevented him from leading the attack, while Radford, possibly the most adventurous county seamer, is playing for the first time since a stomach operation six weeks ago. In the event, Phil Neale won the toss and put his incomplete attack to the test by inserting Lancashire.

If there was a shortage of currents crackling around Lord's as Mendis and the recovered Fowler strode out, then that was attributable to the size of the crowd, condensed in number by the (de)construction of the Compton and Edrich Stands (at one time there had been talk at the TCCB of switching the game to Edgbaston) and the cost of tickets. These ranged from £22 to £30, plus the odd seat beneath the Grandstand for a cut-price £18; a rough estimate for the weekend break was £200, a sum beyond the ken of most of the populace. Fowler didn't tarry long, flipping the bustling Phil Newport to square-leg off a thickish inside edge, and then both his accomplice and Fairbrother departed as unhappy hookers, the former top-edging to square-leg, the latter inside-edging Stuart Lampitt into his stumps. Atherton stabilised matters, breaching the perimeter just the once in his two-hour stay for 40 as he and Watkinson put on 88, but all of a sudden both were gone within the space of a run, Atherton run out by Lampitt's throw from mid-wicket, Watkinson spooning a return catch to Botham upon reaching 50.

Then came Lancashire's not-so-secret weapon, Akram, who entered at an unpropitious 136 for 5 in the forty-second over. Recalling Mark Greatbatch's inventive stroke during the Lord's Test, he propelled Radford for 6 over fine-leg. Then, in the same over, he launched an unerringly guided missile into the top tier of the pavilion. Not since Mike Llewellyn hoisted John Emburey into the guttering beside the commentary box in the 1977 Gillette final had a shot of such magnitude been witnessed in St John's Wood. But while Llewellyn quickly returned to anonymity, there seems little chance of the best left-handed all-rounder since the eminently spirited Sobers doing likewise. DeFreitas and Hegg followed his cue, 102 runs gushing from the last dozen overs, one of them contributed by David. It was his first 55-over knock of the season.

A total of 241 for 8 looked even more impressive by the twentieth over of the Worcestershire reply. Again, it was Akram, tippy-toeing to the popping crease like a puma with scalded feet, who made the critical incisions. Curtis, the rock, attempted to steer his second, rising, delivery and was caught by Hegg. Then at 41, Akram now in his third over, Hick, the redeemer, failed for the second time in his two performances on a major stage, nicking another lifting ball that left him off the wicket. Hegg exultant, Lancashire halfway there. There was still Botham, mind, and while there is Botham there is always hope. A frugal spell from Watkinson kept him at bay and accounted for two lesser mortals in Damian D'Oliveira and Martin Weston. A ration of three boundaries in ninety-five minutes underlined Botham's determination to endure, but seeing a passive Botham is like hearing Paul, George and Ringo in harness; you can admire the content, even the sentiments, but it doesn't move you. It was therefore almost as much of a relief for the neutral as for the carousing Lancashire supporters when he missed a pull off DeFreitas and had his off-bail tipped off. Akram returned to spear one under Newport's groping bat, and when Austin struck a blow for Haslingden and unsung cricketers everywhere by bowling Lampitt with the last ball of the penultimate over, Lancashire had won. For only the fourth time in eleven Benson & Hedges Cup Finals, the side batting second had lost. On the other three occasions the winning margins were 6, 4 and 2 runs. Lancashire had bucked a trend with their 69-run advantage.

The closing ceremony was dotted with *déjà vus*. Usually, the man of the match award is not one that triggers controversy; the most influential participant is glaringly obvious for the most part. In 1990, as in 1984 at the end of Lancashire's only previous 55–over final, querulous voices accompanied the announcement. Six years ago, Peter May, then chairman of the selectors (and presumably a bit punch-drunk after seeing his Test nominees pummelled by the West Indies), contrived to nominate the Lancashire captain, the splendid John Abrahams, as the outstanding individual contributor. True, his team had beaten Warwickshire, but his own input had amounted to a dashing duck. The choice had been hard to comprehend, although it had a certain logic. In abridged cricket such as this, the man at the helm has to think a good deal harder and swifter than the full-length version dictates. In low-scoring games (of which this one was a crushingly tedious example), he is often the difference between dominance and subservience. This time it was Watkinson (an invaluable half-century followed by 2–37) who stepped forward. At least in Abrahams's year there were no clear candidates for the award, but what of Akram now? His effortless thwacks had been the catalyst for Lancashire's late-innings explosion, while his dismissal of Curtis and Hick had removed the opposition props.

David draped on his Solomon robes. 'In terms of figures Watkinson deserved it. People tend to forget about Mike, but he went to the Netherlands with MCC last year because England were seeking a seamer after the South African withdrawals. Perhaps he is not a first-class No.5, even though I put him there. His natural slot is No. 6 or 7. But today, from number five, he made 50 at a critical time and then picked up 2 crucial wickets, although those of Curtis and Hick were the most vital.'

Hmm, young master Hick, how to dispose of. David has a couple of theories. 'Like so many fine batsmen, you fancy your chance early on against him because he looks to go back in front of middle and leg, and so leaves a gap through which you can see middle and off. His other Achilles heel, so far as he has one, is that he doesn't seem to hook or duck and so sometimes gets himself into a tangle. Akram didn't bowl him a bouncer, but, significantly, the one he got him with did lift. I still think Hick will make it at international level, however, although whether he should be allowed to do so in an England cap is another matter.

'All in all, though, I don't know that I want to single out individuals. As usual, I gave Atherton *carte blanche* to bat through – he doesn't give it away ten or fifteen overs before the end as some do –and he confirmed what the other specialist batsmen had indicated, that 230 to 240 would be a good score. I tend to go by their feelings, so I suppose we always felt we had enough, even if that was mainly a tribute to the depth of our batting order. The only member of the line-up without a first-class century is Allott, and besides an 88 for us, he hit 52 not out against Lillee and Alderman in his first Test innings.

'Our bowling and fielding was simply the best I've seen since I took over the captaincy. Not one bowler took stick, and they all got wickets. But the only time I felt convinced we would win was when Daffy bowled Botham. I like the man, and I'd have liked him to have come to Old Trafford after he left Somerset to bring the buzz back. Cedric [Rhoades] wouldn't have him at any price, but he's a genius. His record speaks for itself, but he still has a determination to play for England again. He can, too. Very few players would have recovered from the injuries he's had to his back. He's certainly lost none of his powers of swing, but sadly a yard or two of pace. Maybe there will never be an all-rounder like him again. No longer is he head and shoulders above the rest, but he is still very good. Age takes its toll, though.'

So it was, a Final shorn of the drama of Eddie Hemmings's last-ball 4 for Nottinghamshire last year, or Norman Cowans bowling Neil Foster in the fifty-fifth over six years earlier with Essex five short of victory, but blessed with enough to-ing and fro-ing to be better than most. David stayed in the dressing-room with the rest of the Lancashire players until 9 p.m., drinking, bobbing around to a ghettoblaster and holding court to all manner of well-wishers from fans to committee members. 'I had a chat with a couple of Worcestershire players during the presentations, but we didn't mix afterwards. I remember losing here in 1974, and hearing cheering from the Kent dressing-room. That was a terrible feeling, so I imagine how they felt this evening.'

All the Lancashire players bar Mendis ('I can't say I've ever really got to know him off the field') popped off to Covent Garden to meet wives and girlfriends for a bop at Stringfellow's as the owner's special guests. 'Peter's a Yorkshireman. We can't all be perfect.' Champagne flowed, cricket, for the moment, be blowed. No excess, mind. 'There wasn't a lot of drinking because of tomorrow's game, and I said to the lads that if any of them did stop out late, they shouldn't take too much drink. In any case, the volume of drinking at Lancashire is not what it used to be. We have a responsibility to each other to be fit and everyone is aware of that. That said, the players are here to have fun, not just pick up their bags and get on the coach when it's all over.'

One down, three to go.

Friday 20 July, Colchester

Essex v. Derbyshire (County Championship, 3 days)

'Signs of Essex bouncing back' pronounced the *Guardian* after the first day of the match against Derbyshire. Forty-eight hours later it is already tempting to congratulate the headline writer on his prescience, so too the author of his inspiration, David Hopps.

Third from bottom at the start, and with 4 fewer bowling points to their credit than any other county, Essex were still licking the wounds inflicted by Hampshire's astonishing – and successful – pursuit of 307 in the NatWest second round the previous Wednesday. They needed a leg-up and, on a bouncier pitch than most had been used to this season, the Derbyshire batsmen supplied that and more. Bursting away with Sunday vigour, they were 50 to the good inside half an hour. Kim Barnett, in Hopps's words, 'tore to 38 with the gusto of Edmund Kean on an intoxicating night at Drury Lane', but his exit, stage right, set in train the first of two collapses: 67 for 0 to 85 for 3. Then, after Bruce Roberts and Chris Adams had conspired for 85, both were caught close to the wicket attempting to pull the slippery Andrew, Nadeem snaring Roberts, and 170 for 3 cascaded into 203 for 8. Geoff Miller, late of this parish and now back with his hometown club, orchestrated a rally, but 268 seemed woefully insubstantial.

Stephenson was hastily knocked over by Ian Bishop, who was currently topping the bowling averages, but not once did Derbyshire exert any vestige of control thereafter. Dragged up the order to first drop in place of the injured Prichard, Nadeem accounted for the lion's share of a poker-faced 67–run second wicket stand with Hardie, the mission strictly to blunt Bishop. On 42 he edged Steve Goldsmith's irregular seam-up to Karl Krikken, the Bolton-born keeper with the name that exuded Copenhagen, but Waugh and Hussain capitalised to the tune of 126 and 60, and Essex folded with unusual neatness for 366 when Miller dispatched Andrew with the last ball of the 100th over. Forty-one overs later Hardie and Stephenson were buckling up again. Once Barnett had rocketed the first legal delivery of the innings from Foster to the squarer of two gullies, a pell-mell procession to the pavilion was in progress. Spurred by a pitch that had retained the best of its pace, Foster nabbed 6 of the first 8 wickets for 28 in ten overs as brazenness gripped the late afternoon air, Derbyshire barely skittering to 94 for 8 before Krikken directed them to a less ghastly 145 all out. Forty-eight wanted, and duly gathered in the ninth over of the third day by the hearty, perennial Hardie, Nadeem witnessing the winning hit from his vantage point at the non-striker's end.

At Castle Park, a siege had begun. Who would have dared forecast such a renaissance for Pringle and his pals? That Hampshire NatWest defeat was still being pored over by stunned supporters. Their mainspring was elsewhere (having an almost unheard-of brush with mortality, actually, in the Texaco Trophy against India at Trent Bridge). Derbyshire, moreover, were standing 48 points and eleven places distant at the outset of a match conducted on a pitch with enough zest to persuade Bishop to sharpen his claws. It is a tad premature, of course, to start ringing up the bookie and whacking down a tenner on Essex winning the Championship. But with three games in hand of second-placed Warwickshire, whom they trail by 33 points, and only three of their last dozen games against serious contenders, it is easy to get carried away. The batsmen, even without Gooch and Prichard, could look after themselves handsomely, and even though Childs has yet to locate optimum rhythm or a beneficent track, Andrew's 6 wickets suggested that Foster, stalking in with renewed vitality, now had a worthy partner.

That last development, according to Nadeem, may turn out to be a critical one. 'We've been foiled by the weather and some exceedingly flat pitches, but Foster and Jimmy – we call Andrew Jimmy Hill because of his long chin – really seemed to bustle in and give us an extra dimension. I was particularly pleased for Andrew. I was a bit fed up after I got out, feeling, again, that I hadn't gone on when I should have, so I put a towel over my head and sat in the dressing-room like that for half an hour. Every once in a while I'm shouting, "Will I ever learn". Then he comes in and puts me straight. "Look," he said, "at least you're only 21. Look at me: I've been in county cricket for eight years. Will I ever learn to pitch the ball up? Just think of it from that point of view. You've got more chance of learning than I have." That made me giggle and relax. Perhaps it wasn't so bad getting a 30 or 40. I could have got 0.

'It was a good cricket wicket, but Derbyshire didn't bat very cleverly. Well as we bowled, in both innings they threw the bat when there was no need. Sometimes it comes off, but more often it doesn't. No one is getting carried away, but we needed that. That's two wins in our last three games now, but Lancashire are here tomorrow. That should give us an idea of our capabilities.'

And what of going in at No.3? 'Well, I didn't have time to put my feet up in the first innings, did I? I think it was a case of Essex wanting to find a place for me. I was originally meant to open – Fletch thinks I'm good against pace – but Hardie was included and so I went in at No.3, after all, which I prefer. It was a real challenge against Bishop, not least since Kevin Thomas had struck me in the jaw when we were in the nets a couple of days ago and chipped three of my teeth. I'd leave four out of six balls from Bishop and score off Simon Base and Alan Warner, but it was Waugh and Nasser who built the platform for victory by really taking Bishop on. Hardie and I were content to keep him out for the most part.'

Friday 20 July, Worcester

Worcestershire v. Somerset (County Championship, 3 days)

Worcestershire, shorn of the lame Botham, Dilley too, renew hostilities with Somerset. Roebuck takes due advantage of an innocuous New Road surface, scoring an unbeaten 201 and adding 258 for the second wicket with Hayhurst to come within 32 of the county record and permit a declaration of 298 for 3. The familiar pattern has been set. Worcestershire's early response is tentative, Adrian and his trusty room-mate, Mallender, getting rid of Paul Bent and Curtis by the time the score has meandered to 13, but from then on Hick commands centrestage with that special aura of invincibility he seems to reserve for Somerset bowlers. Adrian quits after eight overs and when Neale declares 98 in arrears, the shy lad from Salisbury is unbeaten on 171, having swollen his tally against the Dragons to 1,389 runs at an average of 126.27.

Remembering with something less than affection

Worcestershire's successful pursuit of 300 in fifty-eight overs a year earlier, Tavaré's sums have to be just so. Roebuck extends his sequence to 577 runs in the six first-class innings since his return, at an average of 192.33, and the eventual equation is a stiff 340 in sixty. The climax lasts all of ten overs, Curtis's dismissal at 40 snuffing out any ambitions Worcestershire may have harboured. They finish on 181 for 3, Hick 69 not out. Somerset have now drawn ten of their last twelve games in the Championship, losing the other two. Adrian's glut against Gloucestershire could scarcely have been less of a harbinger.

In their room at the Gifford Hotel, Adrian and Mallender decided to get morose over their morning cuppa. 'We decided to count the number of wickets we had taken between us! That didn't take long. We also chatted about the attitude of some of the sponsors. Sometimes it's like we're back at school. Some of them treat us like kids, ordering us about while we're continually briefed to be polite to this one and that one. At Bath this guy who'd had a few too many called me arrogant and ordered me to turn round. I couldn't believe it. Then he reported me to Anderson as if he was my headmaster. I told Anderson that players deserved more respect.'

Even Roebuck was flapping now. 'Anderson promised he would have a collection for Robey's benefit during the NatWest tie against Worcestershire, but in the end nothing happened, so Robey's been ranting and raving and threatening to resign. I told him to calm down. Being in the runs again has helped him. He's been a changed man this season, much more relaxed. When the Big Three left in 1986 he didn't have a grip on the side as captain. At one stage, when we weren't doing well in the Refuge, he dropped a lot of senior players in favour of some youngsters, and it just so happened that the players who were omitted were those who always seemed to be questioning him, or not getting on with him, so there was a bit of unrest that may or may not have contributed to his being relieved of the leadership. I don't think his problem is anything to do with cricket at all. He just seems so bloody lonely, although I should say that I only really know him in a cricket context. He's a very funny man, very good company when in the right mood. Quite good at mickey-taking too. I think he likes to be contrary, but as soon as people react to that he doesn't seem sure whether to back down, laugh it off or come back at you. But the main thing about Robey is that he is the one person here who has the club at heart. From what I know of him, cricket is his life and always has been. And Somerset are his life too.'

New Road did prompt one happy thought at least. 'Seeing Dilley's swollen knee reminded me of how lucky I've been with injuries down the years.' Lucky. Now there's a word you don't hear too often from Somerset lips at the moment.

Saturday 21 July, Colchester

Essex v. Lancashire (County Championship, 3 days)

'England's Oldest Town', proclaimed the sign as we drove down the Avenue of Remembrance towards Castle Park. Inside the entrance to the ground, a dash of youth seasons the predominantly middle- aged hubbub; a dainty girl in bleached Levis and a T-shirt at least three sizes too big is swallowed up in the arms of a burly boy. He is encased, despite the blissful weather, in one of those trendy American hooded tops so beloved by the hepcat rapsters currently swamping the pop charts. With a mobile scoreboard and what looks like a white-sheet sightscreen, the playing area reeks of austerity. It is flanked, however, by three monuments to Thatcherism: the towering B&Q, the heavily-scaffolded embryo of another gigantic shopping park – Sainsbury's someone said – and a sparsely populated sports centre. The car park, peppered with XR3i's and souped- up Capris, is even more redolent of the age of unreason. Out of their bucket seats spill those meejah-devised brothers-in-arms, Loadsamoney and Essex Man, jangling ignition keys, their tribal charms.

What the brimming throng want from their day out is to bathe in the sun and watch their Scipio Africanus, Gooch, ride that dastardly Hannibal, Wasim Akram, out of town. David, teased by all and sundry for his lack of coin skills, scuppers that by deputing Fairbrother to toss up instead. The switch works and Mendis and Fowler pad up. Andy Atkinson, sporting a savage crewcut and a pair of garish pink striped shorts, supervises the final preparations to the pitch. On a bench outside the visitors' claustrophobic quarters at long-leg, an ageing Teddy Boy with grey sideburns and crepe soles, later unveiled as John, the Lancashire coach driver, pores over the *Mirror*. The Lancashire 12th man, Lloyd, sun cream and Grand Prix shades glued to his nose, hovers nearby, anxious to be part of the fray, and just as anxious not to show it. David and I take a pew by a window in the pavilion as Fowler and Mendis begin what must be the longest walk – fully forty yards – from pavilion to middle at any irregular county venue.

David is still smarting from the previous day's events in Coventry, for which a brief resumé seems in order. On Wednesday, Warwickshire, an unconvincing second in the Championship (to Lancashire's third) by dint of a persuasive seam attack including the rapid South African, Allan Donald, and some playful Edgbaston tracks, had battled out of a hole of 117 for 5 to reach 374 for 7 declared (David 17–0–73–0 with Atherton on Test duty). Then came the unquenchable Fairbrother, back in his county palace after an unhappy venture into the wilds of the Test forest (seemingly undecided whether to give full rein to that free spirit or convert to puritanism, he had made 59 mostly scratchy runs in five confused innings against New Zealand). 'Harvey' was in regal form. Coming in at 26 for 3, he hauled Lancashire to 203 for 8 almost single-handedly (Jesty was the second chief contributor with 17), then found a durable ally at last in David, who scored 29 of their unbroken stand of 129. On-the-spot opinion had it that Fairbrother's 203 was an epic of Charlton Heston proportions, but also that David may have erred in batting on long after the threat of the follow-on had evaporated.

Andy Lloyd, his opposite number, certainly seemed to agree, the result being a tight-fisted offer of 299 in thirty-nine overs. Most teams would have turned up their collective nose, but Lancashire had a go. Fowler took 12 off each of Munton's first two overs and Fairbrother flayed another 50. Adrian Pierson, a stick-insect of an off-spinner whose feet barely leave the ground during his short glide to the stumps, was twice lifted out of the ground by Akram, but he and Asif Din, the bespectacled Ugandan leg-spinner, generally kept the bashers within bounds and Lancashire pulled up at 173 for 5.

'It was suggested to me that I had killed the game by going on too far, but I thought the wicket would deteriorate, so I knew we couldn't afford too big a deficit on first innings. One end turned, but that was probably only through the rough outside the right-hander's off-stump caused by Akram's follow-through, and it did not become as awkward as I'd imagined. Lloyd felt it was a difficult ground to set a declaration on, but in that case, why did he bat if he wanted to chase? Then he said he didn't have any bowlers because Reeve was injured and could only bat. Then why pick the extra batsman instead of Donald in the first place?'

Just as David hits the peak of his indignation, Nadeem catches Mendis at short-leg. 'Jesus Christ! Must have bounced a bit.' Fowler is soon bowled neck and crop by Foster, who would not have been playing had the Labour group on the local council, offended by his South African dalliance, succeeded in banning him from the premises. When Pringle's movement off the seam produces another catch for Nadeem, this time to get shot of Atherton, David mumbles another oath. Allot sidles by. 'You should have tossed,' he hisses, not entirely seriously. 'We would have been bowling by now.' Akram prises himself out of his semi-slumber and hurries away to pad up. The players left on the bench begin to fidget.

Back to Coventry before David starts to follow suit. 'In my innings I just tried to support Fairbrother, who was magnificent. I felt sorry for him after his experiences in the Tests. After the first at Trent Bridge, where he fell foul of an unsatisfactory pitch that seamed around, we chatted and I told him to play his natural game because that was what had got him there in the first place. Because Old Trafford is shorn of grass the ball comes on to the bat, which is what he likes, but that wicket at Trent Bridge was harder to judge. At Lord's Neil said he tried to get down the wicket to John Bracewell but the ball was too close to him and he was caught. As a No.6 you might cop the second new ball, but generally the ball is old when you arrive, which is ideal for a strokeplayer like Neil. He has waited a long time for a second chance and I fear that what happened in those three Tests may have taxed the selectors' trust. Maybe he needs to change his style and occupy the crease, and to play with the full face of the bat rather than the open face that gets you runs to third man. Mind you, I've been an occasional No.3, I've spent two seasons at 4 and 5, but am essentially an 8 or 9, so who am I to judge? I'm going in as low as 10 at the moment because I want to give Akram and Daffy a chance higher up the order. Whether I bat at 8, 9 or 10 won't have an effect on me. I've been all over the order.'

Feeling a shade guilty for being indoors on such a luscious day, we make a circuit of the ground. The Fairbrother discussion continues, David explaining that he regards him as the connection between the two generations in the Lancashire dressing-room, Allott, Fowler, Mendis, Jesty, Watkinson and Patterson on the one side, Akram, DeFreitas, Hegg, Atherton, Lloyd, Austin and Fitton on the other. 'He also favours the democratic approach to captaincy, always consulting Allott, Ormrod and Fowler before making a decision.' That we are talking about the next Lancashire captain is indisputable.

Every twenty yards or so David halts to sign a cluster of autographs, in well-thumbed books thrust nervously forward by small boys, on scorecards proffered with fake adult cool by their boyish fathers. 'From time to time I bring captains of industry into the dressing-room. They're like little kids. It's my workplace but I forget what it means to people. I never refuse autographs, though. I used to sit outside the dressing-room at Old Trafford as a boy and be disappointed whenever someone refused to sign for me. Admittedly, it's not always possible to oblige because of the sheer weight of it, what with all the benefit ephemera, ball sponsors and what have you.' Two elderly women offer David a copy of the legendary Lancashire calypso record, recorded in 1971, the B side of which went by the title of 'The Ballad of David Hughes'. With great politeness he turns them down. 'Johnny Walker played it on Radio One but it sold about ten copies and I never even got one at the time. I've probably got one in the loft somewhere, mind. Those women will be upset, but I couldn't take something that they presumably hold dear. You have to be so careful how you say no.'

And so to the issue of the moment. What are the wise old pro's views on these docile pitches and that despised seam? 'We've hardly played down south so I can't confirm Adrian Jones's view that there is some disparity between wickets down here and in the north and Midlands, but there has certainly been a general upgrade in standards. The perfect pitch to my mind is one that allows a bit of movement on the first day, but enough pace and bounce to play shots, and aid spin by the third. The one we won on at Derby had many of those qualities except that it lacked a bit of pace. I certainly don't want to revert to the disgraceful pitches of the past few years.

'There is definitely an imbalance between bat and ball, however.

One solution might be to increase the number of strands in the seam to eleven or twelve, midway between what we have now and what we had last year. A bigger seam tends to disturb the surface and encourage spin by the end of a game. We could also do with a tighter-knit ball that doesn't look like a grapefruit and retains its hardness and therefore bounces a bit. Then again, bat dominating ball is not necessarily a bad thing. At least it's making the bowlers work harder, and I believe they will be better for it.'

David has again listed himself at No. 10, and once again his wait is not as long as he would wish. Despite an elegant 66 from Jesty and a spunky 45 from Watkinson, Lancashire are wobbling at 190 for 7 by mid-afternoon. DeFreitas wallops his way to 41 then succumbs to Such, bringing David in to join Hegg and exposing the tail. Some tail. In the next thirty overs, the ninth-wicket pair collect 113. Hegg, an experimental – and useful – first-drop last year, motors to the second century of his career with a sequence of chunky drives and whips through mid-wicket. David, meanwhile, spanks Foster for four 4s in an over with some racy strokes to set a personal season's high. In Foster's next over, Hegg sustains a resounding crack on the foot. 'Run, run,' exhorts David, keen to get stuck in again while his victim is still groggy; a couple of balls later he carts Foster over mid-wicket. After making his highest Championship score for two summers, an ebullient 57 from eighty-two balls with eleven 4s, another cheeky bid for a single sees the lag's legs fail him, leaving Hegg to carry his bat and the final score a healthy 395 for 9 declared. Essex troop off, chins inclined towards chests. David comes into the pavilion battling a grin.

Monday 23 July, Colchester

Essex v. Lancashire (cont.) (County Championship, 3 days)

The omens were far from favourable. Essex had yet to recover from their shellacking at the hands of the Lancashire tail when Nadeem walked to the crease, less than half an hour of the second day having elapsed. Stephenson had just been run out by Fairbrother from mid-wicket after committing the heinous felony of attempting a second off a no-ball. With the score still rooted on 39, Gooch was caught behind off DeFreitas's very next ball; the fifth saw Waugh emulate his captain's lead and Hussain skewed the last in front of second slip, from where it whizzed away to the third-man boundary. From 39 for 0 to 43 for 4 in seven tortuous steps. Nadeem, meanwhile, had been blinking it all in from the sanctuary of the non-striker's end.

The Biryani Brothers turned out to be the aces in this particular hole. With Nadeem driving imperiously in the arc between mid- wicket and extra-cover when the opportunity to poke his head above the parapet arose, and Hussain displaying even less inclination to be shackled, the fourth wicket raised 91 in twenty-five overs before the senior partner was caught by Hegg as he tried to welly Atherton. Allott took care of Garnham, and Essex were 158 for 8, still 87 shy of saving the follow-on, when Pringle drifted to the wicket.

Now saddled with the senior partner's role himself, Nadeem manned the bridge with Horatian fortitude, aided by the consistent spring in a pitch showing signs of dustiness. When Atherton and David tossed it up, he danced to the pitch of the ball and hoisted anything of substandard length over the top. As the landmark approached, his apparent nervelessness was unnerving. On 92 he went down on one knee to loft David over cover. If the shot that took him to three figures, an incompletely middled cut for 4 through the slips, was tainted by fortune, no matter. Pringle, smiling massively, shook his hand. Gooch delivered his congratulations from behind the sightscreen. 'Well played, don't give it away,' he exhorted. Nadeem did though, caught and bowled trying to flat-bat Atherton, though not before he had galloped on to 121, collecting twenty-one 4s in three and a half hours. His sixth-wicket stand of 110 in twenty-five overs with Pringle had wiped out the spectre of the follow-on, but no one had been worried about that for some time. For many of those present Nadeem's century was more important, Castle Park being the headquarters of Colchester and East Essex CC, the Paladin League club for whom he plays whenever he can get away from more onerous duties.

Surprisingly, Nadeem, now averaging 85.20 from five completed innings, was not limbering up to vault the moon after play had concluded. 'I wasn't sure how good I was, and, to be honest, this is the first time I've batted in a way that was pleasing to me. I've had a few games now and I suppose I have acquired certain expectations of myself. When I came in the only aim, as at Maidstone, was survival, but I guess I simply felt confident. The fact that we were in trouble helped me, especially in terms of concentration. Yet I was more nervous coming up to the first 50 because I felt that that much was expected of me. The second one was a bonus.

'Most of my runs came when I went down the wicket to the spinners, but I also laced into Allott a bit, and he didn't like that at all, so I received a lot of abuse, more than I've ever had before. It was Allott and DeFreitas mostly. When I hit one boundary off Allott he said, "I could have bet my mortgage on that one getting you"; another time it was, "Are you picking them out of a hat?" Ironically, given that he was born in Dominica, it was DeFreitas who was the racist one of the pair. I later discovered that he'd picked up some Indian swearwords from Pringle and he was trying them out on me. I don't think there was any malice intended, and, all in all, I didn't let it worry me. People see you cropping up with increasing regularity and they think that since you're not a youngster anymore, you can handle the stick. I was 60-odd at lunch and Gooch, who knew what had been going on, came up and said, "Make sure you get that 100; they'll shut up then". And when I did get there, most of the Lancashire players, even Allott and DeFreitas, came up and said well done. I wouldn't go out of my way for people like that, but I do forgive and forget quite easily. They could have apologised, but they didn't. Then again, abuse acts as a spur to me. But that's not the issue. We, Essex, never say a word to an opponent other than "well played". Why do other counties? Maybe it's the old north-south thing? At times like that it helps having Nasser around.'

Though impressed by Nadeem's skilful defiance, David denied any knowledge of the treatment allegedly meted out by Allott and DeFreitas. 'One or two players try to unsettle the younger ones, but I don't think there are ever any racial overtones, certainly not at Lancashire, because everyone gets on with everyone else on the circuit as far as I can see. People do have a go, mostly frustrated seamers. I would stop it if I felt it had gone too far, but I wouldn't stifle a bowler if he was taking out his frustrations like that. There has to be a cut-off point, and as far as I'm concerned, if anyone had been saying anything to Nadeem, then the fact that I didn't notice means that that point wasn't reached.'

Nadeem stood his ground. 'Well, he's bound to say that, isn't he? I bet I get the same next year too.'

Nadeem celebrated by taking out his new girlfriend ('She actually likes cricket; hallelujah') for a Chinese meal. He felt no need to ring chez Shahid. 'They check Ceefax for the scores all the time and they just assume I'm doing well. Tafweaz comes along to see me sometimes, so do the girls, but I don't think any of them hang on to every run I make or anything. Maybe they just expect good things of me? I still go home for my washing, and my bedroom hasn't been touched, so I don't suppose I've really moved out in the literal sense. I may buy a place next summer if things continue to go well, but for the moment I'm quite happy with the arrangement. Suchy is not blessed with overexcitement. He gets up first thing to do the washing-up or the laundry; he'll even stay in on a Saturday night to do that, although that's only because his girlfriend is in Zimbabwe. Still, there are six years between us, and at least we have more than cricket in common, since we share similar tastes in music. Buddy Holly's my passion at the moment. I listen to him in the car all the time.' Unlike his co-tenant, the priority for this brown-eyed handsome young man was to rave on.

An unfamiliar lifestyle was still playing tricks on Nadeem's memory, blurring and sometimes obliterating entire days. This one would remain three-dimensional for a good while yet. So too the next, wherein Essex, set a forbidding task of 348 in fifty-four overs following centuries from Atherton and Fairbrother, cantered in with 6 wickets and six balls left unemployed. Gooch, with a rumbustious 177 from 152 balls, cooked Lancashire's goose, Nadeem, who helped him add 55 in six overs, adding some timely seasoning. Nadeem had overheard Gooch and Fletcher negotiating with David, who had not been inclined to offer a gettable target since Akram had been grounded by that persistent groin injury of his. 'Fletch and Gooch refused to go for 6 or 7 an over, but I knew they would. They always say that to put the pressure on, to stop the other captain opting for 8.' It would be unfair to detract from the resultant hell-for-leathering, however, capping as it did a coruscating contest.

Tuesday 24 July, Uxbridge

Middlesex v. Somerset (County Championship, 3 days)

If that NatWest loss to Worcestershire represented the clinical death of Somerset's season, then today marked its spiritual nadir. Yet in Neath forty-eight hours earlier you couldn't hear yourself think for all the hoorays and back-slapping. Rose had lashed 148 in sixty-nine balls. Cook went demurely to 136 off 110 and Somerset totalled 360 for 3, not so much beating the 40-over record as leaving it simpering in the distance. Glamorgan evidently have some affinity for the patsy role, for they were on the painful end of Essex's 310 for 5 in 1983, the previous benchmark for Sunday swatting. Rose's century came off forty-six deliveries, the fizziest in the tournament's history, and the third-wicket pair pulverised another landmark by adding 223. Richards or no Richards, an understandably shell-shocked Glamorgan went through the motions and folded for 140, Somerset cutting to 4 points the gap between themselves and Kent, the fourth-placed team in the table. With four games still to play, a spot in the Refuge Cup was not unthinkable.

All that had been forgotten, however, by the time the Somerset players filed on to their Scarborough-bound coach this evening. An excoriating assault by Middlesex's erratic prodigy, Mark Ramprakash, had brought them to their knees on the last afternoon of a game that might have done better to have excluded bowlers altogether. On the first day Somerset dawdled to 273 for 2 in 100 overs on the usual Uxbridge Utopia, closing at 445 for 6 on the Monday. Mention of the game between the two at Lord's in 1899 was made in the scorecard notes: the one in which Albert Trott weaved his way through with 7- 13 as Somerset totalled 44 in their second innings to lose by an innings and 7 runs, Middlesex having scaled the giddy heights of 86 all out. Poor old Trott. Like Somerset's own Bertie Buse a few decades later, he had short-changed himself in his own benefit match; the whole shebang was over in a day. Not much chance of that now, of course. Hitherto surprisingly lenient with opposition bowlers in the Championship, Gatting made amends with a furious 170 from 182 balls, his first first-class century since returning from South Africa. For poor Trott read poor Swallow, brought to heel with six 4s, two of them audacious reverse sweeps, in one educational over. No batsman is more contemptuous of spinners than the Neasden Ritz's ballroom dancing bronze medallist of 1974.

Following Gatting's declaration 140 behind, Somerset rattled on to 228-4 and left Middlesex to make 369 in a minimum of sixty-nine overs. Haynes's fifth Championship 100 lit the fuse, but despite some bold blows from Ramprakash, the exit of Gatting for 36 appeared to have made the title leaders think again. With 90 to get off the last nine, shutters were about to be put up when Tavaré took a leaf out of Gatting's book. With Gloucestershire in a similar position in May, Gatting had put on one of his non-bowlers, Keith Brown, in the faint hope of reactivating the chase. The ploy worked a treat. Requiring 40 from eighteen balls with 2 wickets standing, Gloucestershire had a thrash, took 18 off Brown and lost the match with two balls to go. On this occasion, though, Middlesex had 5 wickets left when Tavaré brought himself on in place of Trump, telling Ramprakash that he would give him an over of runs provided he responded in kind by having a go. Ramprakash obliged, smiting 20, and suddenly it was game on again. When Trump returned, Ramprakash swung his first offering over a hamburger stall at long-off, a massive carry. Thirty-three needed off four and Adrian snaps Ramprakash's bat as if it were a twig, as opposed to £90 worth of craftsmanship. In his next over, the penultimate of the match, he breaks the replacement, and then flattens Williams's off stump. With Ramprakash charging on like some runaway rhino, these are but midges on a tough hide. Mallender to bowl the last over and 12 to get. Two off a mistimed hook, 2 more to extra-cover and another 2 to mid-wicket, then an unstoppable off-drive, one that never rises more than a couple of feet from the turf, yet crashes through Rose's grasp on the boundary: 10 so far. Ramprakash aims a joyful air punch at the fading sun, Tavaré and Mallender consult at length before the last ball. Ramprakash drills it straight for 4 and scampers off, king for a day.

The dismayed, incredulous expressions as Tavaré led his team off bore eloquent testimony to their suffering. Defeats may mean zilch in terms of points, but that doesn't mute the sting. Later, while Adrian seeks out Emburey for solace ('That was a horrible way to lose a game, Jonah'), Ramprakash, a little on the bashful side, attends to us boys from the press. 'Yes, that was my first Championship 100 of the season . . . it was obviously nice to get my cap last week . . . maybe that was the encouragement I needed.'

Rose trudges away to collect his kit, muttering to himself as much as anyone else: 'I don't feel as if we lost that.' Adrian, as ever, has been doing his sums. 'That's eight chases we've set now, compared to the three we've been offered, two of which were washed away while in the third the batsmen lost their heads against Derbyshire. And this time we helped them. Tav was a bit premature in putting himself on. I felt that if Middlesex were going to make a real challenge they would get the runs, so it was up to them to take the risks, not us. They should have given us a couple of wickets. The thing is, you've got to set unrealistic targets because you're not going to bowl the other side out on these pitches. In all honesty, the bowlers are also a bit pissed off because we felt we'd performed well considering the conditions. Now people back at Taunton are looking at our wickets and averages and saying, quite rightly, "We're paying a lot for you guys – perhaps we can get someone better". I tell them they ought to write this season off.'

That course of action was the last thing in the minds of Middlesex and their exultant supporters. Holding a handy lead in the Championship, joint top of the Refuge and halfway towards another NatWest Final, they were on course to become the first county to land three trophies in a season. 'Even with Embers and Gatt available all the time, I'm amazed at what they've done,' Adrian admits. 'I think Lord's has helped the bowlers. The slope helps the seamers and spinners, and they've got a wealth of varied bowling to take advantage. In any season, but particularly this one, that's the difference between winning and losing the Championship.'

Saturday 28 July, Old Trafford

Lancashire v. Somerset (County Championship, 3 days)

Try as he might, Adrian cannot remember the last time such a thing had happened to him. 'I've been left out. Admittedly I haven't been bowling well lately, and Birky and Tav told me they thought the same. They said my right arm was too high when I delivered, and whereas it should end up on my left-hand side when I released the ball, it was going straight down on my right-hand side. As a result I have been angling the ball in instead of leaving the bat, which is my talent. They even suggested I bowl in a more round-arm manner. It was different with last year's Reader ball; at least it seamed. I said I deserved to be dropped and accepted their decision to play the extra spinner. Then I saw the wicket was green! Just my luck. It was reported before a ball was bowled, purely for its colour.'

Adrian found a caring listener in the chairman of the Somerset cricket committee, Roy Marshall, who, as Hampshire followers will certainly concur, was arguably the last great white West Indian batsman. Though stricken by skin cancer and the loss of an eye, his enthusiasm and perception for the game remain undimmed. Even more instructive for Adrian was a net with one of his contemporaries. To its eternal credit, cricket remains a game in which giving tips to the opposition is not regarded as a treasonable offence; a reflection of its essential matiness. Alec Bedser is reputed to have taken an opponent into the nets during an Ashes series, while only last summer, Bobby Simpson, the Australian coach, had no qualms whatsoever about passing on a couple of pointers on slip fielding to Andy Moles when the tourists were playing Warwickshire. The grateful pupil later clasped two blinders but there was no question of misplaced loyalty on Simpson's part. 'Wasim Akram isn't playing, so he took me into the nets and showed me how he swings the ball. As Tim Munton and Martin Bicknell have demonstrated, learning how to bowl swing has been a boon this year, but I seem to have lost the knack. Taking wickets would help, of course, because that's the motivation, but I'm not even getting a chance at the tailenders. When I get back to Taunton I'm going into the nets while the rest of the guys have a few days off. I've never had to go and work at my bowling voluntarily before. I just hope I can find someone to throw the balls back.'

Manchester is the music capital of Europe at present, its trendy clubs throbbing to the funky pop purveyed by bands like Inspiral Carpets and Happy Mondays. For Somerset, this was a Sad Saturday. Bowled out for 237 by a half-strength Lancashire side, one deprived of the flu-ridden David as well as Atherton, DeFreitas, Allott and Akram for varying reasons, they managed to get shot of Fowler, Mendis and Lloyd by the close, all falling to Swallow. Fairbrother, though was prowling with ominous intent on 35.

In the wake of his historic 333 against India at Lord's the previous day, however, the runmaker on everyone's lips was the England captain. Gooch's response was typically self-effacing, almost self-erasing: 'It was OK'. The *Sunday Telegraph* leader writer was considerably more effusive, describing him as 'an authentically important phenomenon, the new Briton, forceful, plebeian, undeferential, a winner. He is cricket's Thatcher.' Does that make Gower cricket's Kinnock, or perhaps Botham its Che Guevara? As far as Adrian is concerned, Gooch would be his choice to open alongside Cook for the Earthlings against Mars at Elysian Fields CC.

'Jimmy says his head gets too far over, which means he falls over a bit too much towards the offside, something that contributed to the problems he had last summer when he was repeatedly lbw to Terry Alderman, but all I know is that you've got to be on top form against him all the time or else he'll murder you. Anything slightly loose he hits, and the ball seems to go for 4 every time because he's got brilliant timing. Even when he doesn't time it, he's so powerful that it still goes for 4. None of that is new, of course, but he does seem to have gained enormously in confidence from being the England captain.'

David was more interested in extolling Cook's virtues. 'It's a pity he's not English. He's the best batsman I've seen for a long time. One or two of our lads who had seen him in South Africa said he was *the* man some years ago. He's made nearly 5,000 runs in two seasons, one of which was one of the poorest we've had because of the wickets and the thick seam. And in that time he has made 100s against fourteen counties. Astonishing. I can't see any chinks, either. You just have to wait until he makes a mistake.'

At stumps, Adrian ambled over to the Lancashire dressing-room. 'They are a fine side, although I reckon the Sussex team of 1981–83 would have given them a good run. I had a chat with Mendo, the one man to have played in both those teams. He has a very high opinion of himself, but then he is a very fine player, one of the best batsmen in the country. In fact, if I had to pick an England side to go to the Windies, I'd have him opening with Goochie. He seems very bitter. He has an enormous chip on his shoulder because he hasn't played for England. He should have done. But he's an odd character. He was quoted in *Today* recently, saying that Sussex probably only had themselves to blame for having such a poor record in recent years, and he put it down to all the good players who'd left the club. He was supposed to have said on another occasion that they didn't deserve his talent. I don't remember him ever saying that, but apparently he did.

'Later on I sat down with DeFreitas, Akram and Warren Hegg and they were just moaning endlessly about the ball. It is getting absolutely ridiculous when even someone as brilliant as Akram is struggling to find consistency.' A trouble shared can sometimes be a trouble doubled.

Tuesday 31 July, Chelmsford

Essex v. Sussex (County Championship, 3 days)

Courtesy of a quirky fixture computer, lowly Sussex were the first Championship guests to tread the banks of the Can since the beginning of May. To widespread relief, the pitch was a sight more playful than the one that had doled out wickets at more than 80 runs per head when Leicestershire came to town. A blunderbuss of an innings from Ian 'Gunner' Gould, complemented by the more stolid efforts of Jamie Hall and Tony Dodemaide on an opening day foreshortened by rain, enabled Sussex, 207 for 6 at one stage, to reach 351 for 9 before Paul Parker declared. Essex, chained to the field until the second afternoon, swept to 250 for 6 at more than 4 an over, Nadeem striking 55 from his new launch-pad at the top of the order and Waugh lashing his sixth Championship 100 of the summer.

The calculator was then passed back to Parker. So accurate was Childs, however (a season's best 4–56 from 30 overs), that Sussex dwelt 72.5 overs on their eventual 200 for 8. Mindful of that 6½-an-over demolition job against Lancashire, Parker came up with an even more inventive equation than David: 303 in forty-three overs. This time Gooch was forty miles away at Lord's, doing unto the Indian attack what he had done unto Lancashire's, but Essex gave it a crack anyway. Nadeem and Stephenson sprang out of the stalls with 137 in thirty overs, Nadeem spanking thirteen 4s in sixty-nine balls before he was first to go, bowled by the young off-spinner Brad Donelan for 89. Stephenson went in the next over, but there was no going back now. Five men reached 20 as bats were flailed at anything remotely within reach. Wickets were discarded liberally, yet at 282 for 6 Essex had a hand on the spoils. Then 3 fell for a dozen runs, leaving Topley and Andrew to cling on for a draw, Essex 4 short.

One slice through the slips, one whack over mid-off, and Essex would now be a mere 38 points behind the leaders, Middlesex, with a game in hand. Nadeem's frustration was self-evident. 'If we'd won, that would probably have been my most treasured knock of the summer so far, even more than the 100. In the first innings I was going along at a run a ball until I tried to cut one that bounced a bit and I got a top edge. But I had to attack even more second time up. There was a bit of anger running through the dressing-room because we felt Parker's declaration was diabolical, but Pring told us to forget about blocking, blast everything and then have another look at tea.

'Somehow everything I did came off. Backing away to leg, all those imaginary shots you have in your head, any stupid thing, and I got away with them all. I'd taken 12 off five balls of a Donelan over when I tried to smack the last one over cover instead of running it down to third-man, so I was out for 89 when I should have had a century. But what hurt more was coming so close to victory and failing.'

Norman Gifford, the chummy, knowing Sussex coach, had some words of advice. 'He told me what a good 50 I'd made in the first innings, what a very good 50, but that the next time I got to 50, or 40, or 30, I should walk away from the crease, get away from the play for a second and tell myself to start again. He said I should reprogramme myself, leave the wide ones.' Given the older man's assemblage of 2,068 wickets as a medium-slow left-armer for England, Warwickshire and Worcestershire, the main topic of the conversation between Gifford and Nadeem, not unnaturally, was spin. 'I bowled three overs for 15 in the second innings, my first spell in the first team since May, and he had obviously kept an eye on me. He suggested that I try bowling over my left leg instead of my right, and he also said my pace was a bit too quick. You could get a book out of all the advice I've received over the past three months.'

10 August

Wednesday 1 August, Old Trafford

Lancashire v. Gloucestershire (NatWest Trophy quarter-final)

If Lancashire had been given their choice of NatWest quarter-final opponents, chances are they would have plumped unhesitatingly for Gloucestershire. As a pick-me-up from being Tavaréd yesterday, they would do nicely. Last season Gloucestershire lost half their Championship matches and took an enormous leap from tenth to ninth. Captain Athey passed the buck to Tony Wright, and although they currently occupy a respectable mid-table position in the Refuge, their closest rivals for the Britannic wooden spoon, Sussex, have an 11-point advantage and a game in hand. Asked to cure a patient afflicted with a freshman captain, precious little consistency or experience in the upper batting order and an equally erratic attack, the Eddie Barlow Remedy is taking rather longer to restore health at Bristol than it did at Derby in the mid-1970s.

No one, therefore, is exactly stunned when Lancashire bulldoze their way to 372 for 5 and bury Wright and his team by 241 runs, both records for a 60-over game between first-class counties. Ironically, it was a wayward opening stint from Courtney Walsh, the least erratic of the Gloucestershire bowlers, that unbolted the floodgates. Under-pitched bowling at his pace may be highly effective at Test level, but in this context it can be suicidal. His first four overs cost 29, and Fowler and Mendis had a push start towards their 124-run send-off. The fireworks came courtesy of Fairbrother (86) and Watkinson (90), who cartwheeled to a fourth-wicket stand of 169 at better than 8 an over. The retort was feeble. The first ten overs did produce 57, and there was a fine cameo from the 23-year-old opener, Dean Hodgson, tall, sleek and full of western promise. However, apart from David, who didn't turn his arm over, and

Martin, who did (and suffered the only caning), all the Lancashire bowlers picked up at least 1 wicket as Gloucestershire dwindled from 90 for 2 to 131 all out before the second half of their overs had even started.

The two words now on the tip of every Lancashire follower's tongue, ones never mouthed hitherto in county cricket history, are 'grand' and 'slam'. Second in the Championship, 19 points behind Middlesex; one win to the rear of Derbyshire with three Sunday slogs to go, albeit with only one at home to the leaders' three; into the last four of the NatWest as firm favourites, and, of course, the Benson & Hedges Cup safely stowed away already.

David, as any realist would, put such hubris into perspective. 'I don't believe winning all four major trophies is possible. In 1970 we went for the three that were available, winning the John Player and the Gillette and finishing third in the Championship, but even three is probably asking too much. The pressure right now is tremendous, and it's the sheer volume of cricket that will always stuff you in the end. This is the twenty-second day out of the last twenty-six that we've been in action. We'll have tomorrow off, sure, but then we'll be travelling to Headingley on Friday to start sixteen days' play in the next nineteen. Success keeps you going, but the game is faster and more intense than it ever has been. Whether it's all the young kids coming in that is responsible for the increase in pace and fitness, I don't know, but the rapport between the captains has certainly heightened the intensity of the Championship. For the last four years there has been very little change among the county captains, and so we've been able to build up a bit of an understanding. It doesn't always come off, but most have been willing to play some form of a game rather than let it die.' For those of us who cringe at the production line slapstick on Tuesday and Friday afternoons, enthusiasm for such apparent harmony is less marked.

Tuesday 7 August, Weston-super-Mare

Somerset v. Surrey (County Championship, 3 days)

As passionately as Adrian detests Bath, Weston occupies a similarly low position in his chart of favourite grounds. The pitches, of course, were to blame. Low, slow and uninviting, a stark contrast to the strip of August 1914, on which Yorkshire's Drake took all 10 Somerset wickets inside nine overs.

Adrian's most recent memory of the seaside resort was scarcely better. 'The man from the *Telegraph* chose to ignore a great day's cricket against Middlesex last year. Instead he picked on one lbw shout I had turned down. I was a bit miffed, sure, but he thought I threw the ball down in a fit of pique. Later on he went to the umpires' room and asked them if they were going to report it. No one could believe it when the whole thing was blown up in the paper the next day. It was crap reporting.'

Still, apart from a Sunday loss to Surrey, burying as it did Somerset's chances of qualifying for the Refuge Cup, the 1990 Weston Week had been going swimmingly. Inserted by Surrey, Somerset raced to 441 for 8, then in rumbled Adrian to make short work of the visiting openers, Grahame Clinton and Mark Feltham. Surrey recovered to declare at 302 for 5, Cook moved to his seventh first-class century on castors and Tavaré set 369 in seventy-one overs. Again Adrian wiped out Clinton and Feltham early on, but now Monte Lynch was in residence, swatting Swallow for 6s with contemptuous ease and whittling the target down to conceivable proportions. Around now, near-calamity befell Adrian. 'I was fielding at deep mid-off, and Lynch had slogged the previous ball over mid-off and into a portable loo for 6, but still Swallow kept me ten yards in from the boundary to stop the 2. The next ball was a skimmer going over my left shoulder. I ran at an angle of 30 degrees, knowing Monte had hit it hard. The next thing I knew my head had just missed a wall and I'd blacked out.'

The collision with the boundary boards reverberated around the ground. Catapulted over them and brought to earth with a fearful bump, Adrian lay motionless for a short time until help came. When the ambulance arrived he was carried away on a stretcher, legs tied together. 'People kept coming over and asking what I'd done. Later I heard that one boy went up and told Liz it was my neck. On the news bulletins it was my thigh one minute, my ankle the next. But it was my right leg, and there was a dirty great gash in it. Bloody painful.' Adrian returned to the ground in time to see Rose and Lefebvre ('he looks like a puppet on a string in his delivery stride, doesn't he?') choke Surrey's bid for victory. Playing against Nottinghamshire was obviously out of the question, but he still insisted on Liz driving him to Weston the following day. One lady came over and informed him that he had ruined her breakfast, so saddened had she been at reading about the accident. Another supporter presented him with a large hunk of Dorset cheddar. Smellier than flowers and twice as tasty.

Wednesday 8 August, Southend

Essex v. Glamorgan (County Championship, 3 days)

Hallelujah! We've only just completed the fourth day of the 1990 Southend festival and the pitch still appears to be more pussycat than sabre-toothed tiger, Glamorgan having been turbo-jetted to 356 for 8 declared by Viv Richards's 111. However, Nadeem, sadly, almost tragi-comically, had precious little time to sample it. 'I'm so depressed. I went in for the last five overs, and I was seeing the ball like a football. I'd been left out of the game against Nottinghamshire because Gooch was back and the wicket was expected to take spin on the last day, so Suchy and Childs both played. But I still felt in form. I'd made a single when I went back to a ball from Steve Bastien, and although I'd been standing outside the crease as his arm came over, just as Fletch had suggested, somehow I hit my own wicket, again!

'That's three times now in my last five innings. At Grace Road I played Agnew to mid-on, called for a single, Stevo sent me back and then someone pointed out that a bail had fallen. I'd trodden on the stumps. I accepted it that time, thinking this was the sort of thing that was bound to happen to me once in my career. Then on Monday, playing for the 2nd XI in a friendly against Wivenhoe, I aimed a shot off the back foot to leg and dislodged a bail with my heel. I told myself it was only a freak so it didn't matter, but what about now? Generally I go back and across smoothly, but now I've gained in confidence, if the delivery is short, I jump back and punch the ball through the covers, so it could be my momentum. It will feel weird at first, but I've got to follow Fletch's advice and stand outside the crease. I don't want this to happen to me ever again.'

Essex, however, captained for the first time by Foster due to Pringle's absence with a worrying back complaint, endured a dreadful *déjà vu* on the final day. After Richards's second century had set up a hunt for 333 in fifty-five overs, Nadeem made 46 of a 97-run opening stand with Stephenson, Prichard bounded along to 94 off seventy-seven balls and at one juncture Essex were 200 for 2, before Richards, inexcusably heckled by a tiny, ugly minority, completed his game of distinction by dobbing out Prichard and then Hussain. Quickly 252 for 3 shrank to 317 for 8 and the last over was negotiated by Andrew and Childs with survival uppermost in mind. This time two clumps over mid-on would have worked the oracle.

Earlier on that final day, Nadeem discovered why Boot Hill is so called. 'Richards received a half-volley on his leg stump and he crashed it. I saw the ball leave the bat and I tried to put my hand in the way, but it only crushed my hand and struck the peak of my helmet, in the gap between the grille and the peak actually. The ball singed my eyebrow. It would have been a 6 otherwise. Now you know why I prefer to run around in the outfield.'

Tuesday 14 August, Northampton

Northamptonshire v. Lancashire (County Championship, 3 days)

If there is a more dispiriting first-class venue than the one here in Wantage Road, it has certainly made a point of not making my acquaintance. When the ground is swathed in murky clouds, and the adjoining, all too visible football stand is a-bustle with Northampton Town FC folk preparing for the new season, you wonder how the audacious instincts of Fred Bakewell and Ollie Milburn ever flourished. That both these joyous souls had their careers abbreviated by car crashes underlines the length Him Upstairs had to go to in order to subdue their spirit. Though far from breaking, Lancashire's certainly seems to be bending under the strain. Today's close squeak against mercurial Northamptonshire means that, in the Championship at least, they have still to raise a smile this month.

Since that redoubtable victory dash against Nottinghamshire at Southport on 27 July, a 24-pointer that elevated them to Middlesex's shoulder, 23 points back with eight games to go including five against rivals in the bottom half of the table, Lancashire have made exactly that number in four fixtures. In that time they have been denied an extra 32 points by Tavaré's staunch resistance and by a similarly stern vigil by Ashley Metcalfe after Yorkshire had followed on in the Roses match. On both occasions a top-notch spinner may have proved a double diamond and worked wonders. By Kidderminster disappointment had surrendered to irresolution, Lancashire following on for the first time since the opening game of the 1988 season, finally losing to the same vanquishers by 10 wickets. With Fitton at a loss and Atherton doing Queen and country proud at Old Trafford, David, who last bowled forty-two overs in an innings before Maggie Thatcher had acceded to Downing Street, was now the premier Lancashire tweaker. He sent down thirty overs here on Saturday, dismissing Felton, Larkins and Capel as fellow NatWest semi-finalists Northants rode to 421 for 4 against a slimline attack festooned with niggles. 'I enjoyed that.' He even reeled off six on Sunday as Lancashire moved alongside Derbyshire at the Refuge summit with one game left, and the Peakites (who have gained one more victory) set to make up their match in hand against third-placed Middlesex next weekend.

But for yesterday's bravura century from DeFreitas, Lancashire would have been in a right pickle, and a late collapse on what David described somewhat theatrically as an 'exploding' pitch, almost brought defeat. Embraced by anxiety following a passing shower on a wearing, relaid pitch, Mendis and Lloyd bade adieu with haste, and ambitions of meeting a target of 253 in just under three hours were shelved at tea. David Capel, England's bulwark in Trinidad less than six months ago but ignored since the homecoming parade, later dismissed young Nick Speak for a duck, giving David Hopps a valid excuse to end his *Guardian* report thus: 'One suspects that, had he [Capel] been a Lancashire player in semi-final week, he would in common with many others have been on the injured list.'

Not unexpectedly, our David bridles at such innuendo. Yet, in allowing his aching bowlers some recuperating space before Friday's NatWest face-off against Middlesex, for which all have been selected, had he not also been indicating that that first outright Championship since 1934 was no longer a serious proposition? 'No. They were all bona fide injuries. Akram was a bit stiff and had a sore groin; Daffy has a flaked bone in his foot; Allott has been out a lot lately, mostly with calf problems; Watkinson can't throw because of his shoulder, and Austin had a groin strain. There has been no conscious concession or anything like that, but although we are still only 23 points behind Middlesex, we cannot seem to win in the Championship. Tavaré's knock at Old Trafford was the stonewall of the season, a great knock, but we still should have beaten Somerset and Yorkshire. The good fortune is with us in one-day games, not three-day ones.'

Thursday 16 August, Edgbaston

TCCB Under-25 XI v. India

With Middlesex now within striking range following a resounding innings win over Yorkshire at Middlesbrough (a fair swap for the Sunday defeat that terminated their Refuge Cup aspirations), Essex take a breather while the NatWest semi-finals are in progress. Not so Nadeem. Along with Nasser and Stephenson, the nominated captain, he had been selected to represent the TCCB Under-25s against the Indians. The English selection, essentially a pot-pourri of the best young players in the country, is indeed one to whet the appetite. Aside from the Essex threesome there are two vibrant strokeplayers in Graham Thorpe and Paul Johnson; Richard Blakey to keep wicket and inject a dose of earthiness into a flighty order; the moody Keith Medlycott and the mean Richard Illingworth to purvey contrasting left-arm spin; and Tim Munton, Stuart Lampitt and Martin Bicknell to shoulder the pace burden. It is not that difficult to envisage most of these young men disputing the Ashes four summers hence.

Regrettably, a blustery crosswind and a pitch damned by the watching Fletcher as the slowest he had ever seen renders the contest almost completely devoid of meaning. After Bicknell had checked the tourists with a pinpoint spell, Ravi Shastri declares at 293 for 6 before the start of day two, whereupon Nadeem makes 39 in thirty-seven overs, adding 118 with Stephenson for the first wicket. It was a struggle, but as Micky Stewart peered out from his eyrie in the pavilion he would surely have derived a dash of pleasure from Nadeem's rigorous attitude.

If your skills are being assessed by a jury of employers, the most dastardly crime is to let yourself down, to fail to make a full and proper representation of those abilities that put you on trial in the first instance. Nadeem pleads innocent to the charge, even taking into account the duck he later sustained in the second innings, lbw to Manoj Prabhakar's in-swing, playing back instead of forward, the more obvious route on such a plodding surface.

'I didn't really think of it as a trial as such because Micky must know what I can do, or else he wouldn't have picked me in the first place, and I know he's seen me bat quite a few times this year. Even so, I was honoured to be chosen and a bit nervous before I went in to bat. It obviously helped partnering Stevo, not to mention having Nasser back in the pavilion, and the fact that I'm pretty matey with the Surrey lads meant that there were four players rooting for me. After the first half-hour or so I felt reasonably at ease, but the wicket was awful, very slow, very low. Most of my shots were hit with the bottom part of the bat, and the few I middled went straight to the fielders. Stevo had most of the early strike, but I didn't worry too much about that.

'Then, again after I'd done all the hard work, I played a really rash shot, charging Shastri and getting stumped. Mind you, Shastri's a very clever bowler, cramping you by pushing it through, although he also made the odd one stop. Today I was going to leave the ball from Prabhakar that got me, changed my mind but failed to get fully forward. But I don't think that was of any significance. I felt for Johnson, though. He got 3 and 1, so I could have had a worse time. That duck put the dampers on it a bit, but I still enjoyed the game. Micky came into the dressing-room a little while ago, and, judging by the way he and Fletch were talking to me, they must be thinking about me possibly going on the A tour to Pakistan. After all, this side was meant to be the nucleus for that tour, and five of the players had been to Zimbabwe last winter.'

Nadeem seemed a trifle disappointed to have encountered a fragmented dressing-room, having enjoyed nothing but relaxed camaraderie up to this point in his fledgling professional career. 'So many players had told me about the north-south split, but this was my first experience of it first-hand. There was no animosity, far from it, but the two Worcestershire lads stuck together, Johnson and Blakey stuck together, and the Essex and Surrey boys stayed in a group, although Steve Watkin joined in with us. Medders and Nasser have been on tour together, as have Stevo, Bicknell and Thorpe, but we didn't try to make it cliquey. We all talked to each other during the day, but in the evening we drifted back into our little groups.'

There was one other disquieting element to the game. 'When the captain tells you at the start to keep your shin-pads on all day, you know you're not in his bowling plans. At first I alternated at short-leg with Johnson, but after a while I stopped there for the rest of the match.' If Nadeem was to win a free trip to see his aunts and uncles in Karachi, it seemed self-evident he would not do so in his former guise as an all-rounder. But at least he was £300 richer for his labours.

Wednesday – Friday 15–17 August, Old Trafford

Lancashire v. Middlesex (NatWest Trophy semi-final)

Had it been condensed into eight and a half hours rather than fifty-six, this NatWest semi-final clash of the county giants between Lancashire and Middlesex, a vibrant contest doused in runs, rain and only narrowly avoiding a comic death, might have entered a powerful corner of the memory.

One-day cricket is about runs, partly because, from the spectators' standpoint, runs prolong games, and prolonged games mean more hours to the pound. It is also about runs because its creators invested the dot ball with an immensely greater value than its traditional worth. And to the new cricketing disciples – those converted by the game's Wham-Bam-Thank-You-Ma'am elements and, therefore, accustomed to the concept of men in lurid jammies scuttling around under floodlights and video screens – there is nothing quite as boring as the dot ball. There were few of them in this mini-series, however, far too few to spare the bowlers from some grisly analyses. Six of them, including three with a Test record, conceded runs at a rate of 5 or more an over. In all, the Middlesex scorer, Harry Sharp, put a line through 595 numbers over the three days, noted balls, minutes, 4s and 6s for two notable centuries, put half-a-dozen entries in the 'bowled' column and noted a run-out. His final act was to inscribe the verdict for posterity: Lancashire won by 5 wickets.

The build-up to the game included an example of investigative journalism, Wapping-style: for twenty-eight minutes a tabloid reporter interviewed David on the pretext of a preview, then spent the last two of the allotted thirty trying to lure his subject into indiscretion. ' "By the way, what do you think of Gatting and South Africa?" he asked me. I don't think it's on to criticise your fellow professionals in any walk of life. And I could see it in the papers: "Hughes Slags-Off Gatting". I don't want anyone to run a "Ten Things You Never Knew About David Hughes." But they didn't use the piece on the day of the game. Probably decided it was too tame. I try not to refuse interviews, but, equally, I try not to make those that I do controversial.'

With Old Trafford creaking at the seams under the weight of a near-18,000 crowd, David won the toss and, not unexpectedly, chose to chase. The start, however, was delayed by rain until 2 p.m., and even then prematurely, in the view of the opposing captains, who were patently dismayed by the damp outfield. The pitch, jade-coloured in the middle and puce at either end, was doubtless a factor in Gatting's preference for Simon Hughes as a fourth seamer instead of going for the second spinner, Phil Tufnell, whose clever slow left-arm had been Middlesex's trump card all summer, particularly in a one-sided quarter-final with Glamorgan. But the consequences of that decision would not become apparent until Hughes went for 68 two days later, and the early omens for Middlesex were good.

The insatiable Desmond Haynes, fresh from his 255 not out against Sussex and, at 34, touching the zenith of his powers, was soon clipping through mid-wicket with contempt and punching off-drives with panache. Lancashire made advances elsewhere. Allott chugged in with intent to plug one end for the first hour, his first seven overs yielding 9 runs and the wicket of Mike Roseberry, caught bang to rights in front of his stumps by an in-ducker. Then Akram gave Gatting a hair-raising entrée, singeing his beard before having three plausible shouts for lbw turned down.

Equally unsettling had been the chorus of boos served up to Gatting when he marched down the pavilion steps. 'I own up,' an offender would later confess in a letter to the *Guardian*. 'I booed; a brief, political action on my part, I admit it.' David felt the treatment meted out to his opposite number was in bad taste. 'I don't know whether it was the crowd's frustrations, but when I went out to inspect the wicket at 2 p.m. there were a number of rude, possibly alcohol-induced words flying around in the pavilion. As to the South African issue, it's a question of your point of view. In comparison to the golfers, who are not restricted in the way we are, cricketers are paid so poorly that the money they are offered to go over there can be hard to resist. £90,000 is not a drop in the ocean.'

By the time the rains returned in mid-afternoon, Gatting had recovered his poise and, at 139 for 1, the balance was edging towards Middlesex. Play resumed at 6.35, time enough for a dozen overs. The visitors suffered an immediate and potentially mortal blow when a ball from Watkinson slid off the inside edge and into Gatting's leg stump. Haynes, though, pressed even harder on the throttle and pulled into the pits undefeated on 95, Middlesex on 199 for 2 with eleven laps left on the morrow for the final charge.

Only there wasn't a morrow at Old Trafford, unless you happened to have been born with a bill and a quack. Throughout the hiatus between pitch inspections, David busied himself as best he could, catching up with the mail, working out in the multigym, practising in the indoor cricket centre, watching satellite TV. 'It was an incredible bore. Disruptions like that make it difficult to re-motivate yourself, not to mention a team. The crowd were telling us to get back on, but what could we do? Conditions must be fair for both sides, and there should be no danger of injury whatsoever. And when deciding to start or resume a game under such circumstances, especially when every delivery is significant, you have to allow thirty-five to forty minutes for the groundstaff to make the requisite preparations.'

Both county chairmen approached Lord's about the feasibility of staging a replay there next Wednesday, but neither found satisfaction. With football's World Cup fever still infesting the national health, today's morning tabloids were full of gleeful 'penalty shoot-out' warnings. Should the rain persist and no further play prove possible, the two sides would repair to an indoor net and nominate five bowlers each to bowl two balls apiece at an unattended set of stumps. The quintet gaining the most hits would earn their team a place in the final against Northamptonshire, winners in the Southampton sunset over Hampshire by 1 run in the other, palpitating, semi-final.

Mercifully, the need for such a preposterous tie-break was averted, though only narrowly. At 1.46 this afternoon Haynes and Mark Ramprakash stepped gingerly on to the greasy outfield. Half an hour later and the forty-nine overs played so far would have been annulled and voided. Inaccurate bowling from the A-Team, Allott, Akram and Austin, was properly crashed here, there and everywhere, Haynes (149 not out) and Ramprakash (45) overseeing a stampede to 296 for 4.

On a pitch containing a bit of devil, against an attack of Middlesex's calibre, 5 runs an over appeared daunting. At 23, Fowler chopped Cowans into his stumps. Five runs later Mendis, on 15, drove to mid-off. Hughes spilt the chance, however, and the tenor of the game altered almost instantaneously. Mendis, relieved at his reprieve, took a new mental guard and added 60 in fifteen overs for the second wicket before Hughes reduced his debt by yorking Atherton.

As ever, the spark came from Fairbrother. He scrunched 48 off fifty-two balls against some wantonly wide bowling that made Lancashire's earlier efforts seem die-straight by comparison and, with Mendis, enlarged the score by 102 in seventeen overs despite Gatting's attempts to retard the over-rate. It was no use. As the skies darkened, it was the fielders who became disconcerted; on two occasions one of them set off for a ball whizzing in the opposite direction. Fairbrother nicked Hughes to Downton, but on 90, Mendis was spared again, advancing to Emburey, missing, and turning to see the wicket-keeper do precisely the same. Watkinson promptly sailed into a barely fluttering Middlesex attack, smiting 43 from forty balls, including two 6s in one Emburey over and another to the longest boundary off the hapless Williams (who finished with 0–72 from ten). Fraser, belatedly, collared him and Akram, but Mendis remained embedded until the death, striking Fraser for the winning runs to emerge with 121 not out, his first one-day century for Lancashire, the end coming with 5 wickets and twenty-five balls in hand. By then, more than 5,000 Mancunians had scampered in from work to witness the gayest of last rites. A rout, pure and simple.

David sighed heavily. 'I'm just glad to get it over with. The sad thing was having nearly 20,000 in on the first day when the conditions under foot were not good. The umpires had to get the thing started, but the outfield simply wasn't fit enough. Akram couldn't do anything with the wet ball. To make matters worse, the bowlers were still all unfit to one degree or another. But because none of them would have to bowl all day as he might expect to in a three-day game, and since, therefore, the degree of fitness demanded of bowlers in one-day cricket is different, they were able to play.

'What won us the game, though, was coming back at 6.35 on that first evening and bowling fourteen overs for 50-ish, and getting Gatting out, which allowed me to use my fourth and fifth bowlers. By today the wicket was absolutely flat; we'd made 372 on the same track against Gloucestershire in the quarter-final. I thought we would chase 270 to 280, and Middlesex managed a few more, but I was never really worried about the game being scrapped. I arranged with the Manchester Weather Centre to get a reading from their radar, so I knew we would get our full sixty overs. Mendis held us together and allowed Fairbrother and Watkinson enough scope to play their shots. In my opinion that was the best one-day innings Mendis has ever played for us. In the past he has worked himself into good positions only to smack one in the air. This time I told him to bat through, just as I do with Atherton on a Sunday. Once you are two- thirds of the way through an innings and an early order batsmen is still there, then he has to bat through.'

Those two little words are still floating in the air. Back to the Championship tomorrow against Yorkshire, a chance to claw back some leeway and avenge the frustrations of Headingley. David remained unmoved. 'I still don't think a grand slam is possible.'

Sunday 19 August, Old Trafford

Lancashire v. Yorkshire (County Championship, 4 days)

Flushed with success after yesterday's achievement in becoming the first British television company to instal a camera in a middle stump, Granada TV brought their toy along again today. It rained. All day. Deciding whether no play in the 229th Roses match is preferable to a woodworm's eye view of a pair of unshapely legs is no easy matter.

Tuesday 21 August, Chelmsford

Essex v. Surrey (County Championship, 3 days)

The juggernaut rumbles irresistibly on. Foster's second nap hand of the match brings him figures of 11–76 and Essex victory by 283 runs over a compliant, injury-riddled Surrey. Six wins out of the last nine now, and Middlesex only two points away. And still there is the cushion of that game in hand. On a wicket generally agreed to be sporting (i.e. one that gives bowlers an expectant swagger and batsmen apoplexy), Essex make 236, Foster and Andrew then bundling out Surrey for 114. Nadeem entered at No. 7 to clout 55 and Surrey were left the virtually unattainable task of scoring 404 to win. Again it was Foster and Andrew, abetted by the rich promise of Mark Ilott's left-arm pace, who wrecked the visitors, thus emphasising how much Essex's rejuvenation owed to their mid-season metamorphosis.

Nadeem was doubly satisfied. 'I played really, really well for that 55, out of my skin. I had to get my head down a bit at first because we'd lost our first five relatively cheaply, but it was hard to imagine Surrey getting more than 250 to 300 after the way they batted in the first innings, so I was able to go for my shots. And Micky Stewart saw it all. I think I'm becoming more concerned with that A tour than I am with the Championship. Isn't that terrible? But I must be their man, mustn't I?' That last sentence is loaded with rather more doubt than dogma.

Tuesday 21 August, Old Trafford

Lancashire v. Yorkshire (County Championship, 4 days)

To my knowledge, the New York Yankees baseball alumnus Yogi Berra is the only sporting figure to have had a cartoon bear named after him (although I understand that Hanna-Barbara are devising a Gazza Grizzly). Among Berra's many pithy epithets was the immortal 'It ain't over 'til it's over'. Such undying faith in the possible would have served Lancashire well here today as Yorkshire withstood another flurry of jabs and uppercuts to deny their bitterest rivals for the second time in a fortnight and so drag the Championship even further out of their reach.

Despite five encouraging wickets for Watkinson, reverting to off-breaks and off-cutters on a helpful wicket, Phil Carrick and, latterly, Kevin Sharp – who braved a broken thumb for the final fourteen overs – parried impending defeat, Yorkshire finishing on 266 for 9, still 51 shy of a target of 317 in ninety-five overs but long since satisfied with a draw. Had Lancashire truncated just three (Tavaré, Metcalfe and now Sharp) of the fifty-eight innings played against them in their last three home dates in the Championship, they would now be 29 points clear of the field as they entered the final straight. 'If we had won today I would be really confident,' David asserted. 'But we had ninety-five overs at them on the same wicket that had seen us score that 372 against Gloucestershire and then yielded nearly 600 runs in the NatWest semi-final. There was a bit of turn but the ball didn't bounce much. Yet there is no escaping the fact that it has been our inability to bowl sides out that has cost us.'

Admittedly, Middlesex's long unbeaten record spontaneously combusted yesterday morning on a dog-eared Derby track that incurred the full wrath of the TCCB and its 25-point deterrent. The summer, moreover, does still have a month to run. But from the pained, almost plaintive manner with which David reflected on these near-misses, the Championship, though not the season by any means, may as well be over now.

Tuesday 21 August, Taunton

Somerset v. Hampshire (County Championship, 4 days)

An opportune time for Adrian to return after his leg-gashing accident. At the eighteenth time of asking Somerset have gained their second Championship win of the season after a palpitating chase on the fourth afternoon. Yes, a chase. Although Hampshire had struggled briefly in verdant conditions on the Saturday, Adrian persuading Gower to waft a catch to Burns and later trapping Mark Nicholas for a duck, the pitch had quickly settled into quintessential Taunton timorousness. The loss of all bar a handful of overs on the Sunday converted the game into the usual three-day theatrics.

With his team 29 points and three places behind the leaders, Middlesex, Nicholas had no option but to keep his calculations within the bounds of probability, so Somerset, 100 behind on first innings, were granted a target at last: 302 in sixty-one overs. Cook, as ever, was in the vanguard, striking 77 off 103 balls to set the prescribed tempo, but his exit, leg-before to a Marshall creeper, did little to hearten Hampshire. Twice Hayhurst battered Raj Maru's flighty left-arm spin for straight 6s, and even when he went, stumped off the same apparent meal ticket, Harden and Tavaré put on 91 for the fourth wicket; 139 wanted over the final twenty overs, then 76 from the last ten. Harden pulled Connor to Gower at mid-wicket at 246. At 272 Tavaré's exemplary 64 was foreshortened when he cheekily challenged Paul Terry, the best all-round fieldsman in the land by some distance, only to be shaded by a marvellous throw from short fine-leg. Rose, though, was at hand, shoulders twitching in the glow of derring-do. Nicholas shuffled his attack as if it was a Tory cabinet, even calling on Jon Ayling and his broken toe. Strangely, he saw fit to ignore Marshall, and even though Connor's accuracy in the penultimate over kept the crowd on tenterhooks, Burns sailed into a Maru full-toss to bring the ship into harbour with four balls to spare.

Adrian was more relieved than overjoyed. 'We're all really chuffed. We had to get away from the bottom and now we're going to Hove. If we can win there we can achieve a respectable position. It was a great pitch to bat on, but there was some temperamental batting and we may have been a bit fortunate that Marshall didn't bowl at the end. He and Nicholas had apparently had a bit of an argument.

'I'm delighted for Tav, though. As a Test player he was messed about a bit by the selectors, but when he played he did a great job, doing exactly what he was told, holding up an end. But the press got on his back and gave him some flak for being too slow, and that hurt. He should have had seventy caps and he's ended up with less than half that, but I don't think he's particularly bothered. People at Somerset have seen that he's got all the shots and he's done marvellously in his two years here. Taking over from Vic [Marks] as captain was tough, but he's done well. He's very quiet, not the up and at 'em type at all. He always demands that you do the right thing all the time without him having to tell you, expecting you to be self-motivated. Unfortunately, not everybody is self-motivated and some people need a little bit of inspiration now and again.'

Sunday 26 August, Old Trafford

Lancashire v. Warwickshire (Refuge Assurance League)

Fowler's tenth Refuge 50 of the season may have been enough to ensure a stressless victory over Warwickshire, but it was insufficient to gain Lancashire a record fourth 40-over crown. Derbyshire, washed out against Middlesex last Sunday, needed to win against Essex to pip them and duly did so, so landing their third honour in nearly 120 years. Since the conclusive hit at Derby did not come until four balls from the end, the outcome, as usual in this unfailingly climactic, plastic competition, was in doubt to the last.

David, however, was mystified, and not a little upset, by the reaction of the crowd here. 'They were filing away as soon as they knew the final score from Derby. I can't understand it. Sometimes you think you know your public, but at others . . .' With another Lord's rendezvous just six days away, and Lancashire's second-place finish leaving them with a Refuge Cup semi-final against Middlesex here a week on Wednesday to look forward to, perhaps the faithful flock are becoming blasé?

Lost, momentarily, for words, David scanned the League season. 'It's been such an exciting, fluctuating competition. We could point to two no-results, to our rivals' one, but the worst aspect was our home record. We were unbeaten away, but sustained three losses here, to Middlesex and Derbyshire, which you have to accept, and, more gallingly, to Gloucestershire who made 160 off the last twenty overs.

'This is definitely the hardest one-day competition to win. You need a lot of luck, and, because of the brevity of the game and its physical demands, the margin for error is smaller than in the other formats. But I think we should be marketing it along Australian lines. The Refuge League and Cup would be an ideal vehicle for introducing coloured clothing under a manufacturer's logo. We could merchandise shirts in county colours for people to wear casually. I like day/night games too. About ten years ago we won the first Lambert & Butler Cup playing under lights at Old Trafford and Stamford Bridge, but the sponsors priced themselves out of the market and there was never a second one. I want to be traditional, but the game as a whole here needs to revamp its marketing. There is no point in old players on the committee harping on about how happy they were to be earning £300 a year. That was then and this is now.'

Monday 27 August, Hove

Sussex v. Somerset (County Championship, 4 days)

That inspiration Adrian alluded to after Somerset's win over Hampshire was hardly necessary against basement-dwelling Sussex. Even though they were only 22 points adrift of Somerset and had played a game less, the Brighton beaux were considered something of a pushover, a charge never once levelled against Cook and company. Though rich in promise, four of their top six in this game were under 25; Parker and Smith, their two Test batsmen, were injured, and valiantly though Pigott and Dodemaide strove there was no bowling spearhead to match the Hove heritage of Gilligan, Tate, Thomson and Snow.

From the moment that Adrian awoke at 6 a.m. to see the sea fret from his room at the Dudley Hotel, it was clear that Somerset, given luck with the toss, would dictate terms. The resultant humidity forced the covers to sweat and so Tavaré was greeted by an old-fashioned Hove greentop, a far cry from the blissful pitches that had been force-feeding batsmen there over the past few months. On Adrian's advice, Tavaré went against his natural inclinations and elected to bowl, whereupon his consultant drew first blood by shooting down Jamie Hall, a patient opener of 21 whose assiduousness had been grating on bowlers' nerves lately. Adrian also induced a catch from young Martin Speight, assured and gorgeously reckless. Dodemaide, the cussed Victorian, dragged the score from 78 for 6 to 153 all out, but Somerset were batting before tea. At either end of this decaying ground, with its faded bluey-grey deck chairs, stale odour and pressing need for restoration, stand two outsize eggs. If either is ever hit on the full, the batsman responsible is entitled to a small consideration; for all the zest shown by Sussex during the opening two sessions, they could have been stationed at mid-on and mid-off and still escaped unscathed.

Not so Gareth Townsend. Earlier in the day the opener from Tiverton had received a fax wishing him good luck from Finchley, where his 2nd XI colleagues were playing Middlesex. With the renewal of his contract in the balance, he had been drafted in for his debut after Roebuck had gallantly volunteered to stand down for the rest of the season in order to give some of the fringe players an opportunity. Now, though, reality beckoned, as did Peter Moores's gauntlets, snaffling Townsend off Dodemaide for a blob. As he walked back to the pavilion, wrenching himself from his field of dreams, his doleful face appeared on the brink of tears.

Hayhurst was no happier when speared by the same combination. 'I don't know what happened,' he mumbled when Birkenshaw walked by. The manager did: 'It was a crap shot.' By the end of the third day Townsend's face had regained some of its cherubic gleam and Hayhurst was performing Asian backflips with Lefebvre. Tavaré expanded his overnight 45 into a career-best 219, sharing in a ninth-wicket liaison of 183 with Mallender to equal Greetham and Stephenson's county record set against Leicestershire at Weston in 1963. Even Adrian waded in, outscoring Mallender during their unbroken last wicket stand of 41 to lift Somerset to 525 for 9. Confronted with arrears of 372, only Lenham and Dodemaide resisted at any length as Sussex ebbed towards defeat, Adrian picking up Speight once again and Townsend redeeming himself by catching Hall. By Saturday's close Sussex were still 41 behind, and although Dodemaide proceeded to a well-deserved 112 this morning, Adrian pocketed a return catch, Tavaré secured Rodney Bunting's edge off Hayhurst and Somerset were left needing 11, a task Burns and Anderson expended nine deliveries accomplishing. Townsend nevertheless failed to break his first-class duck.

Adrian, unsurprisingly, had mixed feelings when it was all over. When he was not on the field, his hand was being endlessly pumped by members who recalled with great fondness the days when he was on their side. It was here, after all, that Emily Jones had brought her younger son for his first taste of cricket. 'I was 11 or 12, and Mum took me along to see Glynne play for Sussex Under-16s against Middlesex Under-16s, who were captained by a fat bulldog called Gatting. All I can remember is being fascinated by the perimeter boards. I always enjoy coming back here, but it saddens me to see Sussex in such disarray. Like us they've effectively been penalised for preparing good wickets so, again like us, their Championship position is a false barometer of their season. Still, their 2nd XI look like winning the Rapidline title, and with youngsters such as Lenham, Hall, Speight and Salisbury coming through, a quick bowler might be all it takes to get the club back on its feet.'

After popping to see Liz's parents in Peacehaven and sharing a few jars with some old buddies, Adrian was going to put his feet up for the next nine days.

Wednesday 29 August, Northampton

Northamptonshire v. Essex (County Championship, 3 days)

Essex had earned themselves a couple of extra days off by steamrollering Derbyshire inside two days of the designated four at Derby (Nadeem 55 and a catch, Ilott, Foster and Andrew a composite 19-fer). Now they are about to commence fire against

Northamptonshire with Gooch back on his throne and Middlesex, without a game, about to be unseated from theirs. Happy though he plainly is at the possibility of a Championship medal, Nadeem is still distracted.

'By next Wednesday I should know whether I'm on the A tour. I know the selectors' meeting isn't until the Tuesday, but with Gooch being England captain and Fletch the A squad team manager I'm sure I'll find out early. It happened that way last year. Whether I'm selected depends on what the party is supposed to represent. Is it going to be an England second-string or a side for the future? Older batsmen like Rob Bailey might get in, which could work against me, but there might be only one middle-aged batsman, so to speak, which could let me in. Of course, when I'm on the field I shut it from my mind. I've noticed a bit of tension creeping in lately, as we get nearer the top of the table. People seem to be taking it all much too seriously, but perhaps the reason I'm a bit more laid-back about that is that I've got something else to think about. On the other hand, I don't think I could ever get as serious as Stevo, say. You have to enjoy yourself.

'To be honest, though, I don't think this tour business would be obsessing me if it weren't for all the people who keep telling me I'm going to be picked. Foster keeps saying, when you go on tour you behave like this, you do this, you do that. When we were at Derby, Waugh and I had a good stand together in light that was so poor that they ended up with three fielders at third-man. The night before he had told me I would be on the tour; the next night he said that my 55 would have ensured it. Then, at the end of the game, Chris Adams shouted over "Good luck". I went over and asked him whether he was referring to the A tour, and he said, "Don't worry, of course you'll go". So you can't help but think about it, and start believing you're going.'

And so to the match, from which Nadeem is ultimately excluded so as to accommodate the second spinner. The irony mounts with every omission. All goes well for Essex at first. The fifth ball finds Winston Davis cussing as Gooch survives a strident leg-before appeal from the wiry, whippy St Vincentian. Davis stands, stares and eventually returns to his mark after a full half-minute. At the end of a six-minute over umpire Kevin Lyons slings Davis's sweater back to him and engages in a summit meeting with his colleague David Constant. Gooch muscles on to 174. Davis is later fined and relieved of his duties by his embarrassed bosses, who have already had to put up with Curtly Ambrose's beamers against Dermot Reeve and David Capel's oathing at David Gower during the NatWest semi-final.

Foster rids Essex of Nigel Felton by the end of the first day, then traps Alan Fordham early on the second morning, but a spate of butter-fingered gropes spares Larkins five times and the descent begins. Just as he did on the same ground a year ago, Larkins clinches an England tour berth against the captain's county: 207, which, together with centuries from Lamb and Bailey, scurries the home side to their grandest-ever total, 592 for 6 declared, 202 in front. Gooch, bestriding the season like some Vulcan of the forge, hammering out runs to order, swells his match tally to exactly 300, passing 2,500 as he does so, and piling on his second 200-plus overture of the match with Stephenson, the pair thus becoming the third in first-class history to achieve the feat. The 4 points Essex glean from a draw are enough to steer them past Middlesex and into a 4-point lead. Nineteen down, three to go. However, there was an unavoidable feeling, particularly among Middlesex folk, that Essex had allowed a pivotal advantage to (literally) slip through their fingers.

Thursday 30 August, Blackpool

Lancashire v. Surrey (County Championship, 3 days)

Finding oneself vying for elbow room on the same bill as Dana, Freddie Starr and a tall blighter covered in light bulbs is no laughing matter. The schism with Old Trafford, caused ostensibly by Blackpool CC's staging of a benefit match here in 1984 for Boycott and Botham, has been healed. Yet the first Championship fixture in Stanley Park since then ranks a distinctly humdrum second on the list of current attractions in this dowdy, tawdry town. Of the anoraked torrents who poured off the 1.20 from Poulton-le-Fylde, a few are here for the beer and the cricket, but most are drawn by tomorrow's ceremonial switching-on of the Tower illuminations.

Aside from an intriguing duel between Mendis and the latest under-age Asian superhero, Waqar Younis, the great turn-off occurred in the middle. Watched by a couple of thousand wet masochists slouched in candy-stripe deck chairs, this 18-year-old Lionel Richie clone with the bobbing bouffant hair, gleaming gold necklace and headband swung the old ball at a fair old lick to pluck out Jesty's leg stump with a yorker, then with the very next ball pinioned Watkinson leg-before. He failed, however, to dislodge Mendis, who eventually capitulated to the persevering Martin Bicknell 6 runs short of his fifth Championship 100 of the season and his third dismissal in the nineties. Eight wickets down for 261 represented a reasonable return on David's decision to bat rather than risk valuable legs and thighs on the slippery outfield, but the probability of Lancashire overhauling Middlesex and Essex was shrinking towards infinity.

With the first four sessions having been washed away, Michael Fish forecasting ceaseless sun for tomorrow's final day and Lancashire requiring 17 more points to keep the death rattle going for another few days, the draw is taken as read.

These calculations are academic, however. No one here is seriously discussing the Championship any longer. Atherton's presence on the touchline is voluble enough. Saturday is NatWest Final day, and, so far as David is concerned, these three days are about practice, pride and place money.

'Having a match off this week was something we really needed because everyone was physically and mentally tired. Five of our last seven Championship games have been away from home, and in the midst of all that we've played four Sunday League games, plus a semi-final and a quarter-final in the NatWest. The Championship, obviously, is out of reach now, although there is still some prize money to play for, so we have to get back into the top five.'

The mathematical lifeline was snapped the following afternoon. David declared at the overnight score after the resumption had been delayed by two and a half hours and, with even the double forfeiture pregnant with pointlessness, Surrey batted out time. Essex are now 48 points distant at the top of the table, so, even in the highly unlikely event of the leaders emerging empty-handed from their last three games, coupled with Lancastrian 24-pointers at the expense of Nottinghamshire and Warwickshire, Lancashire, with five wins to Essex's eight, could not win the title.

It was one of the more unusual days in county history.

Notwithstanding the 10.30 start, Lancashire wanted an early finish to enable them to catch the shuttle flight to Heathrow, from where the team bus would transport them to the hotel. David, Ian Greig and the umpires, Barry Meyer and Bob White, therefore agreed to begin the twenty-over countdown at the start of the last hour, 3.30. The rain, bless its soggy socks, made the shift even shorter. For the first county to reach September and still be in contention to win both major one-day titles, Lord's beckoned.

11 September

Saturday 1 September, Lord's

Lancashire v. Northamptonshire (NatWest Trophy final)

As an example of one-day cricket's propensity for premature ejaculations, the 1990 NatWest Trophy final was up there, way up there. The sheer number of the beasts makes recalling limited-overs matches about as simple as choosing a favourite episode of *Coronation Street*. Those that spring most readily to mind – West Indies beating Australia under lights at Sydney in 1989 and below Old Father Time in the 1975 World Cup final, the Bond'n'Asif Gillette final of 1971, the 1984 NatWest semi-final here between Middlesex and Somerset – did not depend on last-ball histrionics for their drama. As with the best movies, each contained climaxes within its scenes, and a quality of plot that did not need an explosive denouement. On the other hand, many a sleeping contest has been electrified by last-gasp derring-do, a telling comment on the vapid nature of the form. It is not difficult to envisage a time, in the not too distant future, when players are competing for the Shake'n'Vac Cup, a one-day bash featuring twenty-four ten-over games in one day (played with luminous balls, natch). As a way of sorting the good bits from the dross, of slimming cricket down into bite-sized TV portions, it would be hard to beat. But since a delayed orgasm tends to be more enjoyable – and certainly less guilt-ridden – than the early one, this year's sixty-over final was every bit as dissatisfying for the neutral observer.

Not for DeFreitas, mind. Cognisant of this traditional opportunity, at the end of the winter tour hustings, for a party political broadcast on behalf of the Me Party, he charged in to knock down the first 5 Northamptonshire bottles in eight overs, obtaining movement aplenty from a complicit surface. First to wobble was Nigel Felton, edging an out-swinger low to Allott's fingertips at first slip. Alan Fordham missed an in-swinger that may or not have struck him too high on the pads; Larkins kissed an out-swinger for Hegg to clasp another low catch; Bailey was also caught by the wicket-keeper, driving recklessly, and when John Holder gave Daffy the benefit of the doubt following an lbw shout against Lamb, Northants were 39 for 5 and going down for the third time. It was still morning and already the requiem was being composed. And all because, as in the 1988 fiasco between Middlesex and Worcestershire, the pitch spat at the team batting first.

When David arrived in the away dressing-room, among the usual splodge of *Telegraphs* and *Independents* lurked a loose back page from the latter organ. 'Hughes's leading walk-on role' bellowed the sly headline. What awaited David out in the middle was considerably more of an eyesore.

'I went out at 9.30 and scratched my boot on the corner of the wicket. Black soil, half an inch down. I put a key in it and it went straight in, so I said to Mick Hunt, the Lord's groundsman, "This looks a bit damp to me." He said, "No, it's a dry surface but we did have a thunderstorm on Wednesday night." I thought, Christ, I've got a wet wicket. This is absolutely ridiculous. I had a word with Alan Ormrod when I got back to the dressing-room, but I didn't tell the players. There was no point. Everyone knows the repercussions of a damp wicket if you don't win the toss. Some of the players don't inspect wickets as closely as they should, and perhaps one or two are not interested, because they will play on anything and back their own ability, but a couple of them went out to the middle and later told me that it looked a bit damp to them. I said, "I don't think so, I'll be surprised if it is."

'I stuffed them on the toss too. All season they've maintained that they can tell whether I've won it or not, but this time I fooled them. When Lamby and I went out to the middle to toss, he asked me who had the honour of tossing the coin. "Well, you're in the home dressing-room," I said, "but perhaps we should toss a coin to decide who tosses for real." Lamby eventually spun the coin for real, I shouted "heads" and when it returned to earth and I'd won it, I just kept my head down and my shoulders hunched, not giving anything away. Without moving my head I could see them all on the balcony, but I didn't let them out of their agony until I looked up just before reaching the pavilion.' The Marquis de Sade would have been proud.

Thanks to some biffs from the loose-limbed Curtly Ambrose and a dedicated exercise in endurance and self-denial by David Capel, Northants managed to ward off total humiliation and survive until the last ball of the sixtieth over. Indeed, the recovery might well have sired more than the eventual total of 171, but for the fact that both saviours expired needlessly, run-out backing up when Allott (Capel) and Akram (Ambrose) deflected withering drives into the stumps.

Sensing the slimmest of chances, Ambrose and Robinson tore out of the blocks and Lancashire were soon reeling, Fowler pushing Robinson to mid-on off a leading edge and Mendis slicing Capel to the wicket-keeper, David Ripley. With nearly a quarter of the innings over and the favourites just into the 30s, Fairbrother on six chipped Nick Cook's left-arm spin to mid-on, where Ambrose, possibly unsighted by the thickly-populated backdrop, somehow downed the offering and so joined Simon Hughes in Lancashire's list of creditors. Fairbrother expressed his gratitude in inimitable fashion, belting a bracing 81 in eighty-nine balls with the aid of nine 4s and a couple of resounding five-irons into the gallery. His latest explosive turn ended with another lofted shot to Ambrose, who pouched it with consummate, richly ironic, ease.

By now Lancashire required another 30. While Atherton continued to keep watch, Watkinson battered two 6s and a brace of 4s to speed the side home with 7 wickets and 14.2 overs in hand. Only twice before, in 1964 and 1982, had a 60-over final produced as comprehensive a margin of superiority. More noteworthy than that, Lancashire had become the first county to win both principal one-day trophies in one season. Happiest of all, DeFreitas was Man of the Match. In the Year of the Runs, on the most eagerly-anticipated day of the summer, his spell of 5–26 had served to constipate one of the most powerful batting orders in the land. That last thought evoked equivocal feelings.

David recalled tipping Northants to feature in the top five of the Championship. 'They've let me down badly. Their line-up is potentially very strong, but as a team they are an enigma. I was still worried before the start today, because they had nothing left to play for. I really didn't feel that, given the amount of ability at their disposal, they would perform badly. But if we had had to bat first, who knows. We could have been all out for 40. If we'd have been using the Reader ball from last year the whole game might have all been over by lunchtime. But it's the supporters that get the rough end of the deal. They're paying £30 and £37 a seat and they demand a good few hours of entertainment. And it's runs they want, not an avalanche of wickets and an early finish.

'Still, Daffy bowled very well indeed. Walter [Allott] gave him extra support and Wasim had on off-day, but that didn't matter. At 59 for 6 I thought we were well on the road to winning if we kept things going, but in that kind of situation in a one-day match it can be difficult to maintain pressure. Your bowling changes are demanded by the overs that are left, so we had to introduce a fourth and a fifth bowler when, ordinarily, in a Championship match, I would have kept Daffy and Walter going and we would have got them out for under 100. But we were quite happy with 171.'

Notwithstanding a haul of 5–53 against New Zealand at Trent Bridge in June, this was DeFreitas's finest hour since his Test debut in Brisbane four winters ago, when, pitched into the maelstrom after a handful of outings for Leicestershire, he scored an able 40 and claimed 5 victims, including Marsh, Boon, Jones and Ritchie. He had left Grace Road for Old Trafford in 1989 following a contretemps or two, mostly relating to an outlook verging on the primadonna and including one celebrated dust-up with Jon Agnew and a bag of salt. In pulling out of the rebel tour to South Africa, however, DeFreitas had at least evinced a morsel of maturity. After two years at Lancashire, moreover, he is beginning to develop into something like the player he always promised to be. His pace, always snappy, has continued to be a weapon, but is now allied to movement through the air and off the pitch. Runs, attractive ones at that, are progressing from a trickle to a useful stream and, though still prone to wanton waves of the wand, he has doubled his career tally of centuries this season.

David gives Alan Ormrod the credit for enhancing his control of the ball, via the Sardine Technique. 'Two winters ago, when Daffy had just joined us, Alan worked on getting him to bowl closer to the stumps. He would stand next to him and leave him about eighteen inches' room. It was quite a precarious business if you were the one next to the stumps because you ran the risk of being banged in the earhole. It had the desired effect, however. Once he had the confidence to get in close, once he knew he wasn't going to smash the stumps over, he started to get more sideways on and obtain some swing, and also move the ball off the seam away from the right-hander. Once you start doing that you become a major wicket-taking bowler. He has settled in and worked hard here. I would have thought he was one of five of our lads who were very conscious of their performances today, but he's stopped worrying after those 5 wickets. He knows he's Australia-bound now. He is certainly in my squad.'

Some of the other responses were elegaic. 'Commiserations, as always, to Northamptonshire,' the Lord's announcer, Alan Curtis, boomed in that plummy basso profundo of his, alluding to their third losing Final in a row at Lord's. Matthew Engel, an unabashed Wantage Road pilgrim, externalised his pain in the *Guardian*: 'Many people tell me they were born in the wrong century. I was born in the wrong county.' A musicologist, he revealed, had delved into the history of traditional Northamptonshire folk songs and unearthed two, then discovered that both were written in Hertfordshire. 'Could someone maybe write one?' Engel pleaded. ' "I belong to Kettering" or "Higham Ferrers here I come".' He went on to bemoan the fact that the county's most magnetic tourist attraction remains the hold-up between Junctions 15 and 16 on the M1; that its best-known poet, John Clare, was certified insane. After ten years in which a bounteous collection of highly skilful players had failed to win a solitary trophy, there would be little opposition, Engel added, 'if someone did the same to our cricketers.' It was hard to disagree with his implicit contention that the blame lay squarely with those at the top. 'Well-led, well-organised counties do not drop catches, because the players feel involved all the time . . . the atmosphere and spirit in the side helps their concentration . . . successful teams have all found the right man to be captain and given him the authority to turn things round – Brearley at Middlesex, Fletcher at Essex and now David Hughes at Lancashire.'

There were few present who would dispute David's right to have been mentioned in the same breath as the two foremost county captains of the modern era. Out of the rubble of that 1986 NatWest Final demolition by Sussex, he, together with Ormrod and Bob Bennett, a charming, businesslike chairman possibly destined to succeed Peter Lush as the England tour manager, had constructed a new, vastly improved Lancashire, one blessed with the deepest well of talent in the club's history. But not even the fourth pot of David's tenure could camouflage, still less compensate for, his repeated failure to win that elusive Championship.

Comparisons with Lancashire XIs of recent yore are all the rage at times like this. I found myself joining in, jotting down a composite team from the one-day era. It comprised a mixture of 1990 batting (Mendis, Fowler, Atherton and Fairbrother) and 1970s bowling (Lever, Shuttleworth, Simmons and Hughes), with Clive Lloyd the batting interloper, Akram the odd bowler out and the agility of Hegg narrowly squeezing him past Engineer behind the stumps. But at the post-match press conference David, the sole active link between the two eras and the putative captain of this dream team, retracted a statement he had made after the Benson & Hedges final, wherein he cited the current team as the best of his twenty-three years at Old Trafford.

Later in the evening he explained his rationale. 'This is certainly the best squad I've played in, and I'd probably have four or five of the current players in any imaginary side to represent the Lancashire of my time. But I had to be tactful. As captain I'm in an invidious position, and there is a great danger of upsetting people if I go around making comparisons, particularly when you are leading a young side. Players coming into the side in the late 1970s and early 1980s had little desire to be told about their predecessors' accomplishments, and I don't have any wish to harp back either. I had some great times and some sad times, but you must look forward.'

In the evening the Lancashire players and their companions returned to Stringfellow's and boogied the night away. Yet the prevalent mood of relaxation was no more nerveless than it had been all day. Just before the 10.15 team talk, Jim Bowen, the host of an enormously silly, hugely popular TV quiz called *Bullseye*, rang the dressing-room to wish the team good luck. 'Jim told me that if we won, he would give us all a bendy bully, which is the consolation prize he gives you if you don't win any money. When I told the lads what he was proposing, they all shouted, in unison, "He knows what he can do with his bendy bully." However, that was an important moment for us; in an instant the tension had evaporated.' That message of support reminded David of a call prior to the Benson & Hedges final. 'Jack Simmons rang up and wished us the best, so I said, "Thanks Jack, are you coming down for the game?" He said he couldn't because he was playing in one himself, so I said: "It's good to hear from you. In fact I thought about you this morning." He asked me why, so I said, "Because this is the first final for which the Lancashire bus has left the hotel on time." Jack was a terrible timekeeper.'

Winners of the 60-over (for a record fifth time) and 55-over competition, runners-up in the 40-over affair, this Lancashire squad are unquestionably the finest exponents of one-day cricket to grace the county circuit since Richards, Garner and Botham galvanised Somerset in the late 1970s. In winning twenty-two out of their twenty-five completed games in 1990 they have reduced an awkward science to a manageable art.

Wednesday 5 September, Old Trafford

Lancashire v. Middlesex (Refuge Assurance Cup semi-final)

Thereafter, the anticlimax. In indifferent weather before a meagre crowd, Lancashire were outplayed by Middlesex in the Refuge Cup semi-final, their riposte to their opponents' useful but reachable 272 for 6 a spotty 227 for 7. Such was their struggle to contain Haynes and Roseberry during an exhilarating opening stand of 153, that David slipped his leash, bowling six overs and eliciting catches from both to atone for his earlier insertion. After the swift demise of Fowler and Atherton, Lloyd and Fairbrother revived the pursuit in a duet worth 81, but 188 from the last twenty overs proved too stiff against Emburey's spin. Long before Lloyd had holed out amid rain and half-light in the fortieth, Middlesex were contemplating a bully-off against Derbyshire. With no Gatting on hand to jeer, it was a bad day all round for the home supporters.

To sceptics, the decision to site the final at Edgbaston rather than Lord's merely emphasises the lowly status of the fifth county competition. David deems it a worthwhile addition to the canon, pointing to the meaning it adds to the latter stages of the League campaign, but queries its format. 'I'd like to see people support this competition a bit more, but in a long summer, one with a lot of major matches, the cost to the Lancashire supporter is mounting. I know this is a very insular profession, but we're all aware that interest rates are high and so people don't have as much money as they did for following us around. We had five or six thousand in today, which isn't particularly good by our standards, but you have to take into account those factors, and the fact that this is a Wednesday. Why the hell can't we play the semi-finals of a Sunday competition on a Sunday? We had a spare one after Derbyshire had won the League, so it was certainly possible.' Not for the first time, English cricket's marketing policies defied comprehension.

Thursday 6 September, Lord's

County captains' meeting

Just as David and his fellow county captains sat down to pass verdict on the season (and come up with some recommendations that are almost certain, as usual, to be ignored by the TCCB), the England party to tour Australia was unveiled. It was much as predicted, with two interesting draftees (Phil Tufnell and Martin Bicknell), one lucky stiff (Wayne Larkins) and one notable dropout. In among the debris of discards from the semi-successful tour of the Caribbean lay DeFreitas, presumed to be a banker after last Saturday's NatWest show. To their credit, Lord Ted and his pals had disregarded a one-day feat in favour of the three-day consistency of Bicknell, whose current record of 65 wickets at 26.93 makes him the leading bowler in the sixteen-strong squad. Atherton, in fact, is the sole Lancastrian included, a state of affairs that meets with little approval from Ormrod. To him, the selection 'smacks of southern bias', even though its impartiality extends to eight representatives covering Essex, Middlesex, Hampshire, Gloucestershire and Surrey, and another eight from Lancashire, Warwickshire, Northamptonshire, Nottinghamshire, Derbyshire and Leicestershire. A Lancastrian, Colin Snape, wrote to *The Times* suggesting that the north declare UDI and play the south in Tests.

Though particularly unhappy for DeFreitas and Hegg, David reacted more dispassionately. 'I don't sit back and count how many southerners are in an England side and how many northerners. You try and pick sixteen players on merit, and if they all happen to come from one county, then so be it. I hope that the selectors don't have any areas of favouritism. Having said that, however, it does seem that, during my career, certain southern players have been the ones to get more of an extended chance.'

Hegg would be mollified by the selection of one specialist wicket-keeper, the matchless Jack Russell, but consoling DeFreitas would be difficult. 'He has a good temperament for a fast bowler. He's fiery on the field and a bit volatile off it too, so he has probably taken his omission harder than, say, Hugh Morris. But I want him to be bitterly disappointed. All I can do is commiserate with the lad and tell him I thought he should have gone, which isn't much consolation, I know. He was successful in Australia on his first tour, had a bloody good time in fact, and I think he had set his stall out for a return trip. But he will have to accept it and start to look around the corner, to the A tour to Pakistan. Although he's only 23, he will be a senior player in terms of international experience, and it would benefit him greatly to have to be a senior pro and take more responsibility. He'll come back a much better person for the experience.'

The captains' meeting touched on most of the conundrums thrown up over the past five months, focusing energies on the ball, relationships with umpires, and registrations. The call for a seam with two or three more strands stitched with thick twine, was virtually unanimous, as was the desire for a more uniform ball. At present, two Kentish manufacturers stationed ten miles apart, Alfred Reader and BCB, vie for business. The former's offering is more tightly bound but is difficult to shine, while the BCB-produced Dukes afford swing but go out of shape more quickly; the stitches on the quarter seams appear to split much more easily. The zeal to maintain a healthy concord with the men in white jackets was equally noticeable.

More vexed was the import issue. David admits to some confusion. 'Lancashire wanted to keep Patterson for next year, but with the new restrictions on the registration of overseas players, that won't be possible. I find it interesting that the counties who voted for this change generally only had one import on their books. I would retain overseas players, the top ones, because, just as I benefited from playing alongside Engineer, Lloyd and Holding, our young players will learn a lot from them. Overall, I think the majority of county cricketers are very concerned about the number of players born overseas who are playing for England, and with Graeme Hick qualifying next April, he was one of the main talking points at the meeting. At Lancashire I've got the best young number three in the country, and unless Atherton has been transformed into an international opener in the last twelve months, he would have to take a back seat to Hick. He wouldn't begrudge Hick the opportunity to play for England, but I would. The trouble is that if you tell people they can qualify for an England cap provided they are prepared to wait seven years, and they do so, as Hick has done, you can't really complain. But that doesn't make it right in my eyes. The difficulty lies in the guidelines. Devon Malcolm may have been born in Jamaica, but he has lived here all his life so his presence in the England XI is fair enough. It would be the same for Nadeem. On the other hand, there is no way I would allow Hick, or any other player who has learned his cricket and been educated overseas, to do so. Craig White is another awkward example because he was born here, spent the whole of his childhood and teenage years in Australia, then came back to Yorkshire. That seems fair enough too, but he has played for the Australian Under-21 team, so where do his loyalties lie?'

During the conflab, word came of the death of Sir Leonard Hutton in a Kingston-upon-Thames hospital, far, far from his beloved Pudsey. At a memorial service in York Minster, a former colleague, David Sheppard, now the Bishop of Liverpool, would note that many people who had never met this most diligent, dignified and technically accomplished of English batsmen, nonetheless felt a personal loss. For someone such as myself, weaned on tales of his upright grit and polish in Australia and the West Indies, the generation gap was narrowed at a stroke. 'This,' Sheppard proffered, 'is one of the bewitching properties of cricket.'

Our David encountered Hutton on a couple of occasions, but was unable to form any lasting impression or attachment. 'I didn't know Len, but I do know his son Richard well, and having a father of such standing must have been a burden to him in cricketing terms. Cyril

Washbrook always spoke highly of Len and we all owe him something because he was our first professional Test captain. I have a couple of videos of him in action, and he seems to have been the complete player of his era. But it was a different era.'

Friday 7 September, Chelmsford

Essex v. Northamptonshire (County Championship, 4 days)

To most of us Graham Gooch is an implacable sort, that seemingly impervious bat of his serving as a translucent mirror to an unemotional, stoic demeanour. For those not privy to the England dressing-room, the mind's eye picture of his team talk lies somewhere between Gower's fabled do-your-best-chaps and Gatting's let's-nobble-the-bastards. So much for uninformed supposition. The Championship was brewing up to a heady froth, and Essex had to rectify their lapses against Northamptonshire, pronto. And what better way to do so than by putting the same county in their place?

What ensued at 10.40 this morning nonetheless took the dressing-room by surprise, Nadeem especially. 'I was putting shin pads on, trying to make as little noise as possible, when Gooch stood up and really let go. He banged the table in front of him a couple of times and said that if we were content with being second-raters then we didn't deserve to win the Championship. Then he said that that just wasn't good enough and that we had to think like winners, that this match was crucial and that we had to approach it in the right way, a positive way. Because he's a winner he likes to win everything. We do try, but playing every day makes it hard to get geed up. Usually, if there's an important game coming up we still behave normally, but then I suppose we haven't had as important a game as this all season. He tried to bring the aggression out of us. And it made me quiver a little bit. He's been more communicative this year, probably because he's happier in himself and also because he has to deal with players in a Test context now. His enthusiasm for the game is incredible. I've never met anyone more professional towards this sport than him.'

Sadly, for Essex if not for Middlesex, Gooch's broadside proves futile, though this does not become apparent until midway through another oscillating match. The first day certainly augurs well, Foster and, of all people, Waugh sending down Northamptonshire for 196 in 51.2 overs, that colander of the crease, Mark Robinson, belying his status by remaining unbeaten, if scoreless, his eleventh zero in a row. This ousts Jim Griffiths from the top of the all-time list of batting bozos. The one tremor thereafter that day is Gooch's clip to mid-wicket when 8 runs short of his twentieth century in all formats this summer. Nadeem had kept pace with him by making precisely half of a third wicket alliance worth 52, one that steers Essex from the murky depths of 29 for 2 towards a deficit of just 11 by the close with five wickets intact.

A cluster of miserable clouds greets the players the next morning and Essex lose their last 5 wickets for 52. The cumuli had dispersed by the time Northamptonshire resume 48 to the rear on a benign pitch, and Alan Fordham flings caution from his make-up to reach three figures from 139 balls. Lamb and Bailey repeat their Northampton spree, and by the end of the third day Northamptonshire have rewritten their own scoring record for the second time in nine days, running up 636 for 6 before Lamb's merciful closure 588 in front. Essex, clearly shaken by successive drubbings from the most fitful order in the land, drip to defeat. Following an opening partnership of 83, careless strokes from Gooch and then Prichard, exacerbated by Ambrose's subsequent dismissal of Waugh and the nightwatchman Ilott, leave them teetering on 134 for 4. Despite Stephenson's 76 and a watchful 43 from Nadeem, Northamptonshire win by 276 runs. Middlesex, meanwhile, trounce Nottinghamshire by 10 wickets at Lord's to leapfrog back to the apex, now 14 points clear and beginning to believe that Essex's late spurt on the rails is running out of puff.

Friday 7 September, Edgbaston

Warwickshire v. Somerset (County Championship, 4 days)

Adrian was sleeping soundly in his room at the Strathallen Hotel when he was abruptly awoken by the fire bell. As an alarm call it certainly knocked BT's efforts into a cocked hat.Earlier in the season the same thing had happened, only for the alarm to be declared false. This time, though, the reveille was for real. Braving the Birmingham rain the Somerset team accompanied the rest of the eye-blinking guests into the hotel courtyard, where the fire officer took a roll call. Only later was it disclosed, rather shamefacedly, that the source of the alarm was a white powder. No, Richard Pryor had not been freebasing cocaine in the gents, but there was a female guest with a similar addiction – for talcum powder. So intent had she been on dousing every last inch of her body in the stuff that she had set off the alarm, activated by what it interpreted as smoke.

Somerset's penultimate game of the season began just as inauspiciously. Adrian, anxious to finish with a flourish, bowled fourteen overs off the reel and shrugged aside the Warwickshire openers, Andy Moles and Jason Ratcliffe (at last, a contemporary cricketing Christian name). But from a pit of 91 for 5, the county lying third in the table were salvaged by Reeve, the acting captain, and their wicket-keeper, Keith Piper, respectively the best cricketer ever to come out of Hong Kong, and the most impressive graduate out of the nine so far primed for a county career by the Haringey Cricket College, an enterprising North London venture currently in danger of being poll-capped out of existence. Burns gave them a helping glove, dropping Reeve off Hayhurst in the last over before lunch when he lunged for a nick that was heading for first slip, then sparing Piper. Reeve was eventually run-out for 58, but at 215 for 7 Piper found another durable ally in Paul Booth, the former Yorkshire slow left-armer, who accompanied him to his maiden century.

Rose tidied up the next morning as Warwickshire's last 3 wickets fell for the addition of 19 runs, but on a pitch offering variable bounce, none of Somerset's specialists were able to reach 60 in the face of some tight bowling from Paul Smith and Tim Munton. However, Burns made amends for his lapses in the field with a sparky 88, and Somerset ultimately led by 37. Adrian again accounted for Moles and Warwickshire slipped to 75 for 4, but some more jaunty resistance from Reeve, aided this time by Smith, enabled him to set 254 at a shade over 5 runs an over, Adrian emerging with 4–72, his first 4-wicket haul in the Championship since 29 April. A breeze at Taunton undoubtedly, but here the order was a tall one and, after some early alarms, parity became the only feasible objective. Somerset finished on 138 for 4 and a little classic was over.

Despite the fact that Somerset had relinquished control after twice appearing to have the game by the scruff of the neck, Adrian headed back to Taunton in good humour. 'In a shit year that's the second time I've actually enjoyed myself, and not just because the season's finishing and I'm happier as a result. I bowled off a shorter run for a bit, a touch longer than my Sunday run, and found I was achieving the same pace without working my body as hard, which is important because the key to taking wickets now seems to be simply bowling as many overs as you can. I bowled more than sixty in the match and got 6 wickets, so the theory held up, even though my knee is still painful and I can't play without painkillers, which bugger up my digestive system so it feels as if I've got constant indigestion. And I still couldn't feel my fingers on the seam after forty overs. The stitching was gradually being worn away, and it was so bare that it felt as if I was holding a hard lump of cork. When he came back from the captains' meeting at Lord's last week, Tav told us that complaints were made about the state of the ball, that people thought it was leading to boring cricket, but he wonders whether the TCCB will take any notice. How can they do that after all the long-standing records that have been broken this summer?

'On this occasion, however, it didn't matter that much. The Edgbaston pitch was a bit uneven and deliveries either bounced more than expected outside off-stump, or skidded through. At last, a wicket on which you could reasonably expect to bowl the other side out twice. So, from an overall point of view, we were very pissed off at the end. Had Burns not dropped Reeve and Piper on the first day we would have won. Then we would have been tenth with a game to go, and in with a chance of finishing in the top half. I know we've left it a bit late, but we're just starting to play well. Four-day cricket suits us because it's proper cricket. The side that plays better usually wins, without recourse to collusion on the first morning, something that has been happening with increasing frequency this season. A few more four-day games, please.

'Anyway, at least I've got a target for the last match: I need 3 wickets for my 50. I'd feel semi-content with that. Perhaps I lost interest in the middle of the season because I wasn't enjoying it, but if I can salvage 50 wickets it would be the fourth season in a row I'd have managed it. I'd be fairly satisfied with that.'

Adrian may have undermined Moles's defences twice in this match, but he remained a fervent admirer of the stocky opener. Along with Gooch, Gatting and Tim Robinson he is one of four

English-born batsmen with a career average in excess of 40, and the only member of the quartet yet to receive Test recognition. 'Every year Warwickshire tell him to lose weight but I don't think that's the point. Maybe he's slightly unfashionable. He certainly didn't go to the right school and he's had to come up through the leagues. Not like Atherton; he's got an easy ride because they, the powers that be, want him to succeed. Moley has played in South Africa, and he's married to a South African girl, but he knows the consequences of going there to play now, so he decided to hang on and see if England gave him a chance. Unfortunately for him, they haven't done so, at least not so far.'

To most eyes, Warwickshire appeared to have made a strange decision in jettisoning Tom Moody, who had muscled his way to eight centuries and an average nudging 90, preferring to retain their South African express train Allan Donald (28 championship victims at over 35 apiece). To Adrian it made sense. 'You can make as many runs as you like, but bowlers are the matchwinners, and Warwickshire know how rare they are, which is why they're hanging on to Donald. He's the quickest white bowler in the world and he still has two years of his contract to go. Warwickshire have invested a lot of money in him and he deserves it. Anyway, Moody will go to Worcestershire, mark my words.'

As at Trent Bridge, the talk of the dressing-room at Edgbaston was the English Ashes party. Adrian gave it the thumbs-up, with reservations. 'It's a good squad, and Martin Bicknell is an excellent choice. He impressed me at Weston. He seems to have thickened out and gained in pace. But I do wonder about our attack as a whole. We'll be very dependent on Malcolm taking advantage of the extra speed and bounce out there. The Australians are a good unit, and they're on a high, but from their perspective a lot will depend on whether Geoff Lawson, Carl Rackemann and Bruce Reid are fit. We've got more confidence now, mind, so the series should be closer than it was last year. We might even salvage a draw.'

Wednesday 12 September, Chelmsford

Essex v. Kent (County Championship, 4 days)

The world will find out tomorrow, but by then Nadeem will be well entrenched in melancholy. He has not made the A tour. 'I know this has only been my first full season, so perhaps I was expecting a bit too much, but I'd be disappointed if I wasn't disappointed. Mind you, at least I know now. On Monday I rang Fletch three times at Enfield, where he was with the 2nd XI, and finally got hold of him on Tuesday. He said he was supposed to have known the Ashes and A teams by now, but that as soon as he did know he would let me know. I was feeling quite nervous at practice today, and when he called me over he had a sad look on his face, which is very unusual for Fletch, so I knew right away that I wasn't in. He took me for a walk and he said he'd assumed Stanley [Stephenson] would be in the party, and perhaps Prichard too. Then he said that, unfortunately, in answer to my next question, I wasn't in either.

'He said he'd had his say, that I should have been chosen, but unfortunately the selectors didn't agree. I couldn't help thinking that if I'd played more things might have been different. The funny thing is that I'd overhead Fletch talking to Mark Nicholas and he said there would be more youngsters in the squad this year, so I took heart.' [Nicholas had captained the A tour to Zimbabwe and, as an exemplary ambassador, was a fair bet to do so in Pakistan, scene of the shameful Gatting shenanigans three winters ago, until the malaria he had contracted in Kenya during that tour wrecked his season.

'Knowing Stanley wasn't in made me feel better, though, because I knew someone was suffering more than I was. A few days ago I tackled him about it, and when I said that Nasser had been told he was going he said, maybe I won't go. I told him not to be stupid, but then he said he didn't really care if he went or not. Again I told him not to be stupid, saying that he'd be disgusted if he wasn't picked, and eventually he admitted I was right. I suppose we should have known really. Gooch had told Nasser he would be in, but he hadn't said anything to me or Stanley, and if anyone would know, he would.

'Fletch explained that although Nasser was not in form, to have dropped him could have proved a destructive blow to his confidence. I'm not so sure I agree with that. Nasser's so relaxed. He knows he can do it. What gets me is that he's the first to admit his luck. At the start of the season he told me that the gap between county and Test cricket was very thin and he kept saying that throughout the summer to encourage me. He would say that taking that step is a combination of applying yourself and having the desire, telling me how Lamb and Smith would do TDs for hours, urging each other on, full of determination. Maybe I haven't quite got that yet. Mind you, Nasser said the other day that he thought he'd find it difficult to be selected for England again because the top six batsmen are doing so well at the moment. He also feels Hick's availability will work against him, but I don't think Hick should automatically come in. They should wait until someone loses form. It's the same with Waugh and the Australian team.'

Stephenson's peeved countenance at the close was that of a man who had scored nigh on 2,000 runs and could not for the life of him comprehend how he could have done more to advance his case. Nadeem, with half that number and no track record to speak of, had rather less cause to feel aggrieved. The seven specialist batsmen were Fairbrother and Hussain, two Test players; Darren Bicknell, Graham Thorpe and Richard Blakey, each of whom had enhanced their reputations in Zimbabwe; Mark Ramprakash, perhaps the most exceptionally gifted of that generation, and the captain, Hugh Morris, studied compiler of a record ten 100s for Glamorgan and the summer's second heaviest scoring home-grown opener. The really galling inclusion was that of Ian Salisbury, the combative Sussex leg-spinner. Had Nadeem's efforts in that department remotely reflected his abilities, he would have surely been selected. Instead, he would return to Perth, to Gosnells, where he would seek out Bob Paulsen and Tony Mann, two highly respected Western Australian wrist-spinners of recent vintage. 'Last winter I had told the club I would be available again, so that was always at the back of my mind. I was looking forward to it until a month ago. Now it will just seem like second-best.'

With Pringle's dicky back still hindering him, Essex took the field against Kent without their most experienced seamer for the eighth game running. However, a far more fearful blow befell them before the game was an hour old. Trevor Ward, the free-hitting Kent opener, edged Foster low to second slip, where Gooch's attempt to squeeze his left hand under the ball resulted in a yowl of pain and, as was later diagnosed, a broken thumb. Had Essex's recent errant catching received the cruellest of come-uppances? Not according to Nadeem.

'It's true, our slip work has let us down lately, but I wouldn't put that down as a chance. It was going at a 100 miles an hour. He tried to disguise both the physical and mental pain, but I could see he was distraught. And, understandably, our heads went down a bit too, if only for a short while. We had to show him we could still play. Because Prichard and Nasser aren't in form we'll probably miss his batting more than his captaincy. He's been the best batsman I've seen this season, by far. Consistent, always attacking, always on top. I think he may have failed twice for us all year. He can control his life a lot better now as England captain, and that seems to have had a beneficial effect, but he still works desperately hard at his game. Probably because he's essentially quiet – there's no one in the dressing-room he takes into his confidence – I didn't think he was quite as caring as he is. But he shows his feelings when you bowl a bad ball. When I bat with him I really want to show him what I can do.'

Gooch, who only a few days earlier had hosted a raucous Essex end-of-term knees-up at his Brentwood home (Nadeem recalls 'going loopy'), thus rested his laurels at 2,746 runs, the most anyone had mustered since the Championship programme was abridged in 1969. With four innings left and that irrepressible scythe showing no signs of dullness, he had been on target to become the first batsman to rack up 3,000 since Bill Alley in 1961. He had hit twenty centuries, twelve in first-class play, become the first man to make 400 runs in a Test and 1,000 runs in a Test season, and averaged 101.7. Statistically speaking, no batsman had ever thrived so. As a captain he had led England to their first successful summer since 1985 and their first undefeated one since 1979. He had also extended the longest unbeaten start by a skipper from these shores since Ray Illingworth went seventeen Tests between 1969 and 1971 before springing his first leak.

More important than all that, though, had been the manner in which he trampled on those records. Having personally seen no more than a few glimpses of King Wally, the comparison may be open to ridicule, but for much of the season Gooch has resembled a blue-collar Hammond in his patrician authority and mastery of stroke. Against a New Zealand side in transition and an Indian one with what is most charitably described as a friendly attack, neither

Gooch's tactical acumen nor his man-management were overly tested. Being perceived as a winner is what matters, however, and the selectors had been seeking one of those since Brearley took up full-time mind-reading and Fletcher was sacrificed to the arbiters of acceptable behaviour for brushing off a bail with his bat. The least newsworthy event of the summer was therefore Gooch's appointment for Australia. Nothing could have been more inevitable, nor more deserved. Those three years in exile, the surrender of the Essex captaincy and the disappointment of being named as captain for a tour that never took place (India in 1988–89) then sent back to the ranks the next summer; all these lows had been glossed over in the high summer of 1990.

The players Gooch left behind when he trudged off to hospital carried on as normal, downing four, arguably five chances, Kent advancing to 358 for 6 by the close of an unhappy day.

Saturday 15 September, Chelmsford

Essex v. Kent (cont.) (County Championship, 4 days)

How horribly, how speedily, anticipation dissolves into resignation. With Gatting following Gooch to hospital after sustaining a searing blow on the elbow first ball from the prodigal Waqar Younis, Middlesex trailed on first innings at the Kennington run emporium. In the meantime, on the second day at Chelmsford centuries from Prichard and Waugh secured Essex a lead of 99 before Foster declared, Nadeem, filling in for Gooch, having been bowled by Richard Ellison for 20. Ilott, Andrew and Waugh pegged Kent to 129 for 4, but from an unpromising 185 for 4 going into today's final day, the lower order have stalled Essex, Ellison taking up from where he left off first time around. Then he had inched to 44 not out in three hours; now, joined by Richard Davis in a ninth-wicket stand of 115, he crawled for nearly five hours for his undefeated 68. Foster was serving up donkey drops by mid-afternoon, and Nadeem had his longest spell of the season, 17–5–43–0. On the evening TV news, there he was, plopping the shortest of long-hops into the path of Ellison's bat and just about spotting the ball as it departed into orbit. Some first night! 'We'd been told about the cameras and I decided to bowl a bouncer – with eight men round the bat!' When Foster nudged Steve Marsh's off-stump with the penultimate delivery of the morning session, the deficit had been less than 200 with just 3 more wickets to fall. By the time Ellison, and Kent, were done, however, there was barely time for one more over. Surrey held Middlesex, but with one match remaining, 14 points to make up and the leaders promenading off to Hove to conclude their programme against the county dunces, the game was just about up.

Nadeem's reaction was fatalistic. 'We know Middlesex are going to beat Sussex, and if they do, that's that. Just as no one would have predicted we'd be thwarted by Ellison and Davis, you never know what could happen. It could rain, or one of the Sussex guys could play out of his skin, but the odds are against us winning, really. All we can do is do our best. What we don't want to do is think that the race is over and we've lost, then suddenly find out that Middlesex are struggling. We don't want to do that. Surrey haven't lost at the Oval all summer in the Championship and their batting is very strong, so we must make sure we get full batting points to make up for the bowling points we might lose. And I want those 1,000 runs.' He needs 39.

Saturday 15 September, Taunton

Somerset v. Worcestershire (County Championship, 4 days)

The Somerset end-of-term party on the final day of the Worcestershire match splinters into two factions. 'It was a right cock-up,' Adrian admits. 'Neil Burns asked Vanessa, Tav's wife, to book a few tables at Porter's Wine Bar, our regular haunt in town, but Burns's wife had organised a surprise birthday party for him on the same night, so half of us went to that, and the other half to Porter's.'

Not that there was much to celebrate. Somerset completed their season with a splendid sense of symmetry, outshone by the New Road All Stars (minus Dilley and Botham, just for a change). Curtis, who only seems to put his skates on when he sees Somerset arms on the horizon, forged his way with relative briskness to 156, but the first day laurels, unsurprisingly, went to Master Hick. A leg-side 6 off the last ball before lunch brought him his 2,000th run of the season, and when, on 154, Mallender finally nipped an edge for Tavaré to accept the second of his three slip catches, it was the first time Somerset had dismissed him in the Championship since Adrian had managed the feat at Worcester the previous August. The price had been heavy: 1 for 530. Adrian, who had also started with scant regard for exchange rates, conceding 10 from his first over, took the other 3 wickets to fall during the day, Gordon Lord and Curtis unhinged by balls that jagged away, D'Oliveira bowled neck and crop. He later picked up the obdurate Illingworth during Worcestershire's pre-lunch barrage on the Thursday, yielding a final analysis full of philanthropic zeal: 35–6–154–4.

Fortunately for the hosts, anything Hick could do, Cook could do just as well. His ninth first-class century of the summer took him past 2,500 runs and into the money: an equal share with Gooch of the £10,000 from National Power for those reaching 2,500 runs. How would Adrian seek to curb him? 'I wouldn't pitch it short, for one thing. If he gets out, it's mostly through catches. You don't see him lbw and I've only seen him bowled when he's got a 100 and is getting a bit lazy so he plays across the line or something. He's so confident about hitting the ball outside off-stump, square of the wicket, that he goes for it all the time. If one bounces a little more, though, he has a tendency to get caught in the slips, so I would concentrate on bowling a tight line on off stump with a wealth of fielders on the off-side square of and behind the wicket.'

Ricky Bartlett, fresh from a bountiful harvest on behalf on the 2nd XI, marked his first Championship innings of the summer with 73, but when Adrian loped out to join Harden at 372 for 9, Somerset lagged 148 behind. 'I'd bowled a lot of bouncers during their innings. As soon as Neale had come in I bowled three straight off, and he didn't play them very well so I thought I'd have a chance of getting him out that way. I persisted, alternating between over and round the wicket and just kept bouncing him. It was Mallender who ultimately trapped him, but as soon as I came in I knew pretty much what to expect. Lampitt had two balls left in the over and the first one was short – and I hooked it, well, top-edged it, for 6. I got down the other end and they're obviously thinking about wrapping things up quickly, so Newport bowls me a bouncer, but I'm a No. 11, aren't I, so John Harris, the umpire, warns him. I knew the next ball wouldn't be a bouncer, so I came down the track a little bit and had a swish and missed. So the next one is another bouncer and Harris no-balls him. Newps had a bit of a moan and I said, "Well, you've bowled enough of those," that sort of nonsense. It was very tame, very mild, nothing in it. We had a good chat afterwards: no problem. Anyway, I should have got my first 50. I missed out on a dreadful over from Hicky which I didn't lay a bat on, and then Illy bowled me for 41. I enjoyed it, though.'

So did Somerset, who, thanks to a last-wicket stand of 70, now trailed by a comparatively insignificant 78. Back came Hick with another 81, assisted this time by Lord, breathing more freely after being assured of another contract. Adrian, who had dismissed Hick for 29, 8 and 11 in successive innings at New Road over the previous two seasons, duly pinned him leg-before, the fifth occasion he had claimed his scalp in Championship games. He also sent back Curtis, D'Oliveira, Lampitt and Illingworth to earn himself 5–76, but Somerset never once appeared up to the task of making 400. They fell 174 short, Harden gritting it out for 90 against Neal Radford's cunning stunts while Adrian took out his late-flowering bat for 2, thus securing his 100 for the season at the highly commendable average of 25.

So, despite all those months of discontent and disillusionment, Adrian was again Somerset's leading wicket-taker, just as he had been during each of his previous three seasons at Taunton. Fifty-six wickets at 36.69: presentable in the joyless circumstances. Only nine English seamers had procured more victims.

Did that make him indispensable? Did it heck. 'A year ago Somerset were talking five-year contracts, but all they're offering me now is another year. What good is that at this stage of my career? I've taken over 30 per cent of all wickets taken by Somerset since I arrived, for heaven's sake! I might be offered two years if I come back in the spring fitter than ever before, but I don't think that's entirely fair. I was training every single day from January to the start of the season this year. If I do any more I'll come back like a butcher's dog. It was never like this when I started. Back then you just turned up for a net, ran around a bit and loosened up. I'm going to run a lot more this winter, and hopefully lose about a stone and a half, but I need security. I noticed that the TCCB have brought forward to October the date from which counties can make approaches for players, which seems sensible.

'I'd be very sad to leave. I've made some great friends among the players and leaving this time would be even more difficult than it was when I left Hove because I'm married now, and I've got a home and family to consider. I know Liz feels even more strongly about staying in Taunton than I do, but I also know it's not too late for me to fulfil myself elsewhere. I feel as if I'm being pushed out here.'

Tuesday 18 September, Olympia

Welcome, my friends, welcome to the machine. The Sports and Leisure exhibition, to be precise, a monstrous maze of stalls and slick salesmen. Looking more like Grandad than Corporal Jones, a creased Clive Dunn chats up a hulk in a Miami Dolphins jersey. A few yards away, a sizeable collection of leerers and shakers ogle a goose-pimpled young woman clad in a clinging swimsuit. At the Slazenger exhibit, a man in a grey suit effects an introduction: 'By the way, I don't know if you know David Hughes, the Lancashire captain . . .'

The purpose of David's visit is to sort out Lancashire's equipment requirements for 1991. As an alibi for not being at Old Trafford for the final match of the summer against Warwickshire, he could do better. He had sat out the penultimate game at Trent Bridge, which featured a couple of lively passages, one savoury, the other bitter. With Fitton still out of sorts and propping up the averages with 14 wickets at 103.35 apiece, Gary Yates, aged 22, had been introduced as an off-spinner, yet marked his debut with a stylish 106 from No. 9. Fairbrother, filling in for David at the helm, was later warned by umpire John Hampshire after a few overly-sensitive home fans had complained about some characteristically zealous exhortations in the field when Nottinghamshire began their second innings.

Where was the Lancashire Bodhisattva, their selfless leader? 'I decided, and Ormrod eventually went along with me, that it would do more for the club if I stepped down. Apart from earning some place money and giving a chance to youngsters like Nick Speak, Mark Crawley and Gary Yates, the biggest consideration for the last two matches is to give Fairbrother an opportunity to captain the side in four-day cricket, where things happen a lot slower. He can take stock of situations, take responsibility, without having to look over his shoulder for me all the time. With Atherton on the field as well we had our partnership of the future together at Trent Bridge: Fairbrother captain, Atherton vice. I was there for all four days, but I didn't say anything to Neil without him asking and I purposely kept out of most things. What I did observe I'll discuss with him at some stage during the winter. Perhaps if the game had started to slide away and there were gambits I felt he could have tried, then I would have spoken to him during the intervals, but everything went well. He came over for a chat about one or two things, but it was important for him to rely on himself. We need fresh ideas and the enthusiasm of youth that he can offer. His bowling changes got wickets for him, we won by 10 wickets and all in all he would have enjoyed the experience. If he had felt any pressure he would have told me, so clearly he didn't.'

With his active cricketing days nearing a close, was David not tempted to play as often as possible? 'Yes, but that desire has to be tempered. No matter what individuals may feel or want, Lancashire is the be-all and end-all. My responsibility is first and foremost to the players, not myself.' As he talked, David betrayed few signs of any concern over his personal output. It should be said that his first-class record for the season, now complete, was not as modest as one might have suspected: 237 first-class runs at 23.7, 24 Championship wickets at 38.25 (far better than the returns supplied by Akram, Allott or Austin) and 13 catches. During the course of the Roses match at Old Trafford, moreover, David became only the fourth player in Lancashire history – and the first since 1945 – to score over 10,000 runs and take in excess of 500 wickets, joining Johnny Briggs, Len Hopwood and Jack Iddon. Underpinning his figures for the forty-five matches (first-class and one-day) in which he participated, however, were the eleven occasions on which he neither batted nor bowled, the twenty-eight games in which he didn't bat, and the twenty-six in which he didn't bowl.

'Accepting the fact that, inevitably, I have made mistakes during my four years as captain, perhaps the biggest mistake, in hindsight, is in not batting or bowling more frequently. There have been numerous instances when I could have done both but have chosen to give an opportunity to younger players, and although I believe that to be right in the long run, I feel that it has rebounded on me to an extent. If I thought the players were unanimous in not wanting me to play any more, then I would seriously have to think about packing up, but I don't feel that that is the case. Everybody seems to be enjoying themselves and doing well, and the committee don't want me to finish either. They've just offered me another two-year playing contract, including the captaincy for another year. And that was decided in fifteen seconds.

'What volume of cricket I will play I haven't decided yet, but anyone who can play for thirty-four days with only one day off, as we did in July and August, must still possess a certain love and enthusiasm. I've been coping physically too. There have been no direct approaches, but it has been mentioned to me in other quarters that I might be interested in joining Geoff Cook at Durham. It took me five seconds to realise that not only couldn't I play anywhere else, I could not even be involved anywhere else.' At the end of his twenty-third summer, the lad from Newton-le-Willows is still besotted.

Tuesday 18 September, The Oval

Surrey v. Essex (County Championship, 4 days)

Three p.m., and the sound of silence is deafening. The Essex quarters, usually so bubbly, are about as flat as an empty bottle of Dom Perignon. The bonhomie remains but the fizz has flown. More bottom lips being bitten than upper ones stiffened. Some of the players have a squint at Ceefax; a couple ring one of the myriad of county telephone services; somebody darts downstairs for a *Standard*, and a few simply wait until creatures from the outside world enter their domain below the press box in the spanking new, finally-completed red-brick stand next to the pavilion. The news does not alter in the telling. The good bit came shortly after the start, Neil Williams aggravating a hamstring injury in his third over, but now Simon Hughes and Gatting, an unlikely duo, are on their way to skittling Sussex for 187.

Nadeem, subdued by his standards, is hailed as some long-lost friend by Nick Peters and James Boiling, two of the Surrey reserves, but the banter soon ceases. 'I suppose we were expecting this, so heads aren't down. The weather doesn't look as if it's on our side at Hove, but we've still got a match to win. And Foster wants his 100 wickets, Andrew wants his 50 and Stevo wants his 2,000. And I got my 1,000.' That last, sheepish revelation comes almost as an afterthought, as if he is wary of making any outward representation of inner, selfish, guilty pleasure.

'It was the first time I'd opened at 10.30 in the morning [with the season cruising into uncharted depths of September, this final round of Championship games began half an hour early] and the pitch was a bit damp and slower than usual. I was dropped off a sitter to Waqar Younis at cover early on and I struggled a bit, but Stevo nursed me through and we added 96 before I was out in the second over after lunch for 42. Once again, I'd done all the hard work and should have gone on.' On the greensward Hussain is oblivious to the march of history as he dispenses with all that open-face nonsense, reins in those self-destructive urges and begins to regain a vestige of the staying power that had set him apart from the county brat pack a year ago. So much so that Essex miss that fourth batting point. His friend's progress pleases Nadeem no end. 'He played a loose shot first ball, but look at him now. He's really got his head down. This is his best innings of the season.'

Fletcher, not noticeably downcast, endorses Nadeem's assessment. 'That's the straightest Nasser's been all season.'

The next day Hussain returns to his vagabond ways, run out going for a second, though not until he has reached 197, an infant-career-best. 'It sounds better than 200,' he assures Nadeem upon his return. 'And about time too.' More heartening still is a well-organised 116 not out by Jonathan Lewis, who thus becomes the first Essex batsman to score a century in his maiden Championship innings. A 20-year-old bantamweight with a bogbrush hairdo, from the press box perspective he bears more than a passing resemblance, anatomically and stylistically, to Fletcher. Gooch toasts both achievements by popping a couple of corks. The real surprise, though, is Surrey's capitulation to 124 for 8 in thirty-seven overs after Essex, giving few indications of missing Gooch at the crease, have amassed 539 against a bowling attack without Waqar, now injured, and Bicknell.

So consolations abound. They need to. At Hove, Keith Brown's unconquered century places a comfy cushion on Middlesex's high chair and, on Thursday afternoon, at 3.20 p.m., Rodney Bunting stretches forward to Hughes and, to his visible displeasure, is adjudged leg-before. Middlesex are champions.

In 'The Year of the Battered', as the *Guardian* sub-editors would christen the season forty-eight hours later, the chief batterer, Gooch, cited the intransigence of the pitches as the source of Essex's relative failure. 'I am disappointed that we could not play on pitches where there was a more even balance between bat and ball,' he grumbled. 'We had our chances in the last three games, but did not pick up the win points that were necessary to stay at the top. Our catching especially was not good enough.' In as even-handed a tussle as this one has been, little things matter.

There were still four sessions to go at the Oval, lest we forget, and Surrey consumed all of them in saving the match. A significant improvement of 473 on their first innings score was made possible principally by David Ward, he of the pianistic teeth and unextinguishable good cheer, who lambasted his way to 208, his second double hundred of the month and seventh century since mid-May, having managed but two three-figure scores in five prior seasons. He had come in seventy-one overs after Rehan Alikhan and still sped past the opener, who, without one in his four previous summers and his future on the line, eventually crawled to his second motionless, emotionless 100 in a week. A brace of cameos to characterise the Year of the Battered.

Nadeem admired Ward's barbaric biffing but his elders and betters were less convinced. 'When Wardy got to 150, I asked Foster about him, and he reckoned he would have no chance on a wicket that did anything. Nasser and Waugh thought he had no chance of recognition, pointing out that one good year was no big deal. But look at his average. Over 76! Mine is 45, so what can they think of me? Shows you the meaninglessness of statistics.'

Nadeem earned the undying thanks of a sparse crowd by getting shot of Alikhan, caught by Hardie, who later marked his farewell to arms with an over costing 16. Now, if a little belatedly, Nadeem was granted a long enough spell to get into something approaching a groove. 'I still think I'm going to have to change my action, mind. Suchy and I have talked about it a lot at the flat, and everyone's been giving me encouragement, but whereas Childs knows exactly what is going on with his arms and legs and shoulders, so if something goes wrong he can pinpoint it, I'm not sure I know what I'm doing with my action at the moment.' The uncontrolled leg-spinner nonetheless knew enough to clean bowl Monte Lynch and

Jonathan Robinson, all but doubling his season's haul. With Stephenson at last doing for Ward, an Essex win was not inconceivable, Surrey lurching to 514 for 6, a lead of 115 and thirty-four overs left. Lack of concentration then told as Ian Greig ran 4 to the outer reaches to be credited with 8 when an errant return winged to the opposite boundary. No further wickets fell and that, all of a sudden, was the season that was.

After being reminded by Gooch to call him as soon as the England party arrived in Perth, Nadeem showered, talced (though not so much as to raise the fire alarm), brushed all his teeth, and drove back to Braintree. Everyone went their separate ways. Within two weeks Nadeem would be limbering up again by the Fremantle, but for the moment he was experiencing a range of emotions fluctuating between disgruntlement, sadness and pride. A rookie season producing 1,003 runs at 45.59, with 7 wickets at 59, 22 catches (the most by an Essex outfielder) and three hit-wickets in five innings (none in the past six weeks, mind you) suggested those sentiments might err towards self-aggrandisement. But as the smoke of battle cleared, his immediate thoughts were those of a member of the infantry.

'It's been a slightly disappointing summer because coming second in the Championship is a bit of a downer when we should have won it. Our slip catching let us down; by my reckoning we dropped 15 in the second game against Northants.

'Saying goodbye to the guys you've eaten and slept with for five and a half months is difficult, and I really cherish the friends that, thanks to Nasser, I have made on the circuit. I suppose that's a sign that I feel part of things. Doing well helps, they respect that. The main thing to do, it seems, is to find your own identity and stick to it. Even Foster has changed towards me now, takes me for what I am. I went out for dinner with Andrew and Suchy recently and we all agreed how much we love it at Essex. Andrew made the point that while he had to be quiet at Hampshire [his original county], something that goes against his nature, Fletch's biggest asset is the fact that he doesn't want to change you.

'Fletch told me what areas of my batting I need to work on in Perth, mostly relating to tightening up outside off-stump and trying not to throw my wicket away so often. But what scares me is thinking so much about my game, more so even than that operation I'm due for next week. They want to cut off a bit of my right knee and have a look inside. Empa-something-opy they call it. In fact I've been having problems with both knees because of all the jarring that goes on, not so much at short-leg as when you've been told to go to the outfield and you're still wearing shin-pads. The outfields are rock-hard as it is, but when you wear those things the ground feels even harder when you dive around on them.'

Just in case Nadeem needed someone to hold his hand (in the event the probing would result in a clean bill of health, although the anaesthetic made him sick for thirty-six hours), Hussain was also due to be a house guest at Chelmsford Hospital the following Wednesday, to have the pin removed from his wrist. Next stop for him would be Adelaide University, Stephenson's the Gold Coast of Queensland. Nadeem would have a pair of distant bodyguards. 'And who knows, maybe four England players will be severely injured in Perth . . . Did I really say that? I can't believe I just said that.'

12 The Hissing of Summer Lawns

Sunday 25 November, West Hampstead

Critics of all expression
Judges in black and white
Saying it's wrong
Saying it's right
Compelled by prescribed standards
Or some ideals we fight
For wrong, wrong and right.
(Joni Mitchell,
Shadows and Light)

So was it all worth it? From a patriotic perspective, it would appear not. I went to bed at around 12.30 this morning, dismayed that in Brisbane England had slumped to 84 for 6, ahead by 127, but still confident that a lead of 200-plus, given the quixotic scores over the first two days, would be enough. At 7 a.m the radio crackled on. 'Australia have won the first Test by 10 wickets,' announced the Radio 4 newsreader in a tone more befitting the passing of a Mrs Dale or a Dan Archer. Although half-asleep, I inhaled the information and summoned the appropriate degree of disbelief. Aldermanned again. Three thoughts in quick succession:

1: How many teams had ever trailed on first innings in a Test and won by 10 wickets barely a day later?

2: Was this English cricket's response to the resignation of the Prime Minister? A symbol, perhaps, of the country's impoverished state?

3: What on earth was the purpose of all those runs and all those destitute bowlers?

England's Test fortunes, on the upswing following victories over indifferent opposition from New Zealand and India, appear to be on the wane again. From the successes of Sabina Park to bemusement in Brisbane in nine months. The Thatcher Years had embraced Botham and Gower at their peak, and bade a temporary farewell to any lingering conceits about England as a power in the cricket world, let alone the nasty real one. Gooch's absence through injury is no alibi since no one player can make the difference between victory and vilification, and the only possible excuse could be the wicket, which, for the first two days, looks (according to the evidence of *Test Match Special* and the BBC highlights) to have been pretty hairy for batsmen so accustomed to peaceful plunder.

'That's the legacy of the summer we've just had,' lamented Adrian. 'They've been spoilt here. All those runs, all those flat tracks, that seam. No wonder they can't play the moving ball.' David refuses to accept that theory. 'The environment out there is completely different, and that was a poor pitch.' Keith Fletcher was prepared to go further. 'What was the point of us ensuring that our batsmen learn to play on Test-quality wickets when this is what they get? Judging by the scores from there, it's the same in Pakistan.' Nadeem, who had been incorporated into England's practice matches in Perth, and thus witnessed the incident in which Gooch sustained his hand injury, prefers to focus on the debilitating loss of the captain. 'Robin Smith's shot was going at 100 miles an hour and he somehow got a finger to it. Blood was dripping from it horribly when he went off. Jack Russell kicked the stumps down.'

The premise of this book was to examine county cricket as an independent entity rather than a training ground for something higher, so England's fate should not concern us unduly. Yet it would be wrong to delude ourselves that the domestic game can blithely ignore the decay of the national side over the past ten years, one that can only partially be explained by rising standards elsewhere and the side-effects of over-exposure to that antidote to five-day rigour, the 40-over flog. The last Test-free English season was in 1927; the odds on the counties surviving without five-day receipts today are not worth considering.

Intent as they were, for varying reasons, on proving themselves, it must have been difficult at times for Adrian and Nadeem not to feel isolated from all this. David, with fewer mountains left unconquered, was easier to distract. Even though the Manchester rain succeeded in drowning their final Championship game against Warwickshire, leaving them in sixth place, Lancashire had enjoyed a prosperous summer. Two golds, a silver and a bronze in the one-day events are more than creditable in any language.

David's reflections, however, are far from dazzling. 'It takes a while to reflect on a season because your immediate reaction is to try and wind down and forget it. And there is no point in post mortems in the dressing-room because people are tired and fed up with living with each other. All they want to do is shut off. How can you blame us? We've got the blend right with regard to three-day and one-day cricket, but not the quantity. The players are so tired because of the daily grind and the travelling that they can't always give of their best, and by July you can have nothing to play for anyway. In any event, it was not a particularly memorable summer because of the imbalance between bat and ball. In terms of assessing the problems, how could you have a better committee than the captains? But we're ignored. It's the same with the players' union. We have no say at all. On a personal level, people tipped Lancashire to do well, and of course I'm glad we won something, but it wasn't the Championship. All in all, though, despite the seriousness and the hard work, we've had a marvellous season at Old Trafford and I'm thrilled for Alan Ormrod and all the players. I enjoyed every minute. Well, almost every one.'

Nadeem suffered more disappointment, both individual and communal. (In retrospect, John Childs's scanty haul of 25 wickets at 58.88, a far cry from his 67 at 22.70 in 1989, can be seen as perhaps the most critical factor in Essex's narrow failure to win the Championship; Middlesex's principal spinners, Emburey and Tufnell, shared 122 at around 35, throwing Nadeem's struggles with the ball into stark relief.) Not unnaturally for one who profited from the bowlers' misfortune, he seemed untouched by the brouhaha over seam and pitch. Between 9 June and 18 September, he produced at least one innings of 40 or more in eleven out of thirteen games, one sequence yielding 529 runs in ten knocks at an average of 65. But so sound are his temperament and technique that prosperity under less favourable conditions can be assured.

Nadeem's adaptability reinforced this impression. By summer's end he had batted in every position from No. 1 to 7. 'I'm just happy to be playing. I've never had any doubts about whether I made the right choice of career, barring a period in 1989 when I couldn't get the ball off the square, and nothing happened last summer to change that. I enjoyed it. Not being selected for the A tour doesn't seem so terrible now. There will be other chances, I hope.'

Unlike Nadeem and David, Adrian endured considerably more lows than highs. His potency, admittedly, remained undimmed, 77 per cent of his first-class victims being Nos. 1 to 6 in the order, twenty-four of them openers. Yet between duffing up Gloucestershire on 29 April and whittling down Warwickshire on 10 September, he failed to take 4 wickets in a Championship innings, and took 3 just the once. Long before the trading season opened it was clear that he would not be at Taunton come 1991. Part of the problem, as he readily admitted, was the 'slight clash of personalities' between himself and the Somerset chief executive. Formerly with the fraud squad in Hong Kong – 'once a cop, always a cop' – Peter Anderson is said to insist on making all decisions of a cricketing nature himself, instead of relying on the nous of more experienced judges such as Roy Marshall and Brian Rose. Liz empathised with her husband. 'I really hoped we'd spend the rest of our lives in Taunton, but offering Adrian a year's contract means he's on trial the whole time. He can't cope with that kind of pressure. He tries too hard.'

Within a month the wheels were rolling. The cutback on overseas registrations has, as expected, enhanced the desirability and market value of players qualified to represent England, a development underlined when ten counties made bids for Kevin Curran, sacked by Gloucestershire for reasons rather more closely related to character than ability. After apparently giving the go-ahead to Hampshire, Curran signed instead for Northamptonshire in exchange for a tidy pile: a reported £52,000 per annum over five years, plus sizeable signing-on fee. The same county had also written to Somerset to request permission to approach Adrian, joining Sussex in the queue. 'Anderson rang me up to say that he'd received an approach from Sussex. He wanted to know what he should do. I asked him what the procedure was and he said I had to let Sussex know if I want to talk to them. So then he asked whether I wanted to talk to them, and I said, "Well . . .".' Anderson duly authorised the overtures, then sent Adrian a letter confirming Somerset's offer of a twelve-month deal. He also sought to impress on Adrian the need to make a snappy decision since his salary might be needed for another bowler.

'Who is there?' he retorted, incredulously, deeply hurt by the absence of any face-to-face discussion. 'You can count on the fingers of one hand the number of genuinely quick English bowlers.'

In the meantime, Birkenshaw, having been spotted in mid-September driving one of Leicestershire's sponsored cars, duly returned to Grace Road as assistant manager. Happily, Cook signed on for a final summer, but two weeks ago, while Somerset were finalising negotiations with David Graveney (who thus becomes the first player this century to transfer allegiances from Bristol to Taunton), Adrian trotted off to Hove to discuss a three-year deal with Paul Parker and Norman Gifford.

'Giff can't understand why I haven't been picked for England. Perhaps he can do something for me, give me back my self-belief. I've been starting to doubt myself at Somerset.' Adrian returned to Taunton to pack his bags, to all intents and purposes a Sussex player once more. Who knows, if the powers that be are prepared to take into account his previous years in service, perhaps a benefit may not be out of the question after all? Even if it is, competing as they were with the pull of family and friends, the other bidders – and there were a good few – would still never have had an earthly. 'I will miss the Somerset lads terribly, and I will take away fond memories, but it will be nice to go back to friends like the Wells boys. I feel for them as much as I feel for myself. I always wanted to finish my career at Sussex, and I feel rather honoured that a club I left in 1986 have been so keen for me to return. But Liz has mixed feelings as she has enjoyed living in Taunton. I am more worried about her happiness than anything else.'

Adrian's Taunton requiem was unexpectedly memorable. In preparation for next summer's centenary, fittingly a benefit year, Mike Tarr, a local artist, was commissioned by the club to sketch portraits of some 100 foremost players, our departing hero among them, to his undisguised pleasure. Immortalised on a cigarette card!

Flattered wasn't the half of it. Two days ago Adrian went to Hove for a medical, blowing the monitor off the scale during the lung test. Dropping in on his parents on the way back to Taunton, he found out about Thatcher's resignation. 'Mum told me. I couldn't believe it. She's got a lot to answer for. She gave entrepreneurs more of a chance and then took it away. Of the contenders I like the look of Major. He seems honest and trustworthy.'

Weighing against Adrian's new lease of life came the feared news from Lord's. The number of strands used to construct the seam of the ball will remain at nine in 1991. Adrian had to pinch himself, hard. 'The TCCB are so far removed from reality. I don't think anybody enjoyed last season. It was so predictable. Championship games consisted of two days' cricket and a one-dayer. Even Jimmy Cook said the batsmen had too great an advantage and that it was all getting a little silly.'

Part of the TCCB's rationale had revolved around the unnaturally splendid weather – out of 583 playing days, only sixteen were lost – that had covered the season in a duvet of scorched outfields and granite-hard wickets, the like of which had not been seen here for fourteen years. Reasonable enough, except that meteorologists are adamant that global warming will eventually transform that rarest of creatures, the decent English summer, into a regular companion. All the same, Adrian's fury was that of a bowler, a fast bowler at that, the species most threatened by this sliver of a seam. The general view was that the 1989 seam and the 1990 pitches would have presented the ideal combination.

That the batsmen had things too much their own way was indisputable. (In a gesture of dissent, Adrian nominated Neil Foster, taker of 94 first-class wickets, as his player of the year in the annual Cricketers' Association poll.) That said, there were Ten Magic Numbers to conjure with: 26, 32, 48, 863, 752, 1,058, 101.70, 333, 456, 121 .* The temptation to dismiss these – along with the

* (In ascending order of importance): 26: The number of minutes Tom Moody expended accepting the 100 offered him by Glamorgan, thus enabling him to surge past Messrs Fender and O'Shaughnessy to become the fastest century-maker on record (in terms of time rather than deliveries). 32: The number of double centuries in 1990, well clear of the previous high. 48: The number of players averaging 50 or more, 33 up on 1989 and another fresh mark. 863: Lancashire's contribution

myriad other milestones – as no more than freaks, is strong but best resisted. After all, has any editor of *Wisden* ever added an appendix to the first entry in his records selection? Something along the lines of, 'Hanif Mohammed's innings of 499 should be taken with a pinch of salt since the Bahawalpur bowlers were not much cop and the only way they could get rid of the cussed blighter was by dint of a run-out'?

Nevertheless, the consequences of this one-sidedness were manifest. Despite all the scripted finagling and all that sunshine – and bearing in mind that timeless truism about bowlers winning matches – positive Championship results as a percentage of draws fell by 12 per cent on 1989. More than twice as many matches were left undecided as were resolved. In 1967, the season prior to the much-needed introduction of a fully-fledged bonus points system encouraging 'brighter cricket', the ratio was even less attractive; but even in 1973, the year before the current refinement, there was more than one victory to every two stalemates. We must be thankful that cricket, unlike the greater mass of spectator sports, does not depend on so-called 'positive' results for its appeal; a draw that goes to the final over can afford infinitely greater pleasure for the impartial spectator than a two-day demolition.

More relevant was the evidence supplied by the division of bonus points. Between 1974 and 1989, the number of batting points had averaged out at 74.8 per cent of the number earned for bowling, a mean of 825 to 1,103 per season. This year, total bowling points dipped below 1,000 for the first time, a record 1,048 were won by batsmen and the relationship slipped into reverse for the first time,

---

to a senseless match at the Oval and the second highest Championship score ever recorded. 752: Graham Gooch's run tally against India, a three-Test record against a third-class attack. 1,058: Gooch's Test aggregate for the summer, a sixty-year-old Bradman milestone put in its place. 101.70: Gooch's average for the season, making him only the fourth player – and third bona fide batsman, if Bill Johnston can forgive such a slight – to maintain such consistency in an English summer. 333: Gooch's triple nelson against India. 456: The same insatiable's total runs in that Lord's Test. And, finally, 121, small but beautifully proportioned: Azharuddin's dazzling riposte to Gooch behind the Grace Gates, proof that not every figure tells a story. A host of astonishing records, but none as enchanting as Mohammad's Melody.

with bowling marks constituting 86.7 per cent of the batting aggregate. Ironically, although the chasm between bat and ball can rarely have yawned more, this ratio represents the narrowest gap thus far between the two.

In David's estimation the pronounced shift in the balance of power was no bad thing in light of the batsmen's recent struggles, though it did precious little for the prime beneficiaries. Five Somerset batsmen concluded their campaign with more than 1,000 runs and an average in excess of 50, a record unmatched by any other county's batsmen; Somerset were placed fifteenth in the Championship, never in the frame after their first game of the summer. Cook quashed Clive Rice's record haul for a 40-over season with 902 runs, in the process helping run up the biggest total in Sunday League history; Somerset finished eighth. Rose hammered the two quickest one-day centuries ever seen in county competition, the second speeding his side to the highest score in 60-over play; Somerset were knocked out of the NatWest in round two. More tellingly, perhaps, while their scoring rate in the Championship was the third healthiest behind that of Essex and Northamptonshire, their average of 79.31 balls per wicket was comfortably the sickliest. Not that strike-rate is necessarily the final arbiter; Gloucestershire, thirteenth, topped that particular chart, with Middlesex twelfth. Furthermore, while Essex and Lancashire boasted just one bowler between them with 50 Championship wickets, Somerset had three. The falsehood of statistics. One, though, zapped directly to the crux of the matter. Balance, as ever, was all. Only Middlesex had five batsmen with over 1,300 runs to complement five bowlers with upwards of 35 wickets.

Seamers, it is true, had earned exaggerated success for too long. As Mike Selvey put it in the *Guardian*, the severity of their task had become akin to 'cycling downhill with your feet on the handlebars, which is as easy for Eddie Edwards as it is for Eddy Merckx'. The main trouble, in terms of the national interest, was what lay in store at the bottom of that hill, and once it was their turn to prop their size 12s on the handlebars, the batsmen exacted a terrible revenge. Early in the season, Derek Pringle (who didn't take guard for his third first-class innings of the summer until July) suggested that, by simultaneously legislating against over-active balls and under-prepared pitches, there would be no way for the TCCB to know which was responsible for any changes that accrued. If better bowlers – the stated aim – flowed forth, so what? The question is whether the emergence of Tufnell, Martin Bicknell and Tim Munton truly justifies all the palaver.

Furthermore, given current events in Australia, it seems pertinent to emphasise that the confidence a batsman derives from such numerical achievements does not always endure at a higher level. This summer 428 first-class centuries were scored, a new high, ousting the 414 of 1928. No one kidded themselves as to the significance of this. England stomped to a 4–1 series win in Australia that long-ago winter; when Gooch and his footsore infantry left here in October, sharing the spoils against Allan Border's battalion seemed their optimum hope.

More importantly, as regards both aesthetics and commercial viability, county cricket was less entertaining in 1990, as David and his fellow captains stressed so pointedly at their end-of-term get-together. Cook, Waugh, Foster and Fairbrother, Younis, Akram, Tufnell and Ward (D) all submitted moments for the time capsule alongside those inebriated scores, but only in the four-day games was the art of competition not habitually cheapened.

So, again, was it all worth it? Of course it was. Woody Allen's parting monologue in Annie Hall provides an apt summing-up for the defence. A man visits his analyst. 'Doc, my brother thinks he's a chicken.' Analyst: 'Well, why don't you turn him in?' Man: 'We need the eggs.' Despite all its warts, the 1990 county cricket season still threw up more invigorating fare than the past ten years of League football, more suspense than a dozen Wimbledons, and more honesty and humane behaviour than a lifetime of rugby union. There were no mid-pitch brawls, no kiss'n'tell tabloid tattle, no raking and no drug tests, merely quiet dignity in an undignified world.

As for the men who made it all worthwhile, April 1991 seems distant as they temporarily immerse themselves in a more normal form of existence. Nadeem found himself itching to start all over again as he headed for Perth in early October. For Adrian, potential still not fully tapped, the prospect of a fresh start is already beginning to recharge a wilting enthusiasm. As for the *éminence grise*, David, now preparing for his last ride on the merry-go-round, has no hesitation in recommending son James, now nearing 15, to enter the family business. 'He has had a lot of stick at school for being my son, and I have had to be careful not to push him so far that I end up pushing him away from the game, but it's such a great character builder to go in, get a first-baller and walk straight back. And, of course, I'd love him to play for England.'

So, three views from the belfry of the Year of the Bat. The conclusion should come as no surprise if you have read this far. For all the foibles and frustrations, a county cricketer is still something to be. To be part of a bewitching tapestry, an alluring scene, a glamorous profession, one inhabited almost exclusively by decent souls who give their customers much to cherish. How many jobs can you say that about?